Cornell Industrial and Labor Relations Bibliography Series No. 17

LABOR ARBITRATION
An Annotated Bibliography

Charles J. Coleman
Rutgers University School of Business at Camden

and

Theodora T. Haynes
Robeson Library of Rutgers University at Camden

EDITORS IN CHIEF

Paul Barron, School of Law, Tulane University

Mei Liang Bickner, California State University, Fullerton

Gerald C. Coleman, Rutgers University School of Business at Camden

Greg Dell'Omo, School of Business, St. Joseph's University

Stanley J. Schwartz, School of Business, Rider College

Perry Zirkel, College of Education, Lehigh University

ASSOCIATE EDITORS

ILR Press
Ithaca, New York

Copyright © 1994 by Cornell University

All rights reserved

Library of Congress Cataloging-in-Publication Data

Labor arbitration: an annotated bibliography/Charles J. Coleman and Theodora T. Haynes, editors in chief; Paul Barron . . . [et al.], associate editors.
 p. cm. Cornell industrial and labor relations bibliography series; no. 17
 Includes index.
 ISBN 0-87546-322-3 (pbk.: alk. paper)
 1. Arbitration, Industrial—United States—Bibliography.
 2. Arbitration, Industrial—Canada—Bibliography. I. Coleman, Charles J. II. Haynes, Theodora T.
 Z7164.L1L27 1994
 [HD5504]
 016.33189'143'0973—dc20   94-18840

Copies may be ordered through bookstores or directly from

ILR Press
School of Industrial and Labor Relations
Cornell University
Ithaca, NY 14853-3901

Printed on recycled acid-free paper in the United States of America

5 4 3 2 1

Contents

Acknowledgments
vii

Introduction: The Nature of This Book
1

The Legal Foundations of Grievance Arbitration in the United States: Labor Arbitration and the Federal Courts
7

I. BOOKS AND MONOGRAPHS

A. Arbitration and Dispute Settlement
35

B. Arbitrator Characteristics, Careers, and Practices
42

C. Development of Arbitration
43

D. Grievances and Grievance Mediation
44

E. Advocacy
44

F. Arbitrability, Management Rights, and Past Practice
47

G. Discipline and Discharge
48

H. Compensation, Work Rules, and Remedies
50

I. Arbitration and the Law
51

J. Interest Arbitration and Other Forms of Dispute Resolution
51

K. Nonunion Employees and Wrongful Discharge
54

L. Arbitration in Specific Industries
54

II. ARTICLES AND PROCEEDINGS

A. Arbitration and Dispute Settlement
59

B. Arbitrator Characteristics, Careers, and Practices
66

C. Development of Arbitration
71

D. Grievances and Grievance Mediation
75

E. Practice and Procedure
77

F. The Arbitration Hearing
85

G. Advocacy
89

H. Decision-Making and Decision-Writing
101

I. Arbitrability
106

J. Principles of Contract Interpretation
111

K. Management Rights and Past Practice
113

L. Discipline and Discharge
115

M. Seniority Rights, Compensation, Work Rules, and Remedies
133

N. Arbitration and the Courts
144

O. Interest Arbitration and Other Forms of Dispute Resolution
179

P. Nonunion Matters and Wrongful Discharge
210

Q. Arbitration in Selected Industries
216

Subject Index
229

Author Index
241

About the Contributors
271

ACKNOWLEDGMENTS

This volume would not have been possible without the approval of the National Academy of Arbitrators Board of Governors and without the support and encouragement provided by three NAA presidents. The book was conceived under the presidency of Howard S. Block and the work was performed during the presidencies of Anthony V. Sinicropi and David F. Feller. Financial support for the project was funneled through the offices of Dana Eischen, secretary-treasurer of the Academy. We thank all of these people for their help.

We particularly want to thank our consulting editors, Paul Barron, Mei Liang Bickner, Greg Dell'Omo, Stan Schwartz, and Perry Zirkel. These people provided a good part of the solution to our core problem—the preparation of the annotations. We thank Gerald Coleman for plotting the course of the law, as portrayed in the second chapter. We also give our thanks to the undergraduate and graduate students at Rutgers University who prepared much of the rough copy that led to the final set of annotations.

We thank NAA members George R. Fleischli, Jay E. Grenig, Herbert L. Marx, Jr., George Nicolau, Dennis R. Nolan, and Arnold M. Zack for supplying us with lists of their publications so that we could verify the completeness of our literature search. We also thank NAA members David E. Feller, Ira F. Jaffe, Dennis R. Nolan, and Harry Reagan of Morgan, Lewis & Bockius for their incisive comments on the legal foundations chapter.

This work would not have been completed without the financial and in kind assistance provided by the Rutgers University School of Business at Camden. We are indebted to Dean Milton Leontiades for his generosity in allowing the use of secretarial time and in providing funds for student assistance. We thank Business Manager Larry Gaines for *always* finding a way to solve our production problems. Many thanks go to Professor Kenneth Peffers for helping with the bibliographic programs and to his son, Simon Peffers, who produced the complex diagram found in the second chapter. We thank Jeffrey Haynes and Joanne Santry, who entered the bulk of the information into the bibliographic program (and retained some of their sanity in the process), and Lauren Weber for helping with the proofreading. We owe a great deal to Linda Baker, our student assistant, for her help with a wide variety of tasks.

We wish to acknowledge the special help provided by the director of the Robeson Library, Gary Golden; by Libby Hart for her tireless acquisition of materials from other libraries; and by Elaine Adair for her help with word processing. We are deeply indebted to Dean Roger Dennis of the Rutgers Law School at Camden, who permitted us to tap into the talents of some of his faculty in connection with the literature search. We particularly thank Associate Dean Alan Stein, Library Director Anne Dallesandro, and Librarian Gloria Chao for their cooperation and assistance. Whenever we needed something, they found some way to help.

Finally, we want to thank our spouses and children for putting up with us during the process and our friends for pretending to be interested when we discussed the project with them.

    Charles J. Coleman   September 1994
    Theodora T. Haynes   Camden, New Jersey

INTRODUCTION

THE NATURE OF THIS BOOK

This is the second annotated bibliography of labor arbitration that has been prepared under the direction of the Committee on Research of the National Academy of Arbitrators. The editors of the first volume, Howard Foster and Mario Bognanno, set out to "prepare a bibliography on labor arbitration that Academy members could use as easy reference to published literature on subjects relevant to their practice." Because we could build upon their work, the current editors were able to put together a much more exhaustive set of annotations and, in the process, create something that could be directed toward a broader audience.

Objectives and Audience. The primary audience for this volume consists of Academy arbitrators, non-Academy arbitrators at various stages of their careers, and union and management advocates and representatives. The editors set out to prepare a volume that these women and men could use when they needed more than case citations or general reference material to help them with a problem they confronted in their practice. We wanted this to be *the* volume they would turn to when the cases or standard references proved to be inadequate.

We also wanted to supply people who were contemplating a career in arbitration with a guide to the literature in the field and to provide students and professors with a starting point for research. Finally, we wanted to put together the most comprehensive effort of its kind, a work that would be a necessary reference source on labor arbitration for libraries of business schools, law schools, and related professional institutions in North America and abroad.

In determining what was to be included in this work, the first decision was to use the 1985 bibliography as its foundation. Almost every one of the 590 entries in that report is included in this volume. The next important decision concerned the kind of expansion to be undertaken. We decided not only to add works that have been published since the appearance of the original volume, but to broaden the coverage of the older literature as well. In addition to the contents of the 1985 volume, this bibliography includes books and monographs on arbitration and related topics published since 1950; journal articles in non-legal periodicals published since 1970; and articles in law journals published since 1980. These cutoff dates are tied to considerations about the length of the manuscript and, as will be explained later, the beginning dates of certain computerized data bases.

Selection Criteria. Although this bibliography is extensive, it does not exhaust the literature. The goal was to create a guide to the most important information on labor arbitration—to create a volume that would provide a sense of history, institutional development, and the abiding questions that have been raised in and about labor arbitration. A great deal of material had to be eliminated.

The first selection decision was to focus on labor arbitration and closely related processes. This focus meant that general studies of labor law or labor relations were omitted as well as most of the works that discuss arbitration as part of a broader topic (for example, reviews of recent court decisions on labor matters). While works such as these play an invaluable role in labor relations scholarship, this volume focuses on studies whose central concern is labor arbitration.

We also crossed off newspaper articles, editorials about arbitration, book reviews, and articles on arbitration in periodicals that specialize in current developments, such as the *Chicago Daily Law Bulletin, Los Angeles Daily Journal, Legal Times,* and the *Preview of United States Supreme Court Cases.* We felt that discussions of current events would expand the book unduly, and if one of these topics did take on lasting importance, it would soon be examined in a scholarly article and enter this volume through that venue.

Works that examined forms of alternative dispute resolution (ADR) other than arbitration have been omitted from this study, except for inquiries into fact-finding and grievance mediation. Although ADR is increasing in importance, it has not yet become a central concern to the people who practice labor arbitration. Grievance mediation and fact-finding were included because of their close relationship to grievance and interest arbitration.

Geographically, the focus was on the United States and Canada. Material written in a foreign language was eliminated and we did not systematically search the English language literature on arbitration outside North America. Although some may feel that it is shortsighted to ignore what is happening abroad, the primary audience consists of North American arbitrators and advocates, who are most interested in developments in their own countries.

Because most of the audience will be familiar with arbitration, we also eliminated articles that were less than four pages, primarily descriptive, or written at the introductory level. For example, William Lissey has prepared an excellent series of articles on arbitration from a line supervisor's viewpoint for *Supervision* magazine. We did not include these in the belief that they were too fundamental for this audience. Finally, this bibliography includes a large number of books and monographs, but in cases where individual authors sign specific chapters within a book, we did not single out those authors and their contribution.

As a result of our selection criteria, undoubtedly many fine pieces either have been overlooked or have fallen through the cracks. With these selection criteria, the bibliography consists almost entirely of annotations of works that focus on labor arbitration and have been drawn from books, monographs, analytical articles in professional and academic journals, and selections from the proceedings of the meetings of academic and professional societies. Perhaps the next edition of this bibliography will fill the gaps we have left, particularly those that deal with ADR and developments outside of North America.

The annotations themselves are quite brief, reflecting only the basic theme, character, and approach of each entry. They are not evaluative but rather attempt to provide a guide to the contents. The goal was to provide enough descriptive material to help a reader decide whether to pursue the source further.

The Search Strategy. The strategy was to search the most relevant computerized data bases broadly and narrow the field manually by applying the criteria listed above. The data bases were ABI/Inform, the Legal Research Index (LRI), and the Research Libraries Information Network (RLIN). Because we had to limit the length of the manuscript we made the assumption that most of the very old works of lasting value had been picked up in the 1985 bibliography, and established the following cutoff dates: 1970 for ABI/Inform; 1980 for LRI (when that index first appeared); and 1950 for RLIN. The last search was conducted in the summer of 1992.

We started with everything in the data bases that seemed to be related to arbitration and winnowed from there. The phrase—de ("arbitration and award" "arbitration industrial" "grievance arbitration" "arbitrators industrial") or de ("grievance procedures" "strikes and lockouts" "collective bargaining" "collective labor agreements" "labor-management committees") and arbitrat!—may not mean very much to the layperson, but it was the phrase used to tap into the literature of labor arbitration in one of the data bases. That phrase produced over 3,000 citations of journal articles, which turned into some 300 entries in this bibliography.

The Contents. Although the bibliography is selective, it is extensive. Almost 1,100 authors contributed to the 1,336 lead citations contained in this book. The new bibliography contains 148 percent more items than the 1985 version, and if the additional works cited within some of the annotations were added, this bibliography would nearly triple the size of the previous one. Furthermore, the entries are not concentrated in a single time period. There are large numbers of entries in each of the three periods listed in Table 1. The entries from the pre-1970 period were drawn almost entirely from the 1985 bibliography. The years 1970–1985 were covered by both bibliographies and the post-1985 entries came from the current survey alone.

Table 1. The Contents of This Bibliography

1. Comparison of 1985 and Current Bibliographies

Title of Entry	1985 Volume	Added	Current Volume
Books and Monographs	78	76	154
Articles	331	630	961
Proceedings	134	87	221

2. Contents by Time Period

Title of Entry	Pre–1970	1970–1985	1986–1992
Books and Monographs	27	100	27
Articles	52	561	348
Proceedings	65	77	79

Total numbered citations	1,336
Number of authors cited	1,093

The bibliography contains annotations of 154 books and monographs and almost 1,200 journal articles and proceedings from professional meetings. The articles and proceedings make up the heart of the bibliography and the *Arbitration Journal*, the *Proceedings of the Annual Meetings of the National Academy of Arbitrators*, and the *Labor Law Journal* have played a highly significant role. These three sources have produced over 40 percent of the contents of this volume (535 of the 1,336 cited entries). Ten journals and sets of proceedings have yielded almost two-thirds of these citations (see Table 2).

Table 2. Sources of Articles and Proceedings (10 most frequently cited)

Name of Source	Number of Cites	Percent of Total
Arbitration Journal	223	18.9%
NAA Proceedings	187	15.8%
Labor Law Journal	125	10.6%
Jrnl. of Coll. Neg. in Publ. Sec.	54	4.6%
Industrial and Labor Rel. Rev.	48	4.1%
Employee Rel. Law Jrnl.	35	3.0%
Monthly Labor Review	30	2.5%
Industrial Relations	29	2.5%
IRRA Proceedings	27	2.4%
Indl. Rel. Law Jrnl.	21	1.8%
Total from these sources	779	66.0%
Total from other sources	402	34.0%
Total number of articles and proceedings	1,182	

The third table provides three loose "quantity control checks." To satisfy themselves that they had done a thorough search, the editors made a request for individual lists of publications at a meeting of the Board of Governors of the National Academy of Arbitrators. Six arbitrators provided lists of their publications, and the first part of this table deals with these responses. While the bibliography picked up a large percentage of the books, articles, and proceedings that these arbitrators provided, we can probably learn more from the items that we missed.

Most of the limitations are tied into the coverage of the computerized data bases. Of the five books on arbitration that were missed, four were not included in the computerized data bases—three were monographs published either by the federal government or the International Labor Organization in the 1970s, and the fourth was a handbook published as part of a series on arbitration and collective bargaining.

This same limitation also showed up in the journal articles. Five of the ten that were missed were published in law journals before the 1980 appearance of the LRI computerized data base. As far as proceedings are concerned, the coverage of the NAA and the IRRA proceedings was quite good. The search picked up just about everything that these authors had published in these outlets. This is not surprising: the editors of the previous volume undoubtedly paid careful attention to the NAA proceedings; the current editors went through the NAA proceedings from 1985 to 1992 from cover to cover, and we found many entries from the IRRA proceedings, which are published in the *Labor Law Journal*, in LRI. But very little was picked up from the proceedings of other meetings.

The twenty "other" items that were *not* related to arbitration were typically law review articles on topics other than arbitration and works by one arbitrator on training and economic development. The 38 arbitration-related items that were not included were book reviews, short articles, articles in "current-event" periodicals, and book chapters. We later added all of the missing works by these authors that were consistent with the selection criteria and that we were able to locate.

The second and third parts of Table 3 are based on 100 footnotes randomly selected from the three-volume reference work compiled by Tim Bornstein and Anne Gosline, entitled *Labor and Employment Arbitration*. The results show that this book included roughly two-thirds of those references and that the coverage was especially complete for the post-1970 period.

Table 3. Publications Cited

From the Vitae of Six Members of the NAA Board of Governors

Title of Entry	Total	Related to Arbitration	Number Included	Percentage Included
Books and Monographs	12	11	6	55%
Articles	62	36	26	72%
Proceedings	26	18	7	39%
Other	58	38	0	0%

From 100 References in Bornstein and Gosline

Title of Entry	Total	Number Included	Percentage Included
Books and Monographs	8	6	75%
Articles	55	36	66%
Proceedings	37	24	65%

Percentage of the 100 References from Different Time Periods

Time Period	Total	Number Included	Percentage Included
Pre–1970	38	16	42%
1970–1985	44	33	75%
1986–1992	18	17	94%

The Structure. After much of the bibliographic information had been gathered, it became apparent that the development of labor arbitration has been influenced profoundly by court decisions and that large parts of this book were tied to those decisions. The editors felt that it would be helpful to include an introductory chapter that would give readers a summary of the principal court cases and some idea of their flow and development. After this chapter on the law, the next section consists of books and monographs and the last one, by far the largest, of journal articles and proceedings.

The book takes its overall structure from *Labor and Employment Arbitration*. After the initial material on arbitration and arbitrators, the major divisions of the book were taken directly from that study—practice and procedure; arbitrability and contract interpretation; discipline, discharge, and resignation; seniority rights, compensation, and benefits; arbitration and the courts; public sector arbitration; nonunion issues, wrongful discharge, and arbitration in selected industries. Within each section, many of the subheadings tie into chapters or topics in that work, but the final shape of the book was dictated by the entries that were annotated.

The bibliographic entries are organized first by subject area. Entries that overlap one or more topics are presented only once in the section that best fits the entry's primary focus. The book takes a novel approach to the organization of entries within each subject area. Every bibliography known to the editors organizes the entries according to the last name of the first author. *In this book, the entries are organized according to date of publication within each subject area.* We do this for two reasons: the first is to provide a better sense of the chronological development of particular topics; and the second is to help the reader who wants to get to the most current material easily. All that reader has to do is start the search at the end of the section and work backward.

Most of the citations are in Chicago A style from the thirteenth edition of *The Chicago Manual of Style*. In order to save space we have adopted a "modified law journal" form for the citations of proceedings. After listing author and title, the citation includes only meeting number, abbreviation for the name of the society, year, and pages. Thus, "43 NAA (1991): 218-231" means "Proceedings of the Forty-third Annual Meeting of the National Academy of Arbitrators, published in 1991, pages 218–231."

THE LEGAL FOUNDATIONS
OF GRIEVANCE ARBITRATION IN
THE UNITED STATES

LABOR ARBITRATION AND THE FEDERAL COURTS

This bibliography is devoted to the literature of labor arbitration, particularly as it has developed in the United States since the seminal *Lincoln Mills* decision in 1957. Labor arbitration may be based on the principles of contract, but in many respects external law specifies its scope, power, and influence. In the 35 years that have passed since *Lincoln Mills,* the contours of the institution itself and the condition of the practice of arbitration have been shaped substantially by a number of the decisions that have come from the federal courts. In those years, the federal courts have determined issues such as the obligation to arbitrate, the powers of the arbitrator and the courts, the enforcement and the finality of awards, the degree of deference given to awards, and the relationship between arbitration decisions and external law.

Because these cases have had such an impact on arbitration and because so many of the references in this volume deal with them, this chapter provides an overview of the case law and annotations of the leading cases. The reader who is not sure of the holding in a particular case cited in one of the annotations, therefore, can secure more complete information from this chapter.

The digest of cases has been selective. We have identified several streams of cases on labor arbitration and concentrated on those that defined the law, changed it, or contributed significantly to its development. Except in the area of National Labor Relations Board deferral policies, no administrative cases are included, even though their impact is reflected in many of the cases that have been discussed. We have not used any state court decisions or local regulations even though they have had a profound influence on labor relations in state and local government. But these cases do not constitute a uniform body of law and should be considered within their separate areas of authority. That task may wait for the editors of later editions of this volume.

The "Genealogy of U.S. Federal Court Cases on Labor Arbitration" (figure 1) provides the outline for this discussion. These cases fall into six broad categories: those cases that established the foundations of labor arbitration; those that have dealt with the enforcement of the obligation to arbitrate and with arbitrability; deferral

8 LEGAL FOUNDATIONS OF GRIEVANCE ARBITRATION

Figure 1. Genealogy of U.S. Court Decisions on Labor Arbitration

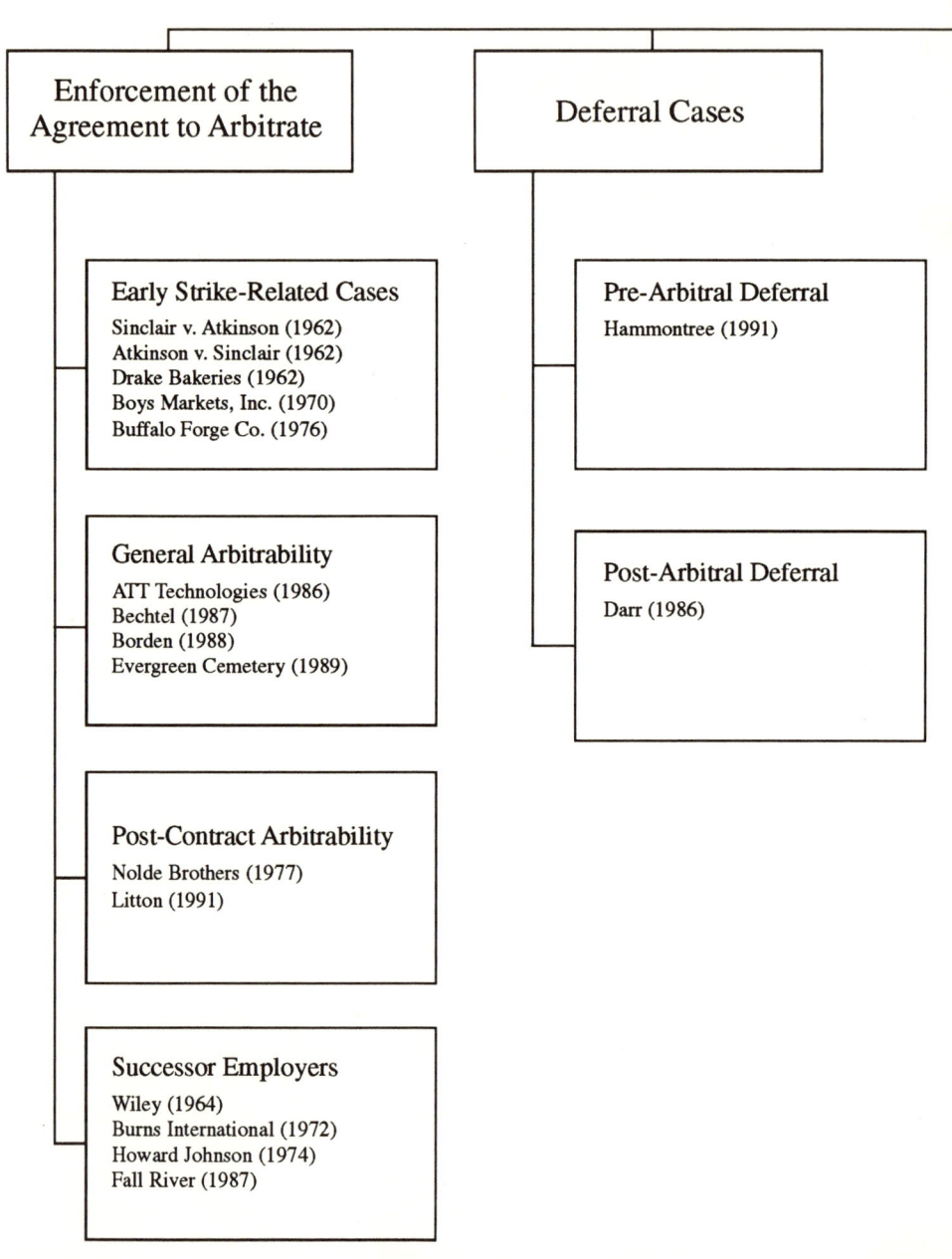

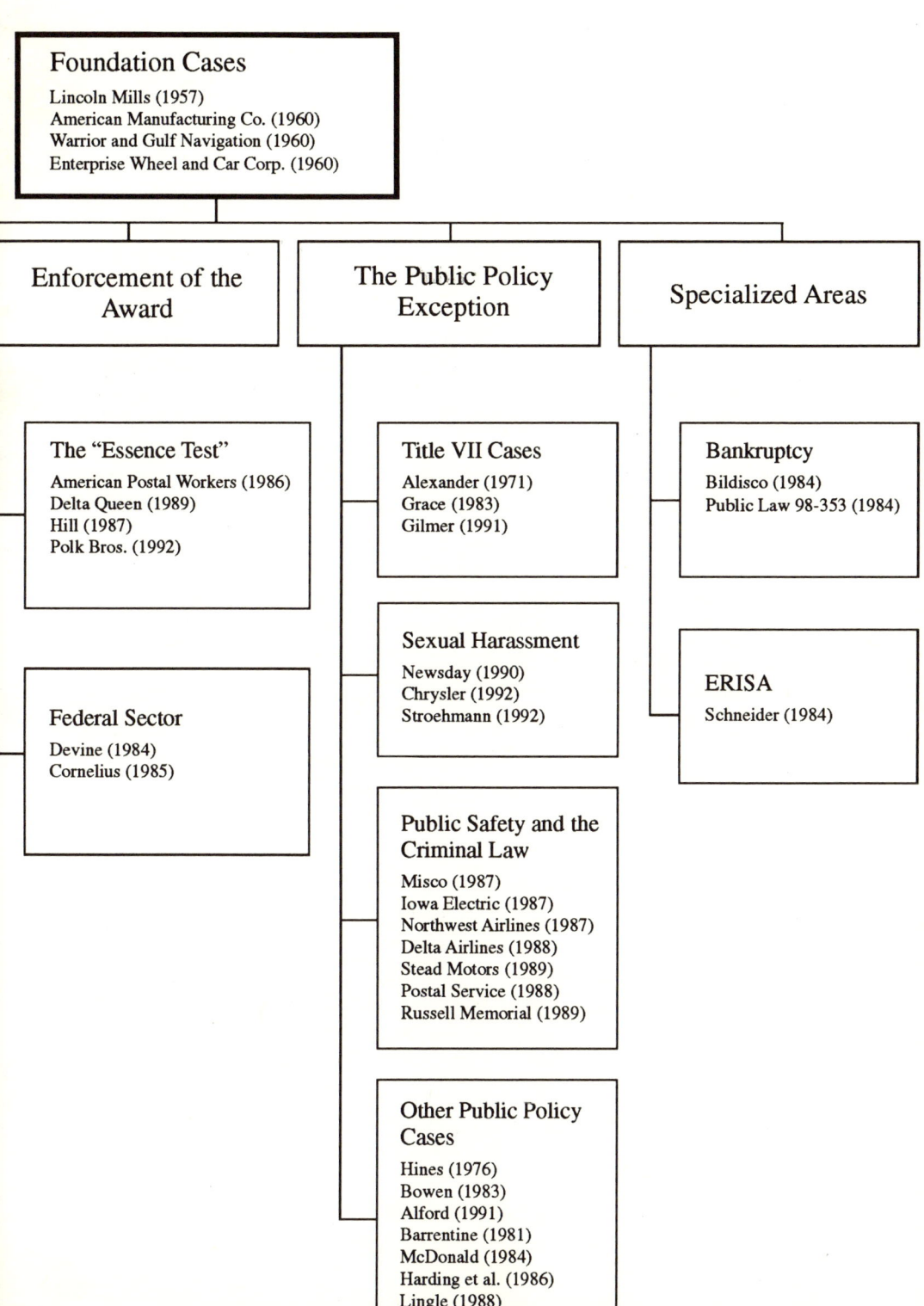

issues; cases that have focused on the enforcement of the arbitration award; those that have turned on the "public policy exception"; and specialized cases in the areas of bankruptcy and the Employee Retirement Income Security Act (ERISA).

The Foundation Cases

Four Supreme Court cases have provided the foundation for labor arbitration as it exists today in the United States. The *Lincoln Mills* decision authorized federal courts to fashion a body of law for the enforcement of collective bargaining agreements and it promoted the view that the agreement to arbitrate is a quid pro quo for an agreement to refrain from striking during the term of the contract. This decision was based on the premise that arbitration provided the best route to industrial peace. This view provided the support necessary for the development of labor arbitration in the United States.

The *Lincoln Mills* concept that the federal courts would mandate the performance of arbitration provisions contained in collective agreements was given substance in the *Steelworkers Trilogy* cases decided by the Supreme Court three years later. These cases set forth five principles to govern the arbitration of grievances under collective bargaining.

> 1. Arbitration is a matter of contract. The parties are not required to arbitrate a dispute that they have not agreed to submit. The courts determine whether there is a duty to arbitrate a dispute.
>
> 2. In determining whether there is a duty to arbitrate a dispute, the courts should not examine the merits of the underlying grievance, even if it appears to be frivolous.
>
> 3. In labor contracts with an arbitration clause there is a presumption of arbitrability unless there is positive assurance that the arbitration clause is not susceptible to an interpretation that covers the dispute. Doubts should be resolved in favor of coverage.
>
> 4. As long as an arbitration award is based on the bargaining agreement, a court should enforce the award without examining its correctness.
>
> 5. In interpreting the labor agreement, the arbitrator is not limited to the words of the contract. The arbitrator is empowered to consider factors such as past practice, parol evidence, and "the common law of the shop."

Enforcement of the Agreement to Arbitrate and Arbitrability

Enforcement. One of the early challenges to the *Trilogy* came in cases where (1) the contract contained an agreement to arbitrate and a no-strike clause; (2) the union struck in violation of the no-strike clause; (3) the employer tried to enjoin the strike and arbitrate the issue; and (4) the union, citing the anti-injunction provisions of the Norris-LaGuardia Act, sought to avoid arbitration. The question concerned whether the court would enforce the broad obligation to arbitrate that it had announced.

In a series of 1962 cases, the Supreme Court ultimately refused to grant the requested injunction because of anti-injunction provisions in the Norris-LaGuardia Act. In permitting the strike to continue, the Court essentially refused to enforce the contractual arbitration provision. However, eight years later the same Court overruled its previous stand and established the current doctrine. In *Boys Market*, the Court ruled that the Norris-LaGuardia restrictions on injunctions did not apply as long as the unresolved dispute was covered in the arbitration provision in the bargaining agreement. The court provided the injunction and ordered the parties to arbitrate any unresolved grievances. This principle was affirmed in the 1976 *Buffalo Forge* ruling.

General Arbitrability. The *Warrior and Gulf* decision established a presumption of arbitrability: if the contract provides for the arbitration of grievances, a grievance is presumed to be arbitrable as long as the agreement does not specifically exclude the topic under consideration. The courts have consistently enforced this broad concept of arbitrability, reserving to the courts the power to determine substantive arbitrability and yielding the determination of procedural arbitrability to the arbitrator (*AT&T Technologies,* 1986).

Postcontract Arbitrability. Does the duty to arbitrate extend to cases where the contract has expired or the ownership of the company has changed hands? In 1977, the Supreme Court held that the duty to arbitrate can extend beyond the life of the contract. Where a dispute is over a provision of an expired contract, the presumption favoring arbitration must be negated expressly or by clear implication. This presumption still exists although the Court narrowed its ruling in 1991, when it held that a postexpiration grievance is arbitrable only when it involves facts and events that occurred before expiration, where the action infringes a right that vested under the agreement, or where the normal principles of contract interpretation show that the disputed contractual right survives the expiration of the remainder of the agreement.

Successorship. Another question is whether the duty to arbitrate survives a change in company ownership. The basic principle was laid down in *John Wiley* in 1964. Although the Board may not require that the successor employer adopt the substantive terms of the predecessor agreement, the successor inherits the contractual duty to arbitrate as long as there is "substantial continuity" between the old and the new companies.

Taken as a whole, these rulings on the enforcement of the duty to arbitrate and arbitrability make it clear that if the labor agreement requires the arbitration of grievances, arbitration will be difficult to avoid. Arbitrability issues are discussed in entries 491 through 502. Issues of postcontract arbitrability and successorship are examined in entries 503 through 518.

NLRB Deferral Policies

Although this book avoids works that focus on the decisions of administrative agencies, a significant part of the literature of arbitration is devoted to the deferral policies of the National Labor Relations Board. Because of this emphasis in the literature, we provide some background here on these policies and their implications for arbitration. Deferral policies are directed to cases in which an employee's contractual grievance is mingled with an unfair labor practice charge. In such cases, will the NLRB order arbitration, and will it defer to an award that has been rendered by an arbitrator? The first question, which ties into the general subject of enforcement of the duty to arbitrate, refers to the Board's policies of *prearbitration deferral*. The second question, which leads into the next section of this chapter, pertains to *postarbitration deferral*.

Prearbitration Deferral. In 1971 the Board determined that it would enforce a contractual duty to arbitrate such cases when it created standards for deferring consideration of unfair labor practice charges until remedies under the collective bargaining agreement had been exhausted. This policy is known as the *Collyer* doctrine and the standards pertain to the nature of the bargaining relationship and of the relationship between the employer and the union, the willingness of the employer to arbitrate, the nature of the arbitration clause, and the nature of the dispute. The NLRB has extended this doctrine many times.

Postarbitration Deferral. The issue of postarbitration deferral is closely related to enforcement because it refers to the willingness of a government agency to defer to the award of an arbitrator. Even before *Lincoln Mills* and the Trilogy were decided, the NLRB ruled that it would defer to an arbitrator's resolution of an ULP claim if certain conditions were met. The conditions for this process, which is called postarbitration deferral, were first announced in the Board's 1955 *Spielberg* decision and they were refined in many subsequent cases. The NLRB's policies on deferral are discussed in entries 885 through 943.

Enforcement of the Arbitration Award

The Essence Test. While the courts routinely enforce the duty to arbitrate, they have been less consistent in enforcing the award itself. Justice William O. Douglas stated in *Enterprise Wheel* that "an arbitrator does not sit to dispense his own brand of industrial justice...an award is legitimate only as long as it draws its essence from the collective bargaining agreement." We shall see below that these words have opened up the merits of an award to judicial review.

The essence standard is not easy to apply: different courts appear to adopt different standards and sometimes the same court seems to apply different standards at different times. We have chosen four cases decided between 1986 and 1989 to illustrate this point: in *American Postal Workers Union*, the D.C. Circuit affirmed an arbitrator's award that had reinstated a postal employee discharged for wrongful conversion of funds, while in *Delta Queen*, the Fifth Circuit overturned an arbitrator's award that had reinstated a steamboat captain charged with gross negligence. In *Hill*, the Seventh Circuit upheld an arbitration award that called for the discharge of an employee for possession of marijuana. But in *Polk Brothers* the same Circuit held that an arbitrator had exceeded his contractual authority by ordering the reinstatement of employees with back pay beyond the expiration date of the contract.

Enforcement in the Federal Sector. In the federal government, grievance arbitration takes place under the Civil Service Reform Act of 1978 (CSRA). Although this law requires that all contracts provide for arbitration of grievances, the CSRA weakens the finality of the procedure though a provision that permits the parties to file exceptions to arbitration awards for review by the Federal Labor Relations Authority. The courts appear to be willing to enforce a standard of review far beyond that envisioned in the Trilogy for private sector cases. In the 1984 *Devine* case, the U.S. Court of Appeals reversed an arbitration award because the arbitrator had substituted his judgment as to penalty for that of the employer. In *Cornelius* the next year the Supreme Court reversed an arbitration award because the arbitrator had not applied the same standards as the Merit Systems Protection Board.

Private sector and federal sector arbitration are grounded on different premises. According to the *Lincoln Mills* decision, arbitration in the private sector is a substitute for the strike. Because the strike is prohibited in the federal government, it is not surprising to find that the courts view arbitration in the federal government differently. Many authorities contend that, in cases involving contractual violations and public law, the arbitrator's job in the *private sector* is to enforce the contract. In the federal government, however, it appears that the arbitrator's job may be to enforce the law. Arbitration in the federal sector is covered in entries 143 through 147 and 1272 through 1299.

The Public Policy Exception

Assume that an employee has a complaint which fits the contractual definition of a grievance and that this complaint also involves a statutory right. If that employee arbitrates the case and loses, can the case be submitted to a judicial forum? The public policy exception concerns appeal rights in cases that involve both a contractual grievance and a public policy. These cases are important to the advocates because of the issues but they are important to arbitration because of their impact upon the finality of *all* awards.

There are three kinds of public policy cases. One set of cases began with the 1974 *Alexander v. Gardner-Denver* decision. These cases are concerned with employee grievance that also involve the equal employment opportunity (Title VII) laws, including sexual harassment. The second began with the 1987 *Misco* decision and it focuses on public safety and the criminal laws. The third kind consists of a number of diverse cases that are concerned with other policies such as the duty of fair representation, the Fair Labor Standards Act, or Constitutional considerations.

Title VII Cases. The principle that the courts enunciated in the early Title VII cases (*Gardner-Denver* and *Grace*) is clear: individuals may exercise a legal right based on external law that is independent of their rights under a collective bargaining agreement. An individual who takes a grievance to arbitration that involves an EEO matter could be entitled to a trial de novo if he or she loses in arbitration.

However, the 1991 *Gilmer* case could signal a new development. Mr. Gilmer was a securities representative who had signed an individual agreement to submit disputes arising out of his employment to arbitration. After he was terminated, he filed a claim in the courts under the Age Discrimination in Employment Act. Contrary to almost every previous decision involving the civil rights laws, the Supreme Court held that he was bound by his agreement to arbitrate unless he could show an inherent conflict between arbitration and the ADEA's underlying purposes. It should be noted that Mr. Gilmer was an intelligent, well educated, and highly paid individual who presumably understood the agreement which he voluntarily signed and that he was not covered by a collective bargaining agreement.

The public policy exception has lately been extended into the area of sexual harassment. In a number of recent cases, the circuit courts have quoted public policy extensively as they reexamine arbitration awards. (See *Newsday* and *Stroehmann*, below, where arbitration awards were set aside, and *Chrysler* where one was affirmed.)

Public Safety and Criminal Law. The courts appear to be less consistent in enforcing public policy in public safety and criminal law matters. The *Misco* case involved marijuana use, possession, and attendant safety concerns. The Supreme Court, citing the Trilogy at length, upheld the award that reinstated the grievant. In subsequent cases some courts have given priority to public policy and other courts have protected the finality of the arbitration award. See, for example, the contradictory decisions in two public safety cases involving airline pilots who had been discharged for piloting under the influence of identical levels of alcohol. The D.C. Circuit enforced an order of reinstatement in *Northwest Airlines* while the Eleventh Circuit set aside a similar order in *Delta Airlines.*

Other Areas. Public policy seems to prevail over arbitral finality in the remaining cases. The duty of fair representation, which is examined in selections 439 through 456, refers to a union's obligation to represent all members of the bargaining unit fairly. In *Hines* and *Bowen*, the courts have held that if a breach in this duty taints an arbitration award, the decision can be set aside and the person harmed can be compensated by the union and the employer. In matters involving the Fair Labor Standards Act (*Barrentine*), constitutional due process (*McDonald* and *Harding*, and State Workers Compensation statutes (*Lingle*), public policy has been enforced. Judicial review and the leading cases are discussed in entries 795 through 862 and the public policy exception in 863 through 884.

Bankruptcy and ERISA Cases

Bankruptcy courts are not required to defer to contractual labor arbitration provisions. When a company seeks protection under the Bankruptcy Code, the bankruptcy court traditionally permits the bargaining agreement to be rejected or modified unilaterally if it burdens the company. Current law has not modified this situation, although the employer who declares bankruptcy is required to deal with the union in good faith over the modifications of the bargaining agreement. An employer's duty to arbitrate in bankruptcy remains in effect unless the bankruptcy court has allowed the company to repudiate the contractual obligation; and the question of enforcement of awards seems to be in the province of the bankruptcy courts as well.

Most of the cases that confront arbitrators in ERISA matters include disputes between a plan (e.g. pension, severance pay, vacation pay, health insurance, retiree health care, apprenticeships) and its participants. In 1980, Congress enacted the Multi-Employer Pension Plan Amendments Act (MEPPAA). In order to ensure stability to these plans, Congress required continued payments by withdrawn employers, established standards to determine and compute liability, and required arbitration for the resolution of disputes.

But MEPPAA is a different kind of arbitration. The cases occur when an employer wishes to withdraw from a multi-employer plan and the law calls for an arbitrator to adjudicate the matter. The arbitrator is provided with criteria for evaluating liability and provision is made for challenging the award in the federal district court. If the award is challenged, the factual findings and conclusions of the arbitrator are presumed to be correct unless shown to be erroneous by a clear preponderance of the evidence. There are few arbitrations in this area but the cases that are heard typically involve large sums of money.

The presumption of arbitrability is not applicable in disputes between the contributors to the plan and the trustees, even if the disputes raise questions under the Collective Bargaining Agreement (CBA). In such cases the trustees are given a right of direct access to the courts. The law concerning arbitration of ERISA and multi-employer liability disputes is still evolving. Bankruptcy issues are discussed in entries 519 through 521 and ERISA and MEPPAA problems in 716 through 729.

Conclusions

In four cases decided between 1957 and 1960, the U.S. Supreme Court constructed a simple but extremely firm foundation for the practice of labor arbitration. Under these decisions, the arbitrator was the final judge of violations of the collective bargaining agreement. As long as the problem fell within the domain of the CBA, the award drew its essence from the contract, and the arbitrator remained true to his or her grant of authority under that agreement, the courts would enforce that award without even looking into its content.

The Extension of Arbitration. For many years this foundation remained intact despite repeated assaults. The first assault came in the enforcement area, but by 1972 it had become clear that the Supreme Court would enforce without question an arbitrator's award as long as the topic was arguably covered in the collective bargaining agreement. Since the 1960 decisions, furthermore, the reach of the arbitrator was extended by a number of developments. The NLRB established rules under which it would provide the arbitrator with unfair labor practice jurisdiction in certain cases; the courts ruled that the obligation to arbitrate could be extended beyond the life of the CBA and to a successor employer not named in the original agreement;

and Congress gave the arbitrator further powers in deciding cases that arose under multi-employer pension plans.

Where Other Laws Are Involved. Although the courts almost always enforce the arbitrator's award when it is challenged (Feuille et al., entries 815 and 816), there are presently two streams of attack on the authority of the arbitrator and the finality of the decision. The first has come in cases of concurrent jurisdiction—where other laws could claim the territory. A long string of cases has made it clear that the courts will not consider an arbitrator's decision as a bar to the individual's assertion of a statutory claim independent of the bargaining agreement, even if the provision in the agreement is similar to the statutory one. The *Gilmer* case stands for the proposition that an agreement to arbitrate all disputes requires the arbitration of claims based on statutes. But whether this case signals a change in the prevailing doctrine concerning statutory claims remains to be seen.

The courts have also determined that in cases involving bankruptcy law, an arbitration award has only the power that a bankruptcy court gives it. In ERISA cases, a trustee is able to avoid contractually mandated arbitration and the legislation that created an arbitration obligation in multi-employer withdrawal cases expressly provided for court review.

Finally, the prevailing legislation in the federal sector, the CSRA, expressly provides the parties with the ability to take exceptions to arbitration awards to the Federal Labor Relations Authority. In addition, the courts have shown themselves more than willing to look into the nature of the arbitrator's award, modify it where they found error or inconsistencies with federal rules and regulations, and establish decisional criteria.

From the Lower Courts. The second attack has come from the lower courts in matters involving public policy. Although the Supreme Court has used what seems to be clear language to define the "public policy exception" to the finality of arbitration awards, the lower courts have been inconsistent in applying the exception. In some cases, the courts have enforced the arbitrator's decision faithfully even when the award is suspect (e.g., when a postal employee was reinstated after firing gunshots at his supervisor's car), but in others the courts have shown themselves willing to embrace fairly vague public policies to vacate or modify an award. Perhaps the arbitrator's greatest power in these public policy cases comes from his or her fact finding role. The arbitrator's findings in this area are conclusive, that is, if the arbitrator finds that the employee is not guilty of alleged misconduct, the court will not set aside the award.

In sum, the simple but elegant structure created in *Lincoln Mills* and the *Steelworkers Trilogy* remains largely intact. But for those who believe that industrial peace is a legitimate goal of public policy and that final and binding arbitration awards contribute mightily to that peace, the decisions that have brought the courts into the review of the merits of those awards are indeed disturbing.

Annotations of the Leading Cases

The Foundation Cases

Textile Workers Union of America v. Lincoln Mills of Alabama, 353 U.S. 448, 77 S.Ct. 912 (1957). The union brought an action in the U.S. District Court for Northern Alabama seeking an order compelling arbitration of a grievance. The district court ordered the company to comply with the arbitration provisions, but the Fifth Circuit reversed on the grounds that under Alabama law an agreement to arbitrate future disputes was not arbitrable. The Supreme Court reversed, holding that Section 301 of the Labor Management Relations Act of 1947 (LMRA), which provides that suits for violation of contracts between an employer and a labor organization may be brought in a U.S. district court, authorizes federal courts to fashion a body of federal law for the enforcement of CBAs. Included within that federal law is provision for specific performance of arbitration provisions contained in CBAs. As mentioned earlier, *Lincoln Mills* was based upon the premise that agreements to arbitrate grievances are the quid pro quo for surrendering the right to strike.

United Steelworkers of America v. American Manufacturing Co., 363 U.S. 564, 80 S.Ct. 1343 (1960). The CBA contained a clause calling for the arbitration of all grievances. A partially disabled worker sought to return to work under the agreement. When the company refused, he sought arbitration, and the U.S. District Court for Eastern Tennessee refused to compel it. The Sixth Circuit affirmed, holding that the grievance was frivolous. The Supreme Court reversed, deciding that the courts below had erred in attempting to weigh the merits of the employee's claim. The arbitration clause called for submission of all grievances to arbitration, not just those a court would consider worthy.

United Steelworkers of America v. Warrior & Gulf Navigation Co., 363 U.S. 574, 80 S.Ct. 1347 (1960). The CBA provided for arbitration except for strictly management functions. The employees attempted to arbitrate a grievance over contracting out, the employer resisted, and the union brought a suit in the District Court for Southern Alabama. The district court dismissed the complaint, holding that the CBA did not permit arbitration of the employer's business judgment in contracting out work. The Fifth Circuit affirmed but the Supreme Court ordered arbitration, specifying that an order to arbitrate a grievance should not be denied unless it may be said with positive assurance that the arbitration clause is not susceptible of an interpretation that covers the asserted dispute (363 U.S. 582, 583). Doubts should be resolved in favor of coverage.

United Steelworkers of America v. Enterprise Wheel & Car Corp., 363 U.S. 593, 80 S.Ct. 1358 (1960). The CBA provided that the employer was obliged to reinstate and provide lost pay to any employee discharged in violation of the CBA. The union brought an action to compel the employer to arbitrate a grievance about the discharge of a group of workers who left their jobs to protest the discharge of another employee. The court ordered arbitration. After the agreement had expired, the arbitrator reinstated the workers with back pay. When the company refused to comply, the employees sought an enforcement order from the district court. That court directed the company to comply but the Fourth Circuit held that the arbitrator had no authority to award reinstatement or pay for the period after the CBA had expired.

The U.S. Supreme Court reversed, holding that the circuit court had exceeded its function. Although the arbitrator's opinion was ambiguous, it might have been based on his interpretation of the contractual provision requiring reinstatement with back pay. That the court might disagree with that interpretation is immaterial. The proper approach for the courts is to refuse to review the merits of arbitration awards under collective bargaining agreements.

Enforcement of the Agreement to Arbitrate

Sinclair Refining Co. v. Samuel M. Atkinson et al., 370 U.S. 195, 82 S.Ct. 1328 (1962). This opinion arose out of the same case as *Atkinson v. Sinclair,* which follows. In this part of the case, Sinclair sought to enjoin the union's violation of the no-strike clause in the bargaining agreement. The district court dismissed the claim and the Seventh Circuit affirmed. The Supreme Court held that Section 301 of the Labor Management Relations Act, which authorized suits against unions for contract violations, did *not* repeal the Norris-LaGuardia Act prohibition against labor injunctions. Sinclair's action for injunctive relief denied.

Samuel M. Atkinson v. Sinclair Refining Co., 370 U.S. 238, 82 S.Ct. 1318 (1962). In this part of the case, Sinclair sought damages for breach of the no-strike clause from the union and its officers. The district court dismissed the action against the individuals. The Seventh Circuit affirmed the refusal to dismiss against the union but reversed the dismissal against the individual defendants. The Supreme Court held that the officers of the union from which the employer sought damages for breach of a no-strike clause could not be held liable when the union was liable. In 1981, the Supreme Court held that individual employees could not be sued for damages for engaging in a strike not authorized by the union.

Drake Bakeries Inc. v. Local 50, American Bakery and Confectionery Workers International, AFL-CIO, 370 U.S. 254, 82 S.Ct. 1346 (1962). This case concerned another action by an employer for damages for breach of a no-strike clause. The district court ordered the action stayed until arbitration occurred, the employer appealed, and the Second Circuit affirmed. The Supreme Court held that the employer was required to arbitrate the claim against the union because the arbitration provision in the collective bargaining agreement included all complaints, disputes, or grievances and did not exclude claims for strikes.

The Boys Markets, Inc. v. Retail Clerks Union, Local 770, 398 U.S. 235, 90 S.Ct. 1583 (1970). The parties' agreement contained a no-strike clause and a provision for binding arbitration. The union called a strike instead of submitting a grievance to arbitration. The employer obtained a temporary restraining order from a state court prohibiting the strike. The union removed the case to the federal district court, which granted the employer's request for injunctive relief. The Ninth Circuit reversed, holding that under *Sinclair Refining v. Atkinson* (above), injunctive relief is precluded by the Norris-LaGuardia Act.

The Supreme Court reversed and held that the *Sinclair* case was overruled. The anti-injunction provisions of the Norris-LaGuardia Act did not preclude a federal district court from enjoining a strike in breach of a no-strike obligation as long as the bargaining agreement provided for binding arbitration of the grievance that led to the strike.

Buffalo Forge Co. v. United Steelworkers of America, AFL-CIO, et al., 428 U.S. 397, 96 S.Ct. 3141 (1976). Buffalo Forge Company's office and clerical-technical employees went on strike and picketed the company's plants. The company's production and maintenance employees honored their picket lines and stopped work. The company filed suit, claiming that the production and maintenance employees' work stoppage violated the contractual no-strike clause and that the question was arbitrable under that contract. The company sought damages, injunctive relief, and an order directing the union tn arbitrate such questions.

The district court held that the Norris-LaGuardia Act prohibited it from issuing an injunction because the sympathy strike was not an arbitrable grievance. The matter did not fall within the exception established in *Boys Markets*. The court of appeals and the Supreme Court affirmed. The Supreme Court distinguished *Boys Markets* by stating that the strike was not over any dispute subject to the arbitration provisions of the agreement.

Arbitrability

AT&T Technologies Inc. v. Communications Workers of America, 475 U.S. 643, 106 S.Ct. 1415 (1986). The pertinent bargaining agreement had an arbitration clause, a management functions clause, and a clause prescribing the order in which employees would be laid off. The company laid off certain employees and refused to submit a union grievance to arbitration because the management functions clause made the layoffs nonarbitrable. On appeal from the union, the district court ordered arbitration of the layoff issue. The company appealed this decision and the court of appeals affirmed, finding that the district court decision had ordered arbitration of the threshold issue of arbitrability. The Supreme Court reversed, holding that it was for a court, not an arbitrator, to decide whether parties to a collective bargaining agreement intended to arbitrate a substantive contractual issue, unless the parties unmistakably proved otherwise. But if the court determines that the issue is arbitrable, the arbitrator decides the merits. Issues of procedural arbitrability, however, are to be decided by the arbitrator.

Local 106, Service Employees' International Union, AFL-CIO v. Evergreen Cemetery, 708 F.Supp. 917 (ND Ill. 1989). In this case the union demanded arbitration of two grievances. The first dealt with whether a nonbargaining unit employee could be assigned to production work, and the second concerned whether the employer was obligated to fill a position of working foreman. The employer contended that the arbitration provision did not cover these disputes. The district court granted the union's motion to compel arbitration, holding that the only issue was whether the parties had agreed to arbitrate the two grievances. Because the CBA defined a grievance as "a claim or dispute concerning rates of pay, hours, or working conditions, or the interpretation or an application of the terms of the agreement," the court found for the union. For related cases, see *Bechtel Construction, Inc. v. Laborers International Union of North America, AFL-CIO*, 812 F.2d 750 (1st Cir. 1987) and *Borden Inc. v. American Arbitration Association; Retail Wholesale Department Store Union, Local 1034, AFL-CIO*, 677 F.Supp. 248 (D. Del. 1988).

Postcontract Arbitrability

Nolde Brothers, Inc. v. Local No. 358, Bakery and Confectionery Workers Union, AFL-CIO, 430 U.S. 243, 97 S.Ct. 1067 (1977). The Nolde Brothers Corporation entered into a CBA that contained one provision for severance pay on termination of employment and another clause that rendered any grievance arising between the parties subject to arbitration. Negotiations failed and the company notified the union that it was closing its plant. The company paid accrued wages but refused the union's demand for severance pay under the CBA. The company also declined to arbitrate the claim for severance pay on the ground that its obligation to do so terminated with the CBA.

The union brought suit in the U.S. District Court to compel the company to arbitrate the severance pay issue. The district court rejected this demand, holding that the employees' right to severance pay expired with the CBA along with the duty to arbitrate. The Fourth Circuit reversed, concluding that the parties' duty to arbitrate under the contract survived its termination with respect to claims arising under the CBA.

On appeal the Supreme Court held that the union's claim for severance pay under the expired contract is subject to resolution under the contract's arbitration clause. The arbitration clause may survive the termination of the CBA when the dispute is over an obligation created by the expired CBA. The parties clearly expressed their preference for an arbitral rather than judicial interpretation of their obligations. When the dispute is over a provision of the expired CBA, the presumption favoring arbitration must be negated expressly or by clear implication.

Litton Financial Printing Division v. National Labor Relations Board, 111 S.Ct. 2215, 115 L.Ed. 2d 177 (1991). The *Litton* agreement involved an expired CBA, a company decision to lay off a number of workers, a refusal to arbitrate the issue, and an NLRB decision which held that the unilateral postexpiration abandonment of the contractual grievance procedures violated the NLRA. The Board ordered Litton to bargain with the union over the layoffs but refused to order arbitration of the layoff disputes because they did not arise under the expired contract.

The court of appeals enforced the Board's order, adding that the layoff disputes did arise under the agreement and were arbitrable. The Supreme Court held that the layoff dispute was not arbitrable. The Court determined that it would not impose a statutory duty to arbitrate disputes that arise after the termination of a bargaining agreement except where the grievance involves facts and occurrences that occurred before expiration, where the action infringes a right that accrued or vested under the agreement, or the normal principles of contract interpretation indicate that the disputed contractual right survives expiration of the rest of the agreement.

The Successor Employer's Duty to Arbitrate

John Wiley and Sons, Inc. v. David Livingston, 376 U.S. 543, 84 S.Ct. 909 (1964). The union had entered into a CBA with Interscience Publishers. The agreement did not contain any provision making it binding on successor companies, and during its term, Interscience merged with another publisher, John Wiley, and ceased to do business. Wiley refused to recognize the union or to accede to its claims on behalf of Interscience employees. The union brought suit to compel arbitration of the claims under the CBA with Interscience. The district court denied the union's request; the court of appeals reversed; and on Wiley's appeal the Supreme Court held that the corporate employer was required to arbitrate with the union under the agreement between the union and another corporation.

NLRB v. Burns International Security Services, 406 U.S. 272, 92 S.Ct. 1571 (1972). Eight years later, the U.S. Supreme Court dealt again with the issue of the successor employer. Although the obligation to arbitrate did not enter into this case, the principle that it enunciated affects arbitration in successorship cases. The successor employer (Burns) had hired 27 of the predecessor's employees to staff a 42-person unit. The Court held that where the bargaining unit remained unchanged and a majority of the employees hired by the new employer were represented by the predecessor's union, the employer was obligated to bargain with that union. The successor employer, however, was not bound by the substantive terms of the prior CBA.

Howard Johnson Co. v. Detroit Local Joint Executive Board, 417 U.S. 210, 94 S.Ct. 2236 (1974). The company was purchased by new owners under an agreement expressly providing that the new owners did not assume any of the seller's obligations, including a CBA. The company hired 45 new employees and retained only 9 of the former employees. The union brought suit to compel arbitration under the CBA.

The district court held that the company was required to arbitrate, the court of appeals affirmed, but the Supreme Court reversed. The Supreme Court distinguished this case from *Wiley* by pointing out that there was no substantial continuity of identity in the work force hired by the new owners of the company. Further, the Supreme Court found no express or implied assumption of the agreement to arbitrate.

Fall River Dyeing and Finishing Corp. v. NLRB, 482 U.S. 27, 107 S.Ct. 2225 (1987). The predecessor employer laid off all of its production workers and went out of business. A former officer of the company formed the Fall River Corporation, acquired the company, and began to operate. When Fall River refused the union's request for bargaining even though a majority of the employees came from the predecessor, the union filed an unfair labor practice charge. The NLRB concluded that Fall River was a successor employer and ordered bargaining. The First Circuit enforced the order and the Supreme Court affirmed. Although the new employer is not bound by the substantive provisions of the predecessor's CBA, it has an obligation to bargain with the union so long as it is a successor to the old employer and the majority of its employees were employed by its predecessor. Substantial continuity existed between the old and new companies.

Deferral Cases
Pre-Arbitration Deferral

Collyer Insulated Wire, 192 NLRB 837 (1971). This case considered pre-arbitration deferral. It arose from a charge of refusal to bargain over an alleged unilateral change in the workday. The Board ruled that it would require exhaustion of the grievance procedure, including arbitration, before it would consider unfair labor practice (ULP) claims provided: (1) there was a long-standing bargaining relationship; (2) there was no enmity by the employer toward the employees; (3) the employer was willing to arbitrate; (4) the arbitration clause covered the dispute; and (5) the contract and its meaning lay at the center of the dispute. The NLRB has extended this doctrine many times as in *National Radio Co.*, 198 NLRB 527 (1072), and *United Technologies Corp.*, 268 NLRB 557 (1984).

Paul Hammontree v. National Labor Relations Board, 894 F.2d 438 (D.C. Cir. 1990) (rehearing en banc granted March 30, 1990). 925 F.2d 1486 (D.C. Cir. 1991) (argued en banc December 12, 1990, decided February 12, 1991). Mr. Hammontree challenged a National Labor Relations Board order that required him to exhaust his grievance remedies before the Board would consider his ULP complaint. He contended that this exhaustion requirement was inconsistent with the NLRB's authority under the NLRA and the LMRA. The U.S. Circuit Court of Appeals found that both acts permitted the NLRB to require an employee to exhaust grievance remedies before filing ULP charges and that the NLRB's order was reasonable and consistent with its established practices. The Circuit Court denied Hammontree's petition for review.

Postarbitration Deferral

Spielberg Mfg. Co., 112 NLRB 1080 (1955). The NLRB ruled that it would defer to an arbitrator's resolution of ULP claims if certain conditions were met. These conditions, as refined in a series of cases, indicate that the Board's policy is to defer if (1) the ULP issue was presented to and considered by the arbitrator; (2) the arbitration proceedings were fair and regular; (3) the parties agreed to be bound by the award; and (4) the award was not clearly repugnant to the purposes and policies of the NLRA. In *Olin Corp.*, 268 NLRB 573 (1984), the NLRB concluded that it would find that an arbitrator has adequately considered ULP issues if (1) the contractual issue is factually parallel to the statutory issue; and (2) the arbitrator was presented with the facts relevant to resolving the ULP.

In *Darr v. National Labor Relations Board*, 801 F.2d 1404 (D.C. Cir. 1986), Marie Darr petitioned for review of an NLRB decision which deferred to an arbitrator's decision that awarded reinstatement without back pay as a remedy for her discharge. The case is significant in that it offers four ideas in support of the Board's postarbitration deferral policies: (1) collateral estoppel, which is based on the concept that the NLRA issue is sufficiently close to the contract question as to have been fully litigated; (2) that the NLRB's role in reviewing the case is the same as that of an appellate body reviewing an arbitrator's application of the NLRA as incorporated in the CBA; (3) deference to a contract interpretation upon which the application of the NLRA depends; and (4) that the parties have waived the statutory rights that the Board is empowered to enforce and rely on a different body of contract law.

After analyzing the ideas, the court stated that if an arbitrator holds that the parties agreed to incorporate the NLRA by reference (rather than waive it) it might follow that the arbitrator gains authority to apply the act. The court further stated that if the Board proceeds under such theory, it must determine that the arbitrator has in fact so held. Because the basis for the Board's action was not apparent, the court remanded the case to the NLRB for further consideration.

Enforcement of the Arbitration Award

The "Essence Test"

American Postal Workers Union v. United States Postal Service, 789 F.2d 1 (D.C. Cir. 1986). The union brought a grievance on behalf of an employee who was removed from his position for alleged wrongful conversion of funds. Although the employee had implicated himself in statements given to the Postal Inspection Service, he was acquitted in a criminal trial because the investigator had failed to give the required *Miranda* warnings. The issue went to arbitration and the arbitrator ruled that just cause for dismissal was absent. Some disciplinary action was necessary because the employee failed to follow postal regulations. The arbitrator, thus, reduced the discharge to a disciplinary suspension.

The union brought an action in the U.S. District Court to enforce the award. The district court denied the union's motion and the union appealed. The court of appeals upheld the arbitrator's decision, finding that it drew its essence from the CBA; an alleged mistake of law (i.e., misapplication of the *Miranda* warnings) does not alter the standard of review; the Postal Service's argument of an alternative reading of the contract was meritless; and there was no violation of public policy in the reinstatement of this postal worker.

The Delta Queen Steamboat Co. v. District 2, Marine Engineers Beneficial Assoc., 889 F.2d 599 (5th Cir. 1989). The captain of the *Mississippi Queen* had his employment terminated after a near collision between his vessel and a tow of river barges. The union grieved and the matter proceeded to arbitration. The bargaining agreement specifically listed carelessness as a basis for discharge and the arbitrator found the captain to be "grossly careless." However, the arbitrator also concluded that the captain was the victim of disparate company discipline and ordered him reinstated as a pilot.

The company appealed the decision to the U.S. District Court, challenging the *contractual* authority of the arbitrator to order reinstatement after finding gross carelessness. The court agreed and vacated the reinstatement order. On appeal, the Fifth Circuit, citing *Enterprise Wheel*, concluded that once the captain was found to be grossly careless, the arbitrator was without authority under the CBA to reinstate him. The arbitrator's jurisdiction is shaped by the CBA but when he exceeds the limitations of the contractual mandate, judicial deference is at an end.

Morton M. Hill, Jr. v. Norfolk and Western Railway Co., 814 F.2d 1192 (7th Cir. 1987). The plaintiff was a brakeman fired by the Norfolk and Western railroad for possession of marijuana. He took the case to arbitration before a public law board. When the board unanimously rejected his claim, he brought suit in the U.S. District Court to set aside the decision and the court ruled against him.

The Seventh Circuit affirmed the ruling. When a federal court is asked to set aside an arbitration award, the question is not whether the arbitrator erred in interpreting the contract, it is whether the arbitrator interpreted the contract. If the arbitrator interpreted the contract, the interpretation is conclusive. By agreeing to an arbitration clause, the parties agree to be bound by the arbitrator's interpretation. The court also sanctioned appellant's counsel for filing an appeal on frivolous grounds.

Polk Brothers, Inc. v. Chicago Truck Drivers, Helpers and Warehouse Workers Union, 973 F.2d 593 (7th Cir. 1992). Because its distribution center was destroyed by fire, the company laid off 163 employees and contracted out warehousing and delivery services. The union grieved, claiming that the decision to contract out violated the terms of three collective bargaining agreements. These agreements were scheduled to terminate on March 31, 1988, and in April an arbitrator issued an award that reinstated the employees with back pay.

The company challenged the remedy awarded by the arbitrator beyond the termination date of the CBAs. The U.S. District Court found that the arbitrator exceeded his authority in awarding benefits after that date and- the Seventh Circuit affirmed. The CBAs did not allow the arbitrator to award reinstatement beyond the contractual termination date. Citing the "essence" test from *Enterprise Wheel*, the court stated that if the arbitrator's words manifest infidelity to the CBA, the courts must decline to enforce the award.

Enforcement of Arbitration Awards in the Federal Government

Donald J. Devine, Director, Office of Personnel Management v. Joseph M. Pastore, Jr., National Treasury Employees Union, and James Estrella, 732 F.2d 213 (1984). A customs inspector had been removed from his position for theft of merchandise. The inspector was observed removing a shirt from a cargo area and placing it in his car. The union invoked arbitration and the arbitrator found that while the customs agent had placed the shirt in his car, his removal was not consistent with the contractual policies of progressive discipline in the collective agreement. The arbitrator reduced the agent's discipline to a 31-day suspension.

The U.S. Court of Appeals found that the arbitrator erred in substituting his idea of an appropriate penalty for that of the agency. The court also found that the arbitrator may have committed a second error by considering only the disciplinary factors set forth in the labor contract to the exclusion of other factors permitted by federal personnel law. The case was remanded to the arbitrator.

Loretta Cornelius, Acting Director, Office of Personnel Management v. Allison E. Nutt, 472 U.S. 648, 105 S.Ct. 2882 (1985). A federal employee represented by a labor union may challenge disciplinary action either by appealing to the Merit Systems Protection Board (MSPB) or through the contractual grievance procedure. Two bargaining unit employees of the General Services Administration (GSA) were removed from their jobs for falsification of records and other reasons.

The employees challenged their removal under the grievance and arbitration procedures of the union contract. The arbitrator stated that the wrongdoing normally would justify removal, but he also found that the GSA had committed a number of procedural errors (including failure to provide union representation during interrogation). Although the errors did not prejudice the case, the arbitrator concluded that the removals were not for just cause and he reduced the penalties to two weeks' suspension without pay.

The court of appeals affirmed with modification but the Supreme Court reversed. Under the provisions of the Civil Service Reform Act, arbitrators must use the same interpretation as the MSPB in reviewing a disciplinary action. The grievant must show that the error caused substantial prejudice to the grievant's rights and affected the agency's decision.

The Public Policy Exception

Title VII Cases

Harrell Alexander, Sr. v. Gardner-Denver Co., 415 U.S. 36, 94 S.Ct. 101 (1974). After the plaintiff, an African-American employee, was discharged, he filed a grievance under a bargaining agreement that contained a nondiscrimination clause. Prior to arbitration, he also filed a racial discrimination complaint that was referred to the Equal Employment Opportunity Commission (EEOC). The arbitrator ruled that the petitioner's discharge was for cause and the EEOC determined that there was no reasonable ground to believe that a violation of Title VII of the Civil Rights Act had occurred. Alexander then brought an action in the U.S. District Court alleging that his discharge resulted from a racially discriminatory employment practice.

The district court held that the petitioner was bound by the prior arbitral decision and had no right to sue under Title VII. The court of appeals affirmed, but the Supreme Court reversed, holding that an employee's statutory right to trial de novo under Title VII is not foreclosed by prior submission of his claim to final arbitration.

From the standpoint of arbitration, footnote 21 in the decision is its most controversial element because it specifically raises the specter of judicial review. The Court said that:

> We adopt no standards as to the weight to be accorded an arbitration decision, since this must be determined in the court's discretion with regard to the facts and circumstances of each case. Where an arbitral determination gives full consideration to the employee's Title VII rights, a court may properly accord it great weight. This is especially true where the issue is one of fact, specifically addressed by the parties and decided by the arbitrator on the basis of an adequate record. But courts should ever be mindful that Congress thought it necessary to provide a judicial forum for the resolution of discriminatory employment claims. It is the duty of the courts to assure the full availability of this forum (415 U.S. 36, 60 [October 1973]).

W. R. Grace and Co. v. Local Union 759, International Union of the United Rubber, Cork, Linoleum and Plastic Workers of America, 461 U.S. 757, 103, S.Ct.

2177 (1983). The employer signed a conciliation agreement with the EEOC that conflicted with the seniority provisions of an existing CBA. The union was not part of the EEOC agreement. On the basis of this agreement, the employer sued in district court to enjoin the arbitration of grievances over layoffs under the CBA. The district court held that the conciliation agreement should prevail, but the court of appeals reversed and compelled the employer to arbitrate. The arbitrator awarded back pay damages, holding that the district court's order did not extinguish the employer's liability for breach of the collective bargaining agreement.

After further appeals and reversals, the Supreme Court held that the arbitrator's award was to be enforced. A federal court may not overrule an arbitrator's decision simply because it believes its own interpretation of the contract would be better. Enforcement of the contract as interpreted by the arbitrator will not compromise the public policy requiring obedience to a court order. The employer was cornered by its own action and cannot now argue that liability under the CBA violates public policy.

The Court defined the meaning of public policy in this case—"such a public policy is to be ascertained by reference to the laws and legal precedents and not from general considerations of supposed public interests." The public policy must be "well defined and dominant."

Robert D. Gilmer v. Interstate/Johnson Lane Corp., 111 S.Ct. 1647 (1991). Robert Gilmer was required by his employer to register as a securities representative with various stock exchanges including the New York Exchange. His registration application contained an agreement to arbitrate any controversy arising out of employment or its termination. When Gilmer's employer terminated his employment at age 62, he filed an age discrimination charge with the EEOC and brought suit in the district court. His employer moved to compel arbitration, relying on the agreement in Gilmer's registration application. The district court denied the motion based on *Gardner-Denver* and the Fourth Circuit reversed.

The Supreme Court held that statutory claims under the Age Discrimination in Employment Act (ADEA) may be subject to the arbitration agreement and enforced under the provisions of the Federal Arbitration Act of 1925. Since neither the text nor the legislative history of the ADEA explicitly precludes arbitration, Gilmer is bound by his agreement to arbitrate unless he can show an inherent conflict between arbitration and the ADEA's underlying purposes. The Court dismissed Gilmer's reliance on the *Gardner-Denver* line because those cases occurred in the context of a bargaining agreement rather than an individual employment contract and because those cases were not decided under the Federal Arbitration Act.

Sexual Harassment Cases

Newsday, Inc. v. Long Island Typographical Union, No. 915, CWA, AFL-CIO, 915 F.2d 840 (2d Cir. 1990). Newsday attempted to vacate an award issued by a labor arbitrator that ordered the reinstatement of an employee who had been discharged for sexually harassing female coworkers. Newsday sought vacatur on three grounds: the award offended the well-defined public policy against sexual harassment in the workplace; it exceeded the limits of the arbitrator's authority; and it failed to draw its essence from the parties' agreement. The district court granted Newsday's motion and the Second Circuit Court of Appeals affirmed. The circuit court concluded that the district court had properly vacated the arbitrator's award as violating the explicit, well-defined, and dominant public policy against sexual harassment in the workplace.

Chrysler Motors Corp. v. International Union, Allied Industrial Workers of America, AFL-CIO, 959 F.2d 685 (7th Cir. 1992). A male forklift operator was discharged by Chrysler Motors after he sexually assaulted a female coworker (grabbed her breasts). The union filed a grievance, which Chrysler denied, and the matter proceeded to arbitration. The arbitrator rejected evidence that the worker had harassed females in the past because it was acquired after the discharge. He further found that the evidence supporting the discharge did not indicate that he could not be rehabilitated. The arbitrator determined that severe discipline short of discharge would be adequate to deter him from future misbehavior and show Chrysler's opposition to sexual harassment. On this basis, the arbitrator determined that the worker was not discharged for "good cause," reduced the penalty to suspension for 30 days, and directed Chrysler to reinstate the worker with back pay.

Both parties sought summary judgment in the U.S. District Court, but the court affirmed the arbitration award and ordered its enforcement. On appeal, the Seventh Circuit affirmed the district court's ruling because the arbitrator's decision was within the purview of the collective bargaining agreement and public policy. While recognizing the public policy against sexual harassment in the workplace, the court of appeals cited *Misco* for the proposition "where it is contemplated that the arbitrator will determine remedies for contract violations that he finds, courts have no authority to disagree with his honest judgment in that respect" (484 U.S. at 38, 108 S.Ct. at 371).

Stroehmann Bakeries Inc. v. Local 776, International Brotherhood of Teamsters, 969 F.2d 1436 (3d Cir. 1992), cert. denied, December 7, 1992. Stroehmann Bakeries discharged a worker for "immoral conduct" after a customer reported him for sexual harassment. The case progressed to arbitration and the arbitrator reinstated the worker with back pay because the company had not given him a full opportunity to refute the charge or explain his conduct.

The employer brought an action in the U.S. District Court challenging the reinstatement. The court concluded that the arbitrator's award violated public policy against sexual harassment, vacated the award, and remanded the matter to a different arbitrator. The Third Circuit affirmed, holding that an arbitrator's award reinstating an employee accused of sexual harassment without a determination regarding the merits of the allegation violates well-established and dominant public policies.

Public Safety and the Criminal Law

United Paperworkers International Union, AFL-CIO et al. v. Misco, Inc., 484 U.S. 29, 108 S.Ct. 364 (1987). One of Misco's work rules listed as cause for discharge the possession or use of controlled substances on company property. An employee covered by the agreement was apprehended by police in the backseat of someone else's car on the company parking lot. There was marijuana smoke in the air of the car and a lighted marijuana cigarette in the front seat ashtray. A police search of the employee's own car on the lot revealed marijuana gleanings.

Management discharged the employee for violation of the disciplinary rule. The employee grieved and an arbitrator later upheld the grievance and ordered reinstatement. The arbitrator concluded that the cigarette incident was insufficient proof that he was using or possessed marijuana on company property. At the time of discharge the company was not aware of the fact that marijuana was found in the employee's own car, so the arbitrator refused to accept this fact into evidence.

The district court vacated the arbitration award and the court of appeals affirmed, ruling that reinstatement would violate the public policy against the operation of dangerous machinery by persons under the influence of drugs. The Supreme Court reversed, holding that the court of appeals exceeded the limited authority possessed by a court reviewing an arbitrator's award under a CBA. Absent fraud by the parties or the arbitrator's dishonesty, reviewing courts in such cases are not authorized to reconsider the merits of the award. The high court also stated that the CBA left evidentiary matters to the arbitrator: the arbitrator's finding of fact is conclusive. A court's refusal to enforce an arbitrator's interpretation of a CBA is limited to the situations outlined in *Grace*, where the interpretation would violate some explicit public policy that is well defined and dominant and is to be ascertained by reference to laws and legal precedents and not from general considerations of supposed public interests.

Iowa Electric Light and Power Co. v. Local Union 204 of the International Brotherhood of Electrical Workers, 834 F.2d 1424 (8th Cir. 1987). The company appealed a labor arbitrator's award calling for reinstatement of a nuclear power plant machinist who had been discharged for deliberately violating federally mandated safety regulations. The employee had a cast on his leg and, to facilitate leaving his work station for lunch, he defied the control room engineer and defeated the plant's interlock system by opening a secured door.

The arbitration case turned on just-cause considerations. The arbitrator found that the employee's act was "deliberate, improper, foolish, and thoughtless," but termination was too severe and not justified under the total circumstances of the case. The district court vacated the award on public policy grounds and the union appealed. The Eighth Circuit held that public policy precluded enforcement of the arbitrator's award. Citing *Grace,* the court stated that if a CBA, as interpreted by the arbitrator, violates some explicit public policy, the court must not enforce the award. Once the public policy issue is raised, the court must take the facts as found by the arbitrator but it must also review the conclusions de novo. The court also held that it is not required to find that the award itself is illegal before overturning the arbitrator on public policy grounds.

Northwest Airlines, Inc. v. Air Lines Pilots Assoc., 808 F.2d 76 (D.C. Cir. 1987) and *Delta Air Lines, Inc. v. Air Lines Pilots Assoc.,* 861 F.2d 665 (11th Cir. 1988). These two cases involve the discharge of airline pilots for flying while under the influence of alcohol. In each case the pilot's blood alcohol level was .13 percent and the state law had established .10 percent as creating a presumption of intoxication.

In *Northwest,* the grievant was the copilot of the plane. An arbitration board found his discharge to be without just cause because he was an alcoholic. The board ruled that he should be offered reinstatement without back pay or benefits upon certification by the Federal Air Surgeon that he had recovered from the effects of his alcoholism, including total abstinence for two years. The pilot completed the program and when he was recertified by the FAA, the airline filed a complaint in the district court seeking to set aside the arbitration award. The court issued a summary judgment for Northwest, finding that the Board's award was inconsistent with public policy. But the D.C. Circuit reversed, holding that the lower court had no valid basis for setting aside the award and that the lower court's decision was at odds with *American Postal Workers Union v. United States Postal Service,* reported above.

In *Delta,* the pilot was a pilot-in-command. The board of arbitration did not find just cause for the discharge. It ordered reinstatement and required the airline to pay the costs of private alcohol rehabilitation. The district court overturned the award and the Eleventh Circuit agreed. While upholding that portion of the award that required the airline to pay for the rehabilitation, the court held that the board's decision on just cause violated clearly established public policy and could not be enforced.

Stead Motors of Walnut Creek v. Automotive Machinists Lodge No. 1173, I.A.M. 843 F.2d 357 (9th Cir. 1988) argued en banc 886 F.2d 1200 (9th Cir. 1989). A mechanic had been given a written warning for improperly tightening lug bolts while installing a wheel. About a year later another customer reported wheel vibration and an examination revealed loose and/or missing lug bolts on both front tires. The same mechanic had worked on both cars and he was fired for recklessness. The employee grieved and the case came to arbitration.

The arbitrator found that the employee indeed had been reckless but because he felt that discharge was too severe, he reduced the penalty to a 120-day suspension. Stead Motors moved to vacate and the U.S. District Court voided the reinstatement order because it was against public policy. On appeal, the Ninth Circuit sustained the lower court's ruling. However, on rehearing, en banc, the Court held that the arbitrator's award did not violate explicit, well-defined, and dominant California public policy and his award would be upheld.

United States Postal Service v. National Association of Letter Carriers, AFL-CIO, 839 F.2d 146 (3d Cir. 1988). The union appealed a district court ruling that reversed an arbitration award reinstating a postal worker who had fired gunshots at his postmaster's empty parked car. The arbitrator had weighed the single offense against the employee's 13-year record and determined that the CBA required a lesser penalty. On appeal, the U.S. District Court reasoned that the arbitrator's award contravened public policy in that there is an indisputable public policy against permitting an employee to direct physical violence at a superior. The Third Circuit reversed, citing the *Misco* standard of review and concluded that the district court exceeded the scope of its reviewing authority.

Because the parties have contracted to have disputes settled by an arbitrator, it is the arbitrator's view of the facts and the meaning of the contract that they have agreed to accept. The court also dismissed the idea that because the Postal Service is a public employer there was an alternate basis for enlarging the reviewing authority of the court.

Russell Memorial Hospital Association v. United Steelworkers of America, 720 F.Supp. 583 (E.D. Mich. 1989). The employer discharged a licensed practical nurse for negligence in administering medication. The union grieved her discharge under the union contract, and an arbitrator ruled in favor of the union and ordered the nurse's reinstatement with full seniority rights but without back pay. The hospital filed suit to vacate the award, contending that enforcement would violate public policy. The U.S. District Court concluded that enforcement of the arbitration award would violate established Michigan public policy (ensuring safe and competent nursing care) and granted the hospital's motion to vacate the award.

Other Public Policy Cases: Duty of Fair Representation

Charles A. Hines v. Anchor Motor Freight, Inc., 424 U. 554, 96 S.Ct. 1048 (1976). The petitioners were discharged by the employer for filing false expense vouchers. The union claimed that they were innocent, opposed the dismissal, and submitted the matter to an arbitration committee, which upheld the discharges. But when subsequent information indicated that the charges of dishonesty might have been false, the grievants brought a wrongful-discharge suit against the employer and union under Section 301 of the Labor Management Relations Act. They claimed that the falsity of the charges could have been discovered with a minimum of investigation. Because the union made no effort to ascertain the truth, it violated its duty of fair representation.

Although the district court granted summary judgment for the union, the court of appeals concluded that there were sufficient facts to infer bad faith or arbitrary conduct on the union's part and that the grievants should have been given opportunity to prove their charges. The court of appeals reversed the summary judgment in favor of the union but it upheld the judgment as to the employer on the ground that the finality provision of the CBA had to be observed unless evidence showed misconduct by the employer or a conspiracy between it and the union.

The Supreme Court held that it was improper to dismiss the suit against the employer. If the petitioners prove a wrongful discharge and the union's breach of the duty of fair representation, they are entitled to an appropriate remedy against both offenders. The union's failure to represent fairly relieves the employee of any requirement that disputes be settled through contractual mechanisms and, if the integrity of the arbitral process is seriously undermined, it affects the finality of the arbitrator's decision.

Charles V. Bowen v. United States Postal Service et al., 492 U.S. 412, 103 S.Ct. 588 (1983). Mr. Bowen was discharged as a result of an altercation with another employee. He filed a grievance and, when the union declined to take the case to arbitration, he sued both the Postal Service and the union in the U.S. District Court. The court held that the discharge had been without just cause, held that the union had handled his grievance in an arbitrary manner, and divided the damages between the Postal Service and the union. The Fourth Circuit affirmed except for the award of damages against the union. The Supreme Court held that where an employee proves that his employer violated a bargaining agreement and the union breached its duty of fair representation, liability is to be apportioned between the employer and the union according to the damages caused by the fault of each.

Terry Alford et al. v. General Motors Corp., 926 F.2d 528 (6th Cir. 1991). The plaintiffs were employed by General Motors as temporary security guards and they were members of the security guards' bargaining unit. They brought suit against the company for its failure to offer them permanent positions and against their union for failing to give them fair representation. The suits were filed in a state court, but were removed to the U.S. District Court. The district court dismissed the suits and the plaintiffs appealed. The Sixth Circuit affirmed, holding that the grievance procedures in the CBA were final and exclusive. Having had their claims resolved under such agreement, the plaintiffs could not maintain a direct action against General Motors for breach of contract.

The FLSA, the Constitution, and Tort Claims

Lloyd Barrentine et al. v. Arkansas-Best Freight System, Inc. et al., 450 U.S. 728, 101 S.Ct. 1437 (1981). The employees submitted a wage claim for time spent on pretrip inspection and transportation of their vehicles to a repair facility. The claims were submitted to a joint grievance committee and the committee rejected them without explanation. The petitioners filed an action in the district court alleging that the claims were compensable under the Fair Labor Standards Act (FLSA). Further, they claimed the union breached its duty of fair representation.

The district court addressed only the fair representation claim and rejected it. The Eighth Circuit affirmed and also concluded that the petitioners' voluntary submission of their grievances to arbitration barred them from asserting their FLSA claims in a subsequent court action. The Supreme Court reversed, holding that FLSA rights are independent of the collective bargaining process. Such rights devolve on petitioners as individual workers, not as members of the union, and cannot be waived. While courts should defer to an arbitrator's decision where the employee's claim is based on rights arising out of a labor contract, different considerations apply when the claim is based on rights arising out of a statute designed to provide minimum substantive guarantees to individual workers.

Gary McDonald v. City of West Branch, Michigan, 466 U.S. 284, 104 S.Ct. 1799 (1984). The petitioner was discharged from the city police force and filed a grievance contending that there was no proper cause for his discharge. The grievance was taken to arbitration and the arbitrator denied it, finding just cause. The grievant did not appeal the arbitration decision but filed an action in federal district court. The jury returned a verdict against the chief of police but the court of appeals reversed, holding that petitioner's claims were barred because they had been resolved in arbitration. The Supreme Court reversed, holding that a federal court should not afford res judicata or collateral estoppel effect to an award in an arbitration under a collective bargaining agreement. Where the claim is based on an independent statutory right, the claimant may proceed to perfect such right through judicial channels.

John W. Harding, Larry J. Williams, and Robert A. Goff v. United States Postal Service, 802 F.2d 766 (1986). The appellants were former postal employees who challenged their discharge for filing false injury compensation claims (the second appellant was also discharged for failing to meet the physical requirements of his position). Their discharges were upheld in arbitration. They filed suit alleging lack of due process under the Constitution. The U.S. District Court dismissed their claims, concluding that a constitutional remedy was not available to them because they had other procedures available for redress. They had arbitrated their claims under the collective bargaining agreement and they could also have used administrative remedies under federal law. The Fourth Circuit affirmed, holding that the grievance cannot seek to bring a private cause of action against the postal service for alleged constitutional violations connected with their discharges.

Lingle v. Norge Division of Magic Chef, Inc., 486 U.S. 399, 108 S.Ct. 1877 (1988). Lingle was discharged for filing a false worker's compensation claim. The union grieved and, while arbitration was proceeding, the employee filed a retaliatory discharge action in Illinois state court. The employer removed the suit to the federal district court and filed a motion to dismiss the case as pre-preempted by Section 301 of the Labor Management Relations Act (LMRA).

The district court dismissed the complaint, holding that the claim was arbitrable under the collective agreement and that the state law action would undermine the arbitration procedures in that contract. The Seventh Circuit affirmed, but the Supreme Court reversed, holding that the application of the employee's state tort remedy was not preempted by the LMRA.

The application of state law is preempted by Section 301 only if it requires the interpretation of a bargaining agreement. Under Illinois law, in cases of retaliatory discharge for abuse of worker's compensation, the employee must show that the employer's motive for the discharge was to deter the employee from exercising rights under the Workers Compensation Act. Because these elements do not require interpretation of the CBA, the claim is independent of the agreement for section 301 preemption purposes. The interpretation of collective agreements remains firmly in the arbitral realm and judges can only determine questions of state law if such questions do not require construing bargaining agreements.

Specialized Areas: Bankruptcy and ERISA

NLRB v. Bildisco and Bildisco, 465 U.S. 513, 104 S.Ct. 1188 (1984). The Bankruptcy Code provides that a trustee may assume or reject the debtor's executory contracts. Bildisco, a building supplies distributor, had filed for reorganization under Chapter 11 of the code. The company also failed to meet certain obligations under its union contract and it refused to pay the wage increases called for in the agreement. Bildisco requested and received permission to do so from the bankruptcy court's order and the union filed an unfair labor practice charge.

The NLRB found that the company had unilaterally changed the terms of the bargaining agreement and that it had unfairly refused to negotiate with the union. On appeal, the court of appeals held that a labor agreement is an executory contract subject to rejection under the Bankruptcy Code. The U.S. Supreme Court later held that (1) the language "executory contract" contained in the Bankruptcy Code includes collective bargaining agreements, and the bankruptcy court may permit rejection of the contract if it burdens the company; and (2) a debtor does not commit an unfair labor practice when it unilaterally rejects or modifies a CBA before formal approval by a Bankruptcy Court.

Later that year Congress stated in Public Law 98-353 (1984), 11 U.S.C. Section 1113, that the employer petitioning for bankruptcy protection can reject the collective agreement only when it has made a proposal designed to permit reorganization and treat employees equitably, when it has provided the union with relevant information, when it has conferred in good faith with the union over the proposed modifications, when the union rejection is found by the court to be without just cause, and when the court concludes that the balance of the equities favors rejection of the agreement.

ERISA and the Multiemployer Pension Amendments (MEPPAA)

Schneider Moving and Storage Co. v. Loran W. Robbins et al., 466 U.S. 364, 104 S.Ct. 1844 (1984). The employer had entered into collective bargaining agreements that required participation in two multiemployer-employee benefit trust funds. The trust agreements required the employers to contribute to the funds according to the terms of the contracts with the union. The trust agreements authorized the trustees to initiate any legal proceedings that they, in their discretion, deemed in the best interest of the Fund to effectuate the collection or preservation of contributions.

The trustees filed complaints in the U.S. District Court claiming that the employers failed to meet their contribution requirements. The company responded by saying the complaints raised disputed interpretations under the CBA that first must be submitted to arbitration. The CBAs gave no parties other than the union or the employer access to the arbitration process. The U.S. District Court, however, dismissed the suits pending arbitration. The court of appeals reversed, holding that the relevant agreements indicated no intent to require the arbitration of contractual disputes. Thus, the failure to arbitrate could not bar the trustees' suits. The Supreme Court affirmed this decision. Trustees may seek judicial enforcement of trust terms without first submitting to arbitration an underlying dispute over the meaning of a term in the CBAs.

I. BOOKS AND MONOGRAPHS

A. Arbitration and Dispute Settlement

General Studies

1. Office of the General Counsel, American Arbitration Association. *Arbitration and the Law: AAA General Counsel's Annual Report.* New York: American Arbitration Association, 1985-93.

> An annual review of current legal developments surrounding labor and all other forms of arbitration.

2. Braun, Kurt. *Labor Disputes and Their Settlement.* Baltimore: Johns Hopkins Press, 1955.

> A general study of the development of dispute settlement. Arbitration topics include voluntary and compulsory arbitration procedures, the award, its enforcement, and surrounding law.

3. McKelvey, Jean T., ed. *The Profession of Labor Arbitration: Selected Papers from the First Seven Annual Meetings of the National Academy of Arbitrators, 1948-1954.* Washington: Bureau of National Affairs, 1957.

> Selected papers from the first seven annual meetings of the National Academy of Arbitrators, including those by Edwin Witte, George Taylor, Ralph Seward, Archibald Cox, and David Cole.

4. Woods, H. D. *Patterns of Industrial Dispute Settlement in Five Canadian Industries.* Montreal: Industrial Relations Centre, McGill University, 1958.

> An analysis of dispute settlement in the following Canadian industries: coal, men's garments, construction, textiles, and logging and lumber.

5. Cole, David L. *The Quest for Industrial Peace*. New York: McGraw-Hill, 1963.

> An analysis of the roles of labor, management, and government in the collective bargaining and dispute resolution process by one of the important historical figures in the field.

6. Fleming, R. W. *The Labor Arbitration Process*. Urbana: University of Illinois Press, 1965.

> Results of three experiments designed to ascertain the extent to which arbitration outcomes can be predicted. Other topics include problems of cost and time-lag, individual rights and due process, and evidence.

7. Updegraff, Clarence M. *Preemption, Predictability, and Progress in Labor Law*. Monograph Series no. 5. Iowa City: Center for Labor and Management, College of Business Administration, University of Iowa, 1967.

> Analysis of the foundations of and developments in labor law and arbitration.

8. Bernstein, Merton C. *Private Dispute Settlement*. New York: Free Press, 1968.

> Topics include the scope of the grievance procedure, employee representation, grievance processing, time limits, tactics, fair representation, and individual rights.

9. Barnett, George E., and David A. McCabe. *Mediation, Investigation, and Arbitration in Industrial Disputes*. New York: Arno Press, 1971.

> Reprint of the classic 1916 study of mediation and arbitration; based on a report submitted by the authors in June 1915 to the Commission on Industrial Relations.

10. Yaffe, Byron. *The Saul Wallen Papers: A Neutral's Contribution to Industrial Peace*. Ithaca, NY: New York State School of Industrial and Labor Relations, Cornell University, 1974.

> Wallen's view on the role of the arbitrator, the impact of collective bargaining, the system of industrial discipline, mediation, and the responsibility of labor and management to society.

11. Baer, Walter E. *Strikes*. New York: AMACOM, 1975.

> A study of conflict resolution. Arbitration topics include the role of arbitrators, their demographic background, and selection procedures.

12. Landis, Brook I. *Value Judgments in Arbitration: A Case Study of Saul Wallen*. Ithaca, NY: New York State School of Industrial and Labor Relations, Cornell University, 1977.

> Study of the role of personal value judgments in the decision-making pro-

cess of arbitrators via an analysis of Saul Wallen's arbitration decisions.

13. Nolan, Dennis R. *Labor Arbitration Law and Practice in a Nutshell.* St. Paul: West Publishing, 1979.

> Provides a simple but comprehensive description of the origin, development, and practice of labor arbitration in America. Discusses law, form, practice, and decisional standards of interest arbitration.

14. Teple, Edward R., and Robert E. Moberly. *Arbitration and Conflict Resolution.* Washington, D.C.: Bureau of National Affairs, 1979.

> A comprehensive collection of materials on conflict resolution, with emphasis on arbitration.

15. Prasow, Paul, and Edward Peters. *Arbitration and Collective Bargaining: Conflict Resolution in Labor Relations.* 2nd ed. New York: McGraw-Hill, 1983.

> An analysis of the development and operation of arbitration. Includes an analysis of U.S. and foreign collective bargaining systems.

16. Zack, Arnold M., and Richard I. Bloch. *Labor Agreement in Negotiation and Arbitration.* Washington, D.C.: Bureau of National Affairs, 1983.

> Overview of arbitral decision-making, including general principles of contract construction, the impact of external law, and issues.

17. Zack, Arnold M., ed. *Arbitration in Practice.* Ithaca, NY: ILR Press, 1984.
> This book is based upon talks given during a training program for new arbitrators at the University of Michigan Law School in 1975.

18. Coulson, Robert. *Labor Arbitration: What You Need to Know.* Rev., 3rd ed. New York: American Arbitration Association, 1988.

> This book covers arbitrator selection, hearing preparation, case presentation, and the role of the arbitrator. It includes the AAA's Rules, the Code of Professional Responsibility, a glossary of terms, and brief descriptions of NLRB and court decisions.

19. Zack, Arnold M. *Handbook for Grievance Arbitration: Procedural and Ethical Issues.* New York: Lexington Books and American Arbitration Association, 1992.

> Written for arbitrators and advocates, this book examines grievance arbitration procedure, evidentiary problems, and professional responsibility. Contains case studies with questions and answers. For Zack's earlier views, see *Grievance Arbitration: A Practical Guide,* Geneva: International Labor Organization, 1977; *Understanding Grievance Arbitration in the Public Sector,* Washington, D.C.: U.S. Department of Labor, 1974, 1976, 1980; and "Suggested New Approaches to Grievance Arbitration," in 30 NAA (1978): 105-117.

Public Sector

20. Polasek, Robert G. *The Common Law of the Shop.* Public Employee Relations Library no. 24. Chicago: Public Personnel Association, 1970.

> A review and digest of a number of grievance cases in one public sector jurisdiction (Milwaukee County, WI) that utilized the services of a permanent umpire.

21. Ullman, Joseph C., and James P. Begin. *Negotiated Grievance Procedures in Public Employment.* Public Employee Relations Library no. 25. Chicago: Public Personnel Association, 1970.

> An early empirical study of public sector grievance procedures, structure, control mechanisms, arbitration procedures, and scope.

22. Pops, Gerald M. *Emergence of the Public Sector Arbitrator.* Lexington, MA: Lexington Books, 1976.

> Study of the role of the arbitrator in the public sector.

23. Staudohar, Paul D. *Grievance Arbitration in Public Employment.* Berkeley: Institute of Industrial Relations, University of California, 1977.

> A primer on arbitration for practitioners in the public sector.

24. Vause, W. Gary. *Labor Arbitration in State and Local Government.* Monograph no. 3. Tallahassee: Center for Employment Relations and Law, College of Law, Florida State University, 1981.

> An examination of several aspects of arbitration in the public sector, including the history, legal and institutional framework, contract administration, fair representation, and arbitration practice and procedures.

25. Rabin, Jack, Thomas Vocino, W. Bartley Hildreth, and Gerald L. Miller. *Handbook on Public Personnel Administration and Labor Relations.* Public Administration and Public Policy no. 15. New York: Marcel Dekker, 1983.

> This set of essays on personnel administration and labor relations in the public sector includes one chapter on grievance arbitration (by Kurt H. Decker) and another on interest disputes (by D. S. Chauhan).

26. Deitsch, Clarence R., and David A. Dilts. *The Arbitration of Rights Disputes in the Public Sector.* New York: Quorum Books, 1990.

> A basic guide to arbitration written for labor relations practitioners in public employment.

Arbitration and Dispute Settlement Abroad

27. Chang, Ducksoo. *British Methods of Industrial Peace: A Study of Democracy in Relation to Labor Disputes.* New York: Columbia University Press, 1936.

A study of the history of conciliation and arbitration in Great Britain including an analysis of the World War I experiment of compulsory arbitration, the Industrial Courts, the Joint Industrial Council's system, and the negotiation process in several industries.

28. Woods, Noel S. *Industrial Conciliation and Arbitration in New Zealand.* Wellington, New Zealand: R. E. Owen, Government Printers, 1963.

A study of the development of industrial conciliation and arbitration in New Zealand from 1894 to 1961.

29. Brissenden, Paul F. *Settlement of Disputes over Grievances in the United States with Marginal References to Australia and New Zealand.* Honolulu: Industrial Relations Center, University of Hawaii, 1965.

Analysis of rights arbitration in the United States with comparisons to Australia and New Zealand.

30. Furniss, Edgar S. *Labor Problems.* New York: Arno Press, 1969.

Contains an analysis of general arbitration concepts; arbitration in Great Britain, New Zealand, Canada, and the United States; and a comparison of conciliation, mediation, and arbitration.

31. O'Dea, Raymond. *Industrial Relations in Australia.* 2nd ed. Sydney, Australia: West Publishing, 1970.

A survey and analysis of labor relations in Australia supported by a discussion of relevant cases. Updated by Luigi M. B. Lamprati in a 4th edition of *O'Dea's Industrial Relations in Australia* (New York: J. Wiley, 1984).

32. Aaron, Benjamin. *Labor Courts and Grievance Settlement in Western Europe.* Berkeley: University of California Press, 1971.

Comparative study of labor courts, grievances, and dispute settlement in France, West Germany, Sweden, and Italy.

33. Hoffman, Eileen Burkas. *Resolving Labor-Management Disputes: A Nine-Country Comparison.* New York: Conference Board, 1973.

A comparison of dispute resolution in Argentina, Australia, Germany, Israel, Italy, Japan, Sweden, the United Kingdom, and the United States. See also Hoffman's "Resolving Labor-Management Disputes: A Nine-Country Comparison" in *Arbitration Journal* 29, no. 3 (September 1974): 185-204.

34. *Conciliation and Arbitration Procedures in Labor Disputes: A Comparative Study.* Geneva: International Labor Organization, 1980.

A detailed survey of the conciliation and arbitration systems in six European countries, North America, the Philippines, India, and Kenya.

Arbitration and Dispute Settlement in Canada

35. Brown, Donald J. M., and David M. Beatty, eds. *Canadian Labour Arbitration.* Aurora, Ontario: Canada Law Book, 1988.

>A loose-leaf volume designed to provide a "snapshot" of Canadian "arbitral jurisprudence." Covers general topics such as arbitral jurisdiction and the arbitration process, and specific issues such as seniority, discipline, and compensation.

36. Palmer, Earl Edward, and Bruce Murdoch Palmer. *Collective Agreement Arbitration in Canada.* 3rd ed. Toronto: Butterworths, 1991.

>A general reference work on labor arbitration in Canada.

Reference Materials

37. Elliott, Sheldon D. *Materials and Cases on Arbitration.* Mineola, NY: Foundation Press, 1968.

>A casebook of leading Supreme Court decisions supplemented by a review of arbitration systems, historical developments, and procedural and ethical standards.

38. Seide, Katherine. *A Dictionary of Arbitration and Its Terms.* Dobbs Ferry, NY: Oceana Publications, 1970.

>A concise and comprehensive dictionary of labor, commercial, and international arbitration terms.

39. Smith, Russell A., et al. *Collective Bargaining and Labor Arbitration: Materials on the Negotiation, Enforcement, and Content of the Labor Agreement.* Indianapolis: Bobbs-Merrill, 1970.

>A general reference source of concepts and cases in collective bargaining and labor arbitration. Updated in a 3rd edition by Donald P. Rothschild, Leroy S. Merrifield, and Charles B. Craver, 1988.

40. Seide, Katherine. *The Paul Felix Warburg Union Catalog of Arbitration: A Selective Bibliography and Subject Index of Peaceful Dispute Settlement Procedures.* 3 vols. Totowa, NJ: Rowman and Littlefield for Eastman Library of the American Arbitration Association, 1974.

>A three-volume bibliography of the collections of 19 cooperating libraries on arbitration. Volume III contains labor arbitration materials listed by subject.

41. Trotta, Maurice S. *Arbitration of Labor-Management Disputes.* New York: AMACOM, 1974.

>A study of the principles and procedures of arbitration.

42. Fairweather, Owen. *Practice and Procedure in Labor Arbitration*. 2nd ed. Washington, D.C.: Bureau of National Affairs, 1983.

> A standard reference work on labor arbitration. Updated in a 3rd edition of *Fairweather's Practice and Procedure in Labor Arbitration*, Ray J. Schoonhoven, ed. (Washington, D.C.: Bureau of National Affairs, 1991).

43. Getman, Julius G., and John Blackburn. *Labor Relations: Law, Practice, and Policy*. 2nd ed. Mineola, NY: Foundation Press, 1983.

> Relevant cases on quality circles and employee committees, as well as more traditional topics.

44. Elkouri, Frank, and Edna Asper Elkouri. *How Arbitration Works*. 4th ed. Washington, D.C.: Bureau of National Affairs, 1985.

> A standard reference work on labor arbitration. Updated by the *1985-89 Cumulative Supplement to Elkouri and Elkouri How Arbitration Works*, Marlin M. Volz and Edward P. Goggin, eds. (Washington, D.C.: American Bar Association, Section of Labor and Employment Law, and Bureau of National Affairs, 1991).

45. Gifford, Courtney D., and William P. Hobgood. *Directory of U.S. Labor Arbitrators: A Guide for Finding and Using Arbitrators*. Washington, D.C.: Bureau of National Affairs, 1985.

> Biographical sketches of U.S. and Canadian labor arbitrators arranged alphabetically and cross-referenced by state.

46. Kagel, John, and Douglas H. Barton. *The Practice and Law of Labor Arbitration*. 4th ed. Stanford, CA: Stanford University School of Law, 1985.

> This collection of journal articles, typed manuscripts, chapters from National Academy of Arbitrators meetings, case reprints, and other materials provides historical background on labor arbitration, discussion of legal issues, and significant cases.

47. Bornstein, Tim, and Ann Gosline, eds. *Labor and Employment Arbitration*. 3 vols. (loose-leaf) New York: Matthew Bender, 1988-93.

> A comprehensive compilation of essays on labor arbitration written by experts in the field, updated annually.

48. Steiner, Julius M. *The Arbitration Handbook: A Guide to the Practical and Legal Issues in Labor Arbitration*. New York: Executive Enterprises Publications, 1989.

> A general reference guide to the practical and legal issues in labor arbitration.

Casebooks on Arbitration

49. Stone, Morris. *Labor Grievances and Decisions*. New York: American Arbitration Association, 1970.

> Seventy-three cases with awards and discussion questions.

50. Robinson, James W., et al. *The Grievance Procedure and Arbitration: Text and Cases*. Washington, D.C.: University Press of America, 1978.

> Thirty-five arbitration cases with discussion questions, some text on the grievance and arbitration process, and hints on preparing a case.

51. Elkin, Randyl D., and Thomas L. Hewitt. *Successful Arbitration*. Reston, VA: Reston Publishing, 1980.

> Four cases—two discharge and two language construction. Each case includes background and recommended arguments for each party. Also hints for preparing a case and coaching witnesses.

52. Imundo, Louis V. *The Arbitration Game*. Cincinnati: South-Western Publishing, 1982.

> An arbitration simulation of a discharge case with several tear-out sheets for use as evidence.

53. Handsaker, Morrison. *The Case of the Television Game Player and Other Labor Arbitration Cases*. Berlin, MA: Allied Publishing, 1989.

> Popularly written digests of 15 arbitration cases decided by the author, each followed by questions for discussion about the case.

54. Hilgert, Raymond L., and Sterling H. Schoen. *Cases in Collective Bargaining and Industrial Relations*. 7th ed. Homewood, IL: Richard D. Irwin, 1993.

> Forty-two arbitration cases and discussion questions and 32 NLRB cases.

B. Arbitrator Characteristics, Careers, and Practices

55. Gold, Charlotte, and Ruth E. Lyons. *Dispute Resolution Training*. New York: American Arbitration Association, 1978.

> Proceedings of a conference on training labor-management neutrals.

56. Wertheimer, Barbara M., and Anne H. Nelson, eds. *Women as Third-Party Neutrals: Gaining Acceptability*. Ithaca, NY: New York State School of Industrial and Labor Relations, Cornell University, 1978.

> This brief volume is drawn from papers presented at a conference spon-

sored jointly by the NYSSILR at Cornell University and the American Arbitration Association to help women explore entry into the field of arbitration.

57. Barreca, Christopher A., et al., eds. *Labor Arbitrator Development: A Handbook.* Washington, D.C.: Bureau of National Affairs, 1983.

> Reviews arbitrator training programs and outlines steps for planning such programs. Decisions are reproduced to illustrate typical issues arising in arbitration.

58. Bognanno, Mario F., and Charles J. Coleman, eds. *Labor Arbitration in America: The Profession and Practice.* New York: Praeger, 1992.

> An empirical study sponsored by the National Academy of Arbitrators. From a data base of more than 600 arbitrators, the various authors provide information on the characteristics of arbitrators and their careers, caseloads, and earnings.

C. Development of Arbitration

59. Kennedy, Thomas. *Effective Labor Arbitration: The Impartial Chairmanship of the Full-Fashioned Hosiery Industry.* Philadelphia: University of Pennsylvania Press, 1948.

> Analysis of the development, procedures, and operation of the system of impartial chairmanship utilized in the full-fashioned hosiery industry from 1929 to 1945.

60. Aaron, Benjamin, et al. *The Future of Labor Arbitration in America.* New York: American Arbitration Association, 1976.

> Topics include the impact of private sector developments on the public sector, procedural matters and NLRB deferral policies, the effect of legal developments, the duty of fair representation, unjust discipline, and interest arbitration.

61. Shils, Edward B., et al. *Industrial Peacemaker: George W. Taylor's Contributions to Collective Bargaining.* Philadelphia: University of Pennsylvania Press, 1979.

> Authored by a group of Taylor's colleagues, students, and friends, this book deals generally with his contributions to labor relations and includes his role in the early development of grievance arbitration.

62. Oral History Project, National Academy of Arbitrators. *The Early Days of Labor Arbitration.* Ann Arbor: Graduate School of Business Administration, University of Michigan, 1982.

Reminiscences of G. Allan Dash, Jr., Sylvester Garrett, John Day Larkin, Harry H. Platt, Ralph T. Seward, and William E. Simkin. The volume is a verbatim transcript of interviews with these early leaders in arbitration.

D. Grievances and Grievance Mediation

63. Trotta, Maurice S. *Handling Grievances: A Guide for Management and Labor.* Washington, D.C.: Bureau of National Affairs, 1976.

> An examination of the causes of grievances, grievance procedures, and preparing for arbitration.

64. Labor Committee, American Public Transit Association. *Transit Manager's Handbook: The Grievance-Arbitration Process.* Washington, D.C.: American Public Transit Association, 1985.

> A typescript manuscript that provides an introduction to grievances: administration of the process, investigation, evaluation, disposition, and arbitration. Not restricted to the transit industry.

65. Butt, Elizabeth Rae. *Grievance Mediation: The Ontario Experience.* Kingston, Ontario: Industrial Relations Centre, Queen's University, 1988.

> This monograph defines grievance mediation, examines the Ontario experience, and concludes that it has provided a useful alternative in the resolution of midcontract disputes.

66. Lewin, David, and Richard D. Peterson. *The Modern Grievance Procedure in the United States.* Westport, CT: Quorum Books, 1988.

> This volume reports on the use and effectiveness of grievance procedures in basic steel, retail department stores, nonprofit hospitals, and local public schools.

67. *Grievance Guide.* 8th ed. Washington, D.C.: Bureau of National Affairs, 1992.

> This comprehensive guidebook analyzes the grievance procedure and the common causes of grievances.

E. Advocacy

Preparation and Presentation of Cases

68. Baer, Walter E. *The Labor Arbitration Guide.* Homewood, IL: Dow Jones-Irwin, 1974.

> A primer on labor arbitration aimed at the practitioner.

69. Trower, Christopher. *Arbitration at a Glance: A Manual on How to Prepare and*

Present a Grievance to a Board of Arbitration. Toronto: Labour Research Institute, 1974.

>A practitioner-oriented manual.

70. Miller, Erin-Aine, and Rosalind Schwartz. *Grievance Arbitration: Techniques and Strategies.* Los Angeles: UCLA Institute of Industrial Relations, 1977.

>A pragmatic guide to grievance arbitration, written primarily for non-lawyers and with a focus on the public sector.

71. Harrison, Alan J. *Preparing and Presenting Your Arbitration Case.* Washington, D.C.: Bureau of National Affairs, 1979.

>A brief (76-page) treatment of the basics.

72. Rynecki, Steven B., and Marvin F. Hill, Jr. *Preparing and Presenting a Public Sector Arbitration Case.* Washington, D.C.: International Personnel Management Association, 1979.

>A fundamental monograph designed to help labor and management representatives prepare and present arbitration cases. Applicable to public and private sectors.

73. Baer, Walter E. *Winning in Labor Arbitration.* Chicago: Crain Books, 1982.

>This primer on grievance arbitration covers both procedural issues and decisional standards.

74. Lawson, Eric W., Sr., and Eric W. Lawson, Jr. *Essentials of Labor Arbitration: A Practical Guide to the Principles and Procedures for Successful Grievance Arbitration.* Buffalo, NY: Conflict Resolution Educational Services and Training (CREST), 1985.

>Written for the practitioner, this book focuses on proving a case, evaluating evidence, and selecting an arbitrator.

75. Sanderson, John P. *Labour Arbitrations and All That: A Handbook on the Preparation and Presentation of Labour Arbitrations.* 2nd ed. Aurora, Ontario: Canada Law Book, 1985.

>The book explains how to prepare and present a labor arbitration case, with application to both Canada and the United States.

76. Kagel, Sam. *Anatomy of a Labor Arbitration.* 2nd ed. Washington, D.C.: Bureau of National Affairs, 1986.

>A how-to book primarily concerned with the preparation and presentation of grievance arbitration cases.

77. Weatherill, J. F. W. *Labour Arbitration Procedure*. Aurora, Ontario.: Canada Law Book, 1987.

> This book focuses on topics such as the composition of the tribunal, adjournment and cancellation, costs, subpoenas, the order of proceeding, evidence, direct and cross-examination, the conclusion of the hearing, and the award.

78. LaCugna, Charles S. *An Introduction to Labor Arbitration*. New York: Praeger, 1988.

> An introductory book on labor arbitration specifically designed for labor and management practitioners who have limited experience in arbitration.

79. Grenig, Jay E., and R. Wayne Estes. *Labor Arbitration Advocacy: Effective Tactics and Techniques*. Stoneham, MA: Butterworth, 1989.

> A how-to book that provides a set of practical guidelines from the opening statement to the posthearing brief.

80. Zimny, Max, William F. Dolson, and Christopher A. Barreca, eds. *Labor Arbitration: A Practical Guide for Advocates*. Washington, D.C.: American Bar Association, Section of Labor and Employment Law, and Bureau of National Affairs, 1990.

> The result of a project undertaken by the American Bar Association to provide specialized training in labor arbitration.

Witnesses, Evidence, and Proof

81. Jones, Dallas L., ed. *Problems of Proof in Arbitration: Proceedings of the Nineteenth Annual Meeting of the National Academy of Arbitrators*. Washington, D.C.: Bureau of National Affairs, 1966.

> Reports on proof in arbitration from tripartite committees in four cities, together with workshop reports.

82. Scheinman, Martin F. *Evidence and Proof in Arbitration*. Ithaca, NY: New York State School of Industrial and Labor Relations, Cornell University, 1977.

> A short compendium of classic evidentiary rules, with annotations and references to other materials.

83. Gorsky, M. R., and Michael Steinberg. *Evidence and Procedure in Canadian Labour Arbitration*. Don Mills, Ontario: Richard De Boo, 1981.

> A discussion of grievances, procedural matters, handling objections, conducting the hearing, and rules of evidence.

84. Hill, Marvin F., Jr., and Anthony V. Sinicropi. *Evidence in Arbitration*. 2nd ed. Washington, D.C.: Bureau of National Affairs, 1987.

Topics include relevance and materiality, quantum and burden of proof, evidentiary standards, problems of due process, credibility, and new evidence.

85. Levin, Edward, and Donald Grody. *Witnesses in Arbitration: Selection, Preparation, and Presentation.* Washington, D.C.: Bureau of National Affairs, 1987.

> A reference source to assist advocates in the selection, preparation, and presentation of witnesses.

86. Sacks, Howard R., and Lewis S. Kurlantzick. *Missing Witnesses, Missing Testimony, and Missing Theories: How Much Initiative by Labor Arbitrators?* Stoneham, MA: Butterworth Legal Publishers, 1988.

> This book discusses what the arbitrator should do if parties fail to produce a witness whose testimony appears to be essential to the case or when facts and issues are inadequately developed.

F. Arbitrability, Management Rights, and Past Practice

87. Wiggins, Ronald L. *The Arbitration of Industrial Engineering Disputes.* Washington, D.C.: Bureau of National Affairs, 1970.

> Topics analyzed include the impact of change on jobs, production standards, performance evaluation, and workload and crew size.

88. Baer, Walter E. *Practice and Precedent in Labor Relations.* Lexington, MA: Lexington Books, 1972.

> An analysis of the impact of past practice on arbitrators' decisions in such areas as benefits, subcontracting, job assignment, seniority, hours of work, union representation, and overtime disputes.

89. Grossman, Mark M. *The Question of Arbitrability: Challenges to the Arbitrator's Jurisdiction and Authority.* Ithaca, NY: ILR Press, 1984.

> This book examines the duty of a successor employer to arbitrate issues arising out of the predecessor's agreement, procedural arbitrability, the problem of conflicting jurisdictions (e.g., the arbitrator and the NLRB), and the grounds on which a court will vacate an arbitration award.

90. Hill, Marvin F., Jr., and Anthony V. Sinicropi. *Management Rights: A Legal and Arbitral Analysis.* Washington, D.C.: Bureau of National Affairs, 1986.

> This book covers hiring, layoffs, promotion and demotion, organizational change, subcontracting, past practice, employee privacy, medical screening, off-duty conduct, polygraphs, searches, and surveillance.

G. Discipline and Discharge

General Studies

91. Jones, Dallas L. *Arbitration and Industrial Discipline.* Ann Arbor: Bureau of Industrial Relations, University of Michigan, 1961.

>Topics include problems of discipline; effect of discharge upon the individual, the group, and company policy; and the impact of arbitration upon the supervisor, the disciplinary process, and the union.

92. Tobin, John E. *A Positive Approach to Employee Discipline.* Wheaton, IL: Hitchcock Publishing, 1976.

>A two-volume digest of arbitration cases on disciplinary issues organized according to Bureau of National Affairs number, arbitrator, union, the decision, and the issues, facts, and criteria.

93. Seidman, Joel. *A Guide to Discipline in the Public Sector.* Honolulu: Industrial Relations Center, College of Business Administration, University of Hawaii, 1977.

>This book is a training guide prepared for a series of seminars that were designed to familiarize state government officials with the process of grievance arbitration in Hawaii's public sector.

94. Stone, Morris. *Employee Discipline and Arbitration.* New York: American Arbitration Association, 1977.

>Twenty-seven cases with awards and discussion questions.

95. Adams, George W. *Grievance Arbitration of Discharge Cases: A Study of the Concepts of Industrial Discipline and Their Results.* Kingston, Ontario: Industrial Relations Centre, Queen's University, 1978.

>Deals with the substantive, procedural, and remedial principles used by arbitrators and boards in discharge cases and the impact of arbitral decision-making on the workplace.

96. Zack, Arnold M., and Richard I. Bloch. *The Arbitration of Discipline Cases.* New York: American Arbitration Association, 1979.

>Deals broadly with the concept of just cause, in terms of both disciplinary procedure and type of offense, with topical discussions, cases, arguments, and arbitral standards.

97. Redeker, James R. *Discipline: Policies and Procedures.* Washington, D.C.: Bureau of National Affairs, 1983.

>A manual on disciplinary policies and practices, written for the first-line supervisor.

98. Krashinsky, Stephen, and Jeffrey Sack. *Discharge and Discipline.* Toronto, Ontario: Lancaster House, 1989.

> This book provides about 300 pages of tables and summaries of Canadian discharge and discipline cases.

99. Redeker, James R. *Employee Discipline: Policies and Practices.* Washington, D.C.: Bureau of National Affairs, 1989.

> A discussion of discipline policies and the arbitrators' reasoning, with additional material on the creation, design, and implementation of nonpunitive disciplinary systems.

100. Thompson, Douglas H. *Discharge for Cause: Arbitral Enforcement under the Collective Bargaining Agreement.* New York: Praeger, 1989.

> This book is built around a series of advisory letters written by the author in response to inquiries about the merits of actions involving discharge or discipline.

101. Zack, Arnold M. *Grievance Arbitration: Issues on the Merits in Discipline, Discharge, and Contract Interpretation.* Lexington, MA: American Arbitration Association and Lexington Books, 1989.

> Some 50 topics are addressed and 70 cases analyzed. The book examines evidence, witness credibility, remedies, employment-at-will terminations, alcohol and drug abuse, and sexual harassment.

102. Koven, Adolph M., and Susan L. Smith. *Just Cause: The Seven Tests.* 2nd ed. Washington, D.C.: Bureau of National Affairs, 1992.

> Includes a general treatment of the concept of just cause and the seven tests enunciated by Carroll R. Daugherty in *Whirlpool Corp.*, 58 LA 421 (1972). This volume was updated in 1992.

Alcohol and Drugs

103. Denenberg, Tia Schneider, and Richard V. Denenberg. *Alcohol and Drugs: Issues in the Workplace.* Washington, D.C.: Bureau of National Affairs, 1983.

> Discusses arbitral handling of cases involving use, possession, and sale of drugs and alcohol.

104. Koven, Adolph M., and Susan L. Smith. *Alcohol-Related Misconduct.* Dubuque, IA: Kendall/Hunt Publishing, 1984.

> Explicates how arbitrators have applied just-cause standards in cases involving alcohol violations. The discussion is organized around the seven tests of just cause enunciated by Carroll R. Daugherty. Extensive references to published awards.

105. Coulson, Robert, and Mitchell D. Goldberg. *Alcohol, Drugs, and Arbitration: An Analysis of Fifty-nine Arbitration Cases.* New York: American Arbitration Association, 1987.

> This book examines burden of proof, evidence, legal and logistical problems of drug testing, and off-duty and chronic abuses.

Other Disciplinary Issues

106. Leap, Terry L. *Health and Job Retention: The Arbitrator's Perspective.* Key Issues Series no. 26. Ithaca, NY: ILR Press, 1984.

> This book focuses on arbitration awards decided between 1967 and 1983 that involve employees whose employment status was affected by a handicap or medical condition.

107. Marmo, Michael. *Arbitration and the Off-Duty Conduct of Employees.* Public Employee Relations Library no. 64. Washington, D.C.: International Personnel Management Association, 1985.

> This book examines more than 100 arbitration decisions on discipline taken against public sector bargaining unit employees for off-duty behavior.

108. Barnacle, Peter J. *Arbitration of Discharge Grievances in Ontario: Outcomes and Reinstatement Experiences.* Research and Current Issues no. 62. Kingston, Ontario: Industrial Relations Centre, Queen's University, 1991.

> Based on 800 discharge arbitrations in Ontario between 1983 and 1986. The employer and union respondents describe reinstatement of discharged employees as generally successful.

H. Compensation, Work Rules, and Remedies

109. Bernstein, Irving. *The Arbitration of Wages.* Berkeley: University of California Press, 1954.

> This analysis reports wage arbitration cases in the United States and the impact of cost of living, financial condition of the employer, differential features of the work, substandards of living, and productivity.

110. Sherman, Herbert L., Jr. *Arbitration of the Steel Wage Structure: Guides, Principles, and Framework for the Settlement of Job Description and Classification Disputes and Related Problems.* Pittsburgh, PA: University of Pittsburgh Press, 1961.

> Analysis of disputes between the U.S. Steel Corporation and the United Steelworkers on job description and classification disputes and related wage structure problems.

111. Lockett, Cheryl L. *Smoking in the Workplace: A Review of Arbitration Decisions*. Fort Washington, PA: LRP Publications, 1988.

> This book examines arbitration cases on smoking in the workplace.

112. Hill, Marvin F., Jr., and Anthony V. Sinicropi. *Remedies in Arbitration*. 2nd ed. Washington D.C.: Bureau of National Affairs, 1991.

> Topics include the sources of remedial authority, remedies in discipline cases, authority to reduce discipline, and others.

I. Arbitration and the Law

113. McKelvey, Jean T., ed. *Arbitration and the Law: Proceedings of the Twelfth Annual Meeting of the National Academy of Arbitrators*. Washington D.C.: Bureau of National Affairs, 1959.

> This volume of NAA proceedings includes general discussions of the Lincoln Mills decision and a panel discussion of the role of law in arbitration.

114. Hays, Paul R. *Labor Arbitration: A Dissenting View*. New Haven, CT: Yale University Press, 1966.

> Repudiation of the precepts established in the Steelworkers' Trilogy. For a dissenting view see Saul Wallen, "Arbitrators and Judges: Dispelling the Hays Haze," *California Management Review* 9, no. 2 (April 1967): 17-24.

115. McKelvey, Jean T., ed. *The Changing Law of Fair Representation*. Ithaca, NY: ILR Press, 1985.

> Proceedings of the 1983 national conference on the duty of fair representation.

J. Interest Arbitration and Other Forms of Dispute Resolution

Interest Arbitration

116. Johnsen, Julie E. *Compulsory Federal Arbitration of Labor Disputes*. New York: H. W. Wilson, 1947.

> An early examination of compulsory arbitration.

117. *Compulsory Arbitration of Utility Disputes in New Jersey and Pennsylvania*. Princeton, NJ: Industrial Relations Section, Princeton University, 1951.

> An analysis and comparison of the then existing New Jersey and Pennsylvania public utility compulsory arbitration laws.

52 BOOKS AND MONOGRAPHS

118. Clark, R. Theodore, Jr. *Compulsory Arbitration in Public Employment.* Public Employee Relations Library no. 37. Chicago: Public Personnel Association, 1972.

> A critical survey of provisions made in 1972 for interest arbitration in the public sector that closes with a brief discussion of fact-finding and legislation.

119. Staudohar, Paul D. *Public Employment Disputes and Dispute Settlement.* Honolulu: Industrial Relations Center, College of Business Administration, University of Hawaii, 1972.

> An early survey of the literature, the law, and the overall experience of disputes and dispute resolution in the public sector.

120. Loewenberg, J. Joseph, et al. *Compulsory Arbitration.* Lexington, MA: Lexington Books, 1976.

> A comparison of the evolution, structure, and operation of compulsory arbitration in Australia, Canada, Great Britain, Jamaica, and the United States.

121. Kochan, Thomas A., Mordehai Mironi, Ronald G. Ehrenberg, Jean Baderschneider, and Todd Jick. *Dispute Resolution under Fact-Finding and Arbitration: An Empirical Evaluation.* New York: American Arbitration Association, 1979.

> This study recommends that compulsory fact-finding be eliminated, that arbitrators be allowed to mediate if the parties mutually request it, and that the parties have a choice between several forms of final-offer arbitration.

122. Gunderson, Morley. *Economic Aspects of Interest Arbitration.* Toronto: Ontario Economic Council, 1983.

> This evaluation of interest arbitration in Ontario focuses on forms of arbitration, prevalence, impact, criteria, and proposals for improvement.

123. Lester, Richard Allen. *Labor Arbitration in State and Local Government: An Examination of Experience in Eight States and New York City.* Princeton, NJ: Industrial Relations Section, Firestone Library, Princeton University, 1984.

> An examination of compulsory interest arbitration in Iowa, Massachusetts, Michigan, Minnesota, New Jersey, New York, Pennsylvania, Wisconsin, and New York City.

124. Macdonald, Alastair Peter. *First Contract Arbitration in Canada: An Analysis of the Legislation in Five Labour Jurisdictions in Canada.* School of Industrial Relations Research Essay Series no. 17. Kingston, Ontario: Industrial Relations Centre, Queen's University, 1987.

> The study concludes that first contract arbitration has been useful, ought to be available, and can prevent some employers from adopting tough bar-

gaining positions designed to defeat the organizing rights of employees.

125. Patterson, Diane L. *First Contract Arbitration in Ontario: An Evaluation of the Early Experience*. School of Industrial Relations Research Essay Series no. 30. Kingston, Ontario: Industrial Relations Centre, Queen's University, 1990.

> This study evaluates first contract arbitration, the difficulties in the process, its usage, and its effects.

Final-Offer Arbitration

126. Feuille, Peter. *Final-Offer Arbitration: Concepts, Developments, Techniques*. Chicago: International Personnel Management Association, 1975.

> Primer on how final-offer arbitration works.

127. Stern, James L., et al. *Final-Offer Arbitration: The Effects on Public Safety Employee Bargaining*. Lexington, MA: Lexington Books, 1975.

> An analysis of dispute resolution for public safety employees in Pennsylvania, Michigan, and Wisconsin.

Mediation and Fact-Finding

128. Anderson, Wayne F., R. Theodore Clark, Jr., and John T. Weise. *Fact-Finding in the Public Sector: A Case Study*. Public Employee Relations Library no. 29. Chicago: Public Personnel Association, 1970.

> A case study of a single 1969 fact-finding involving the City of Evanston, Illinois, and the International Association of Fire Fighters, Local 742.

129. Clark, R. Theodore, Jr. *Coping with Mediation, Fact-Finding, and Interest Arbitration*. Public Employee Relations Library no. 42. Chicago: International Personnel Management Association, 1974.

> An early examination of the methods of resolving public sector contract negotiation impasses.

130. Zack, Arnold M. *Public Sector Mediation*. Washington, D.C.: Bureau of National Affairs, 1985.

> An exploration of the mediation process, with suggestions on how to do it and an evaluation of results.

131. Kerur, Sharad. *Factfinding, A Dispute Resolution Procedure for Collective Bargaining: A Review of the Existing Literature and an Analysis of Its Use by School Boards and Teachers in Ontario*. School of Industrial Relations Research Essay Series no. 5. Kingston, Ontario: Industrial Relations Centre, Queen's University, 1986.

> This study examines the use of fact-finding in Canada and reports the results of an empirical study involving Ontario teachers and school boards.

132. Jackson, R. L. *Fact Finding under the School Boards and Teachers Collective Negotiations Act of Ontario*. Toronto: Education Relations Commission, 1988.

> The book reports that fact-finding is helpful in averting some strikes or lockouts; fact finders focus on what can be "sold" rather than what is "right"; and fact-finding has raised the importance of equity considerations.

K. Nonunion Employees and Wrongful Discharge

133. Stieber, Jack, and John Blackburn, eds. *Protecting Unorganized Employees against Unjust Dismissal*. East Lansing: Michigan State University, 1983.

> Proceedings of a conference; topics include grievance procedures in nonunion companies, experience in other countries, and the need for and implications of statutory change.

134. Williams, Robert E., and Thomas R. Bagby. *Allis-Chalmers Corporation v. Lueck*. Washington, D.C.: National Foundation for the Study of Equal Employment Policy, 1986.

> In this 1985 case the U.S. Supreme Court decided that "the whole range of disputes traditionally resolved through arbitration," including wrongful discharge suits, lies within the domain of federal rather than state courts. This monograph examines the decision, its background, and its implications.

135. McCabe, Douglas M. *Corporate Nonunion Complaint Procedures and Systems: A Strategic Human Resources Management Analysis*. New York: Praeger, 1988.

> After reviewing the literature, this book examines several kinds of nonunion grievance procedures and a number of underlying issues (e.g., due process).

136. Ewing, David W. *Justice on the Job: Resolving Grievances in Nonunion Workplaces*. Boston: Harvard Business School Press, 1989.

> A series of case studies involving nonunion grievance procedures in large American corporations.

L. Arbitration in Specific Industries

Education

137. Lataille, Ralph H., and Ernest Gross. *Training Resource Manual on Arbitration in the Public Schools*. Washington, D.C.: U.S. Office of Education, 1975.

A training manual intended for the use of school boards and school administrators on the arbitration process.

138. Igoe, Joseph A., and Anthony P. DiRocco. *Teacher Evaluation: Contract Procedures, Contract Clauses, Arbitration Cases*. Albany, NY: Thealan Associates, 1977.

>A guidebook written for administrators in elementary and secondary school districts.

139. Ostrander, Kenneth H. *A Grievance Arbitration Guide for Educators*. Boston: Allyn and Bacon, 1981.

>Discusses substantive areas of dispute that are unique to public education, such as teacher evaluation.

140. Brodie, Donald W., and Peg A. Williams. *School Grievance Arbitration*. Seattle: Butterworth, 1982.

>Combines a discussion of the general body of arbitral law with specific applications in the schools: leave provisions, extra-duty issues, class assignments, and transfers, among others.

141. Lovell, Ned B. *Grievance Arbitration in Education*. Bloomington, IN: Phi Delta Kappa Educational Foundation, 1985.

>A 40-page overview of basic ideas on the grievance procedure and grievance arbitration, written by faculty members and school and college administrators.

142. Coulson, Robert. *Arbitration in the Schools: An Analysis of Fifty-nine Grievance Arbitration Cases*. New York: American Arbitration Association, 1986.

>This book is built around two- to three-page summaries of arbitration cases in education that involve both disciplinary and contractual issues.

Federal Government

143. Elkouri, Frank. *Legal Status of Federal-Sector Arbitration: Supplement to How Arbitration Works*. 3rd ed. Washington, D.C.: Bureau of National Affairs, 1980.

>This reference source on arbitration in the federal sector provides historical background and an examination of the surrounding laws, rules, and regulations.

144. Loevi, Francis J., and Roger P. Kaplan. *Arbitration and the Federal Sector Advocate*. 2nd ed. New York: American Arbitration Association, 1982.

>A handbook for advocates involved in grievance resolution in the federal government.

145. Adams, Arvil V., and José R. Figuero. *Expediting Settlement of Employee Grievances in the Federal Sector: An Evaluation of the MSPB's Appeals Arbitration Procedures*. Washington, D.C.: Public Policy Program, George Washington University, 1985.

> In 1983, the Merit Systems Protection Board introduced an appeals arbitration procedure to provide a less formal, faster way to resolve employee grievances. The monograph concludes that the procedure worked well.

146. Reischl, Dennis K., and Ralph R. Smith, eds. *Grievance Arbitration in the Federal Service*. Huntsville, AL: Federal Personnel Management Institute, 1987.

> This series of essays by academics and practitioners provides general perspectives on federal sector grievance arbitration, special features, leading topics, and advocacy.

147. Celmer, Albert B., and Robert A. Creo. *Federal Arbitration Advocate's Handbook*. 2nd ed. Horsham, PA: LRP Publications, 1993.

> A manual for advocates practicing in the federal sector.

Railroads and Airlines

148. Jones, Harry F. *Inquiry of the Attorney General's Committee on Administrative Procedure Relating to the National Railroad Adjustment Board. Historical Background and Growth of Machinery Set-up for the Handling of Railroad Labor Disputes 1888-1940*. New York: Eastern Printing, 1941.

> Outlines the procedures surrounding formal National Railroad Adjustment Board hearings.

149. Lazar, Joseph. *Due Process in Disciplinary Hearings: Decisions of the National Railroad Adjustment Board*. Los Angeles: UCLA Institute of Industrial Relations, 1980.

> Examines in great detail the requirements of procedural due process in disciplinary actions as determined by the National Railroad Adjustment Board.

150. Gohmann, John W. *Arbitration and Representation: Applications in Air and Rail Labor Relations*. Dubuque, IA: Kendall/Hunt Publishing, 1981.

> Covers grievance arbitration in railroads and airlines.

Health Care

151. Baderschneider, Earl R., and Paul F. Miller. *Labor Arbitration in Health Care: A Case Book*. New York: Spectrum Publications, 1976.

> Thirty-seven arbitration cases. Introduction by Jesse Simon.

152. Petersen, Donald J., Julius Rezler, and Keith A. Reed. *Arbitration in Health Care*. Rockville, MD: Aspen Systems, 1981.

>   Concentrates on the major issues arising in grievance arbitration in hospitals.

153. Metzger, Norlan, and Joseph M. Ferentino. *The Arbitration and Grievance Process: A Guide for Health Care Supervisors*. Rockville, MD: Aspen Systems, 1983.

>   A basic guide, with chapters by Allen H. Weitzman and Herbert L. Marx and a number of disciplinary cases.

154. Adell, Bernard, Gordon Simmons, Megan Slobodin, and Frank Syer. *The System of Labour Dispute Resolution in Ontario Hospitals and Its Application at Kingston General Hospital*. Queen's Papers in Industrial Relations, Kingston, Ontario: Industrial Relations Centre, Queen's University, 1987.

>   The development and operation of the central bargaining relationships between Ontario hospitals and the two largest unions of hospital employees.

II. Articles and Proceedings

A. Arbitration and Dispute Settlement

General Studies

155. Cole, David L. "Arbitration: Whose Responsibility?" In 4 IRRA (1951): 151-156.

> It is the dual responsibility of labor and industry to resolve conflict through the collective bargaining process, rather than arbitration.

156. Manson, Julius J. "Substantive Principles Emerging from Grievance Arbitration: Some Observations." In 6 IRRA (1953): 136-149.

> Analysis of permanent and ad hoc grievance arbitration.

157. "Arbitration of Jurisdictional Disputes." In 8 NAA (1955): 149-165.

> Essays by David L. Cole on the AFL-CIO no-raiding agreement, Nathan P. Feinsinger on CIO organizational disputes, and John T. Dunlop on the construction industry.

158. Shulman, Harry. "Reason, Contract, and Law in Labor Relations." *Harvard Law Review* 68 (1955): 999-1024.

> This timeless essay by a pioneer in labor arbitration explores the fundamental role of the arbitrator.

159. Cox, Archibald. "Reflections upon Labor Arbitration." *Harvard Law Review* 72 (1959): 1482-1518.

> Classic article on the nature of labor arbitration that argues against the routine application of contract law to collective bargaining agreements.

160. Fuller, Lon L. "Collective Bargaining and the Arbitrator." In 15 NAA (1962): 8-59.

> Reflections on the role of the arbitrator—function, conduct of hearings, self-restraint—and principles of decision-making. Comments by Nathan P. Feinsinger.

161. Benewitz, Maurice C., and Marvin Rosenberg. "The Arbitration Reporters as a Reflection of Arbitration Issues." *Arbitration Issues* 18 (1963): 162-170.

> Compares reported cases with all cases decided by the New York State Board of Mediation from 1955 through 1959.

162. Killingsworth, Charles C., and Saul Wallen. "Constraint and Variety in Arbitration Systems." In 17 NAA (1964): 56-81.

> Focuses on "differences in concepts of arbitration and how they originate, and on what seem to be uniformities in the evolution of umpire systems."

163. O'Connell, Francis A., Jr., and Ben Fischer. "Should the Scope of Arbitration Be Restricted?" In 18 NAA (1965): 102-152.

> O'Connell writes about whether the arbitrator is to be a judge or a legislator and Fischer writes on what and when and how to arbitrate; followed by a panel discussion on reserved rights.

164. Shore, Richard P. "Conceptions of the Arbitrator's Role." *Journal of Applied Psychology* 50, no. 2 (1966): 172-178.

> This study of 28 experienced arbitrators and 73 union and management representatives reveals differing expectations by the parties on some key behavioral dimensions.

165. Friedman, Joel W. "Individual Rights in Grievance Arbitration." *Arbitration Journal* 27, no. 4 (December 1972): 252-273.

> Examines the three forums offered an individual employee by the Supreme Court to handle fair representation complaints: the NLRB, the courts, and the arbitrator.

166. Abrams, Roger I. "The Integrity of the Arbitration Process." *Michigan Law Review* 76 (December 1977): 231-264.

> Focuses on the basic elements of arbitration procedure essential to the achievement of accurate results in an efficient manner acceptable to the parties.

167. Graham, Harry, Brian P. Heshizer, and David B. Johnson. "Grievance Arbitration: Labor Officials' Attitudes." *Arbitration Journal* 33, no. 2 (June 1978): 21-24.

> This survey of 235 union officials from 19 unions concludes that 78 percent believed arbitration was the best method of resolving grievances.

168. Getman, Julius G. "Labor Arbitration and Dispute Resolution." *Yale Law Journal* 88 (April 1979): 916-949.

>Discusses the unique character of labor arbitration and argues against its routine application to other situations.

169. Abrams, Roger I. "The Nature of the Arbitral Process: Substantive Decision-Making in Labor Arbitration." *University of California Davis Law Review* 14, no. 3 (Spring 1981): 551-589.

>Presents a model of labor arbitration as a process of rational and principled adjudication based on an established body of arbitral jurisprudence.

170. Fletcher, Betty Binns, and Edward H. Nakamura. "How Others View Us and Vice Versa: Administrative and Judicial Critiques of the Arbitration Process." In 34 NAA (1982): 218-240.

>Essays by Fletcher (Federal Circuit judge) on Title VII claims and Nakamura (Hawaii Supreme Court justice) on public sector grievance arbitration.

171. Loewenberg, J. Joseph. "An Arbitration Timebomb?" *Arbitration Journal* 37, no. 1 (March 1982): 50-53.

>To ensure enduring success, research should determine if arbitration serves long-range and/or short-term interests.

172. Edwards, Harry T. "Advantages of Arbitration over Litigation: Reflections of a Judge." In 35 NAA (1983): 16-29.

>A positive view of arbitration that emphasizes such factors as speed, expense, informality, flexibility, and the intrinsic value of a voluntary process.

173. Seitz, Peter. "The Arbitrator's Lot." *Arbitration Journal* 38, no. 1 (March 1983): 51-54.

>A general examination of the nature and characteristics of the arbitrator's role.

174. Fowler, Aubrey R., Jr. "Responsibilities in Arbitration: A Tripartite View." *Personnel Administrator* 29, no. 11 (November 1984): 83-90.

>A general review of the responsibilities of arbitrators, management, and union in the arbitration process.

175. Stieber, Jack, Richard N. Block, and Leslie Corbitt. "How Representative Are Published Decisions?" In 37 NAA (1985): 170-203.

>Stieber, Block, and Corbitt discuss differences between published and unpublished discharge decisions. Howard A. Cole examines the NAA poli-

cies; Merton C. Bernstein writes about publication procedures; and Earl M. Curry, Jr., comments on the NAA attitudes toward publication.

176. Nolan, Dennis R., and Roger I. Abrams. "The Labor Arbitrator's Several Roles." *Maryland Law Review* 44, no. 3 (Summer 1985): 873-902.

> This article argues that while arbitrators are principally contract interpreters, they may be called upon to apply community values, mediate, eliminate ambiguities, help the parties fill out their agreement, or even apply external law.

177. Petersen, Donald J., and Julius Rezler. "Employer and Union Attitudes toward the Publication of Arbitration Awards." *Arbitration Journal* 40 (June 1985): 38-44.

> The authors conclude that most parties would not be opposed to pre-award publication inquiries and do not believe that this would have a negative impact on the arbitration process.

178. Coulson, Robert. "Expanding Roles for Labor Arbitration and Other Third-Party Dispute Resolution: A Review of Recent Trends." *Stetson Law Review* 15, no. 1 (Fall 1985): 77-85.

> A general discussion of the expanding use of labor arbitration and its advantages over court proceedings.

179. Dunsford, John E. "The Role and Function of the Labor Arbitrator." *Saint Louis University Law Journal* 30, no. 1 (October 1985): 109-132.

> A discussion of arbitrator development, the arbitrator as a mediator, the application of external law, and the arbitrator's responsibility to guide the process and keep the parties focused on the issues.

180. Gilson, C. H. J., and L. P. Gillis. "Grievance Arbitration in Nova Scotia." *Industrial Relations (Canada)* 42, no. 2 (Spring 1987): 256-269.

> An examination of several variables related to grievance arbitration using data from Nova Scotia, 1980 to 1986. Unions won a majority of cases involving seniority, job posting, working conditions, and job property rights.

181. Dilts, David A., and Clarence R. Deitsch. "The Arbitration Literature: Who Contributes?" *Journal of Labor Research* 10, no. 2 (Spring 1989): 207-214.

> NAA members published more than nonmembers and practicing attorneys published more than professors.

182. Zelek, Mark E. "Labor Grievance Arbitration in the United States." *University of Miami Inter-American Law Review* 21, no. 1 (Fall 1989): 197-207.

> A brief discussion of the advantages of labor arbitration along with historical background. Part of a bar conference on labor arbitration in Central America.

183. Sinicropi, Anthony V. "Remedies and Arbitration Decision Making: Responses to Change." *Labor Law Journal* 42, no. 8 (August 1991): 546-550.

> This article discusses the greater and more specific expectations of the parties; court review of awards; the increasing complexity of the labor agreement; the introduction of employee assistance programs in the workplace; and substance abuse.

184. Dunlop, John T. "The Neutral in Industrial Relations Revisited." In 44 NAA (1992): 26-34.

> The author focuses on the roles other than arbitrator that the neutral can play.

185. Rothstein, Mark A. "Arbitration in the Employer Welfare State." In 44 NAA (1992): 94-103.

> Rothstein shows how the government has used the workplace to promote social policy, and he focuses on drug testing and health insurance. George H. Cohen states that the arbitration system should be able to cope with whatever new problems arise.

Public Sector

186. Killingsworth, Charles C. "Grievance Adjudication in Public Employment." In 11 NAA (1958): 149-171.

> Discussion of various systems prior to the advent of collective bargaining in the public sector. Comments by Eli Rock.

187. Rock, Eli. "Role of the Neutral in Grievance Arbitration in Public Employment." In 20 NAA (1967): 260-286.

> Of historical interest. Covers federal, state, local government.

188. Krislov, Joseph, and Robert M. Peters. "Grievance Arbitration in State and Local Government: A Survey." *Arbitration Journal* 25, no. 3 (1970): 196-205.

> Reports management responses to a questionnaire on the differences between grievance arbitration in the public and private sectors.

189. Krinsky, Edward B. "Municipal Grievance Arbitration in Wisconsin." *Arbitration Journal* 28, no. 1 (March 1973): 50- 67.

> Reviews the Wisconsin municipal grievance arbitration experience and how the process is becoming an integral part of collective bargaining.

190. Staudohar, Paul D. "The Grievance Arbitration and No-Strike Model in Public Employment." *Arbitration Journal* 31, no. 2 (June 1976): 116-124.

> Discusses the extent to which the private sector model has been carried over into the public sector.

191. Abrams, Roger I. "The Power Issue in Public Sector Grievance Arbitration." *Minnesota Law Review* 67, no. 1 (October 1982): 261-286.

>In the public sector the employer often questions the arbitrator's jurisdiction or the arbitrator's power to find in favor of the union. This article examines reasons for the importance of the power issue and its impact on the arbitration process.

192. Thompson, Scott C. "The Non-Delegation Doctrine and Massachusetts Public Employee Grievance Arbitration." *Western New England Law Review* 5, no. 4 (Spring 1983): 699-723.

>Explores the difficulty in accommodating arbitral decision-making with the obligation of public employers to retain control over their managerial powers.

193. Sacks, Barbara B. "Arbitration in Connecticut: Issues in Judicial Intervention under the Connecticut Arbitration Statutes." *Connecticut Law Review* 17, no. 2 (Winter 1985): 387-413.

>This commentary discusses how the Connecticut state courts have treated arbitrability, judicial review, requests for pre-award advice from the courts, and late awards.

194. Coleman, Charles J. "Grievance Arbitration in the Public Sector: Status, Issues, and Problems." *Journal of Collective Negotiations in the Public Sector* 17, no. 2 (1988): 89-103.

>The author contends that grievance arbitration in the public sector is limited by statutes or the courts and emphasizes arbitrability, management rights, and problems of finality.

195. LaVan, Helen. "Arbitration in the Public Sector: A Current Perspective." *Journal of Collective Negotiations in the Public Sector* 19, no. 2 (1990): 153-163.

>This general review of grievance and interest arbitration in the public sector concludes that most studies are too narrow and descriptive and that more research is needed on the effect of arbitration on clerical and maintenance employees.

Arbitration and Dispute Settlement Abroad

196. McPherson, William H. "Grievance Settlement Procedures in Western Europe." In 15 IRRA (1962): 26-35.

>Comparative analysis of grievance settlement procedures in France, Germany, Norway, and Sweden.

197. Fleming, R. W. "The Presidential Address: The Labor Court Idea." In 20 NAA (1967): 229-249.

Based on European experiences, particularly in Sweden, Fleming concludes that labor courts "do not offer a ready alternative to the American grievance arbitration tribunal."

198. Fairweather, Owen, and H. D. Woods. "American and Foreign Grievance Systems." In 21 NAA (1968): 1-41.

Essays on British grievance handling by Fairweather and on public policy and grievance arbitration in Canada by Woods.

199. Levinson, David. "The New Zealand Waterfront Industry Tribunal." *Arbitration Journal* 25 (1970): 261-268.

Focuses on a "comprehensive industrial relations system in microcosm, which seems to be dominated by compulsory arbitration but is based appreciably upon informal negotiations and other voluntary processes."

200. Laffer, Kingsley. "Compulsory Arbitration: The Australian Experience." *Monthly Labor Review* 95, no. 5 (May 1972): 45-58.

Although Australia has long provided for compulsory arbitration, arbitration is no bar to strikes.

201. Stern, James L. "Bargaining and Arbitration in the British Civil Service." *Monthly Labor Review* 96, no. 8 (August 1973): 61-62.

Describes the system in nonindustrial civil service as functional despite strife in other areas of British labor relations.

202. Hoffman, Eileen Barkas. "Resolving Labor-Management Disputes: A Nine-Country Comparison." *Arbitration Journal* 29, no. 3 (September 1974): 185-204.

Compares and contrasts the practices in nine countries—Argentina, Australia, the Federal Republic of Germany, Israel, Italy, Japan, Sweden, the United Kingdom, and the United States.

203. Forkosch, Morris D. "Compulsion in Collective Bargaining and Arbitration: A Comparison of American and Australian Industrial Law." *University of Toledo Law Review* 7, no. 2 (Winter 1976): 457-499.

Focuses on interest disputes and concludes that the major difference between the two systems is the greater degree of compulsion in Australia.

204. "Outer Limits of Interest Arbitration: Australian, Canadian, and United States Experiences." In 34 NAA (1982): 68-108.

Essays by Sir John Moore (Australia), Frances Bairstow (Canada), and Arvid Anderson (United States, especially New York City).

205. Ottolenghi, Smadar. "Arbitration Institutions in Israel." *Arbitration Journal* 38, no. 3 (September 1983): 53-60.

> Describes arbitration as used by labor and management, cooperative friendly societies, and religious groups.

206. Miller, Ronald L. "Arbitration in New Zealand: Mediation Plus Decision Making." *Industrial Relations* 23, no. 1 (Winter 1984): 126-138.

> Argues that New Zealand's system of med-arb for both rights and interest disputes may hold important lessons for the United States.

207. Loewenberg, J. Joseph. "International Comparison of the Role of Neutrals in Resolving Shop Floor Disputes." In 44 NAA (1989): 247-265.

> The paper presents overall conclusions drawn from twelve reports on different countries' systems of resolving shop floor disputes. Jack Stieber provides a commentary.

208. Nolan, Dennis R. "Regulation of Industrial Disputes in Australia, New Zealand, and the United States." *Whittier Law Review* 11, no. 4 (1990): 761-782.

> This investigation of the attempts by the three countries to prevent and resolve labor disputes notes that in recent years all three were moved toward free collective bargaining. See also, by the same author, "Does American Labour Arbitration Provide a Model for Australia?" *Monash University Law Review* 11, no. 1 (1990): 21-40; and "R.I.P. Compulsory Labor Arbitration in New Zealand, 1894-1984," *Comparative Labor Law Journal* 12, no. 4 (1991): 441-457.

209. Zack, Arnold M. "Managing International Work Place Disputes: Are United States Techniques Exportable?" *Willamette Law Review* 27, no. 3 (1991): 645-659.

> The author argues that Americans find it difficult to understand why other nations are reluctant to accept our systems in areas such as conflict resolution. He argues for patience and sensitivity on our part. See also, by the same author, "An American Arbitrator in Donetsk," *Arbitration Journal* 45, no. 3 (September 1990) 43-47.

B. Arbitrator Characteristics, Careers, and Practices

Characteristics of Arbitrators

210. Committee on Research and Education, National Academy of Arbitrators. "Survey of the Arbitration Profession." In *The Profession of Labor Arbitration: Selected Papers from the First Seven Annual Meetings of the National Academy of Arbitrators*, edited by Jean T. McKelvey, 176-182. Washington, D.C.: Bureau of

National Affairs, 1957.

> Reports on the demographic, educational, and experiential background of arbitrators, as well as on caseload, method of selection, and income. Based on responses from 115 academy members (58 percent of total membership).

211. Krislov, Joseph. "The Supply of Arbitrators: Prospects for the 1980s." *Monthly Labor Review* 99, no. 10 (October 1976): 27-30.

> This article predicts a shortage of arbitrators by 1980.

212. Brown, Henry K. "Structural Change in the Labor Arbitration Profession." *Personnel Journal* 55, no. 12 (December 1976): 616-620.

> This analysis of demographic data indicates that more lawyers are arbitrating than thirty years ago.

213. Herrick, John Smith. "Profile of a Labor Arbitrator." *Arbitration Journal* 37 (June 1982): 18-21.

> A study published by the National Academy of Arbitrators on the characteristics of arbitrators who handle labor disputes.

214. Heneman, Herbert G., III, and Marcus H. Sandver. "Arbitrators' Backgrounds and Behavior." *Journal of Labor Research* 4, no. 2 (Spring 1983): 115-124.

> Examines the relationship between biographical information and arbitrator behavior for 250 arbitrators. Biographical information accounted for only a small portion of the variance in four measures of arbitrator behavior.

215. Herrick, John Smith. "Labor Arbitration as Viewed by Labor Arbitrators." *Arbitration Journal* 38, no. 1 (March 1983): 39-48.

> This study of 42 percent of arbitrators on the panel of the Federal Mediation and Conciliation Service on 24 controversial concepts reveals no consensus.

216. Sprehe, J. Timothy, and Jeffrey Small. "Members and Non-Members of the National Academy of Arbitrators: Do They Differ?" *Arbitration Journal* 39, no. 3 (September 1984): 25-33.

> This article reports first results from a 1983 survey of arbitrators that set out to determine differences between NAA members and nonmembers.

217. Allen, A. Dale, Jr., and Daniel F. Jennings. "Sounding Out the Nation's Arbitrators: An NAA Survey." *Labor Law Journal* 39, no. 7 (July 1988): 423-431.

> This survey of 296 arbitrators provides data on their background, training, and experience; demographic information; caseloads; procedures and practices; decision-making criteria; and future projections.

218. Bognanno, Mario F., and Clifford E. Smith. "The Demographic and Professional Characteristics of Arbitrators in North America." In 41 NAA (1989): 266-290.

> The initial report on data that later contributed to Bognanno and Coleman (1990), number 58 in this volume.

Arbitrator Selection and Acceptability

219. Ryder, Meyer S. "The Impact of Acceptability on the Arbitrator." In 21 NAA (1968): 94-124.

> "Attempts to analyze and evaluate the influence that the arbitrator's need for joint acceptability may have on the arbitrator's professional services and the arbitration process." Discussions by Herbert Prashker, Bernard Kleiman, and Harry H. Platt.

220. King, Brian L. "Management and Union Attitudes Affecting the Employment of Inexperienced Labor Arbitrators." *Labor Law Journal* 22, no. 1 (January 1971): 23-28.

> Both labor and management advocates have a marked preference for the arbitrator with experience.

221. Westerkamp, Patrick R., and Allen K. Miller. "The Acceptability of Inexperienced Arbitrators." *Labor Law Journal* 22, no. 12 (December 1971): 763-770.

> This study reported that experienced advocates could not distinguish between those awards written by experienced and inexperienced arbitrators.

222. Benar, Herbert. "Woes of a Newcomer Neutral." *Arbitration Journal* 27, no. 3 (September 1972): 186-194.

> A newcomer recounts his experience and problems in gaining acceptability.

223. Seitz, Peter. "So You Want to be an Arbitrator!" *Arbitration Journal* 27, no. 3 (September 1972): 179-185.

> A well-known arbitrator offers observations on gaining entrance and achieving success as a labor arbitrator.

224. McDermott, Thomas J. "Survey on Availability and Utilization of Arbitrators in 1972." In 26 NAA (1974): 261-304.

> This survey of NAA members concludes that there is no shortage of qualified and available arbitrators.

225. Primeaux, Walter J., and Dalton E. Brannen. "Why Few Arbitrators Are Deemed Acceptable." *Monthly Labor Review* 98, no. 9 (September 1975): 27-30.

This study of factors associated with selection of arbitrators reports greatest reliance is on experience.

226. Rezler, Julius, and Donald J. Petersen. "A Study on Strategies of Arbitrator Selection." *Labor Arbitration Reports* 70 (1980): 1307-1320.

> The results of a study to determine the strategies of selecting arbitrators and the factors that affect their continuing acceptability.

227. Briggs, Steven, and John C. Anderson. "An Empirical Investigation of Arbitrator Acceptability." *Industrial Relations* 19, no. 2 (Spring 1980): 163-174.

> A mail survey of arbitrators on AAA's California panels reveals that heavier caseloads are related to background and visibility characteristics of the arbitrators.

228. Lawson, Eric W., Jr. "Arbitrator Acceptability: Factors Affecting Selection." *Arbitration Journal* 36, no. 14 (December 1981): 22-29.

> A study of arbitrators and advocates about the criteria used in the selection of arbitrators.

229. Nelson, Nels E. "The Selection of Arbitrators." *Labor Law Journal* 37, no. 10 (October 1986): 703-711.

> This article outlines the procedures used to select arbitrators and focuses on the efforts of advocates to secure information on individual arbitrators and their performance.

230. Kauffman, Nancy L., and William L. McKee. "Labor Arbitrator Selection and the Theory of Demand." *Arbitration Journal* 42, no. 1 (March 1987): 35-42.

> The article contents that parties often select well- known arbitrators in order to be in style, attain exclusiveness, or because they are concerned with conspicuous consumption.

231. Petersen, Donald J., and Marsha Katz. "Male and Female Arbitrator Perceptions of the Arbitration Process." *Labor Law Journal* 39, no. 2 (February 1988): 110-119.

> An examination of some of the difficulties confronted by women who wish to break into the arbitration field.

232. Berkeley, Arthur Eliot. "Arbitrators and Advocates: The Consumers Report." In 41 NAA (1989): 290-304.

> An examination of the reasons why parties select arbitrators, based on a Federal Mediation and Conciliation Service survey questionnaire. George R. Fleischli comments.

233. Berkeley, Arthur Eliot. "The Other Side of the Mirror: Advocates Look at the Future for Female Arbitrators." *Labor Law Journal* 40, no. 6 (June 1989): 370-375.

>The author argues that although many advocates feel the need for a greater number of female arbitrators, as long as the practice of industrial relations is dominated by men, the preference for male arbitrators will exist.

234. Berkeley, Arthur Eliot, and Susan Rawson Zacur. "So You Want to Be an Arbitrator? Update of a Guide to the Perplexed." *Labor Law Journal* 41, no. 3 (March 1990): 170-174.

>A description of key factors considered in choosing an arbitrator: years in arbitration, background in union or management advocacy, and possession of a law degree.

235. Cox, Garylee. "The Selection Process and the Appointment of Arbitrators." *Arbitration Journal* 46, no. 2 (June 1991): 28-34.

>An examination of arbitrator selection techniques utilized by the American Arbitration Association and a number of specialized industries.

236. La Rue, Homer C. "The Ethics of Disclosures by Arbitrators of Color: Have the Rules Changed?" *Labor Law Journal* 42, no. 9 (September 1991): 619-634.

>The article contends that in cases where the arbitrator is of African-American heritage and the advocates are all white, the disclosure that the arbitrator is of color often leads to a request that the arbitrator be withdrawn from the case.

Training and Development for Arbitrators

237. Dorr, John Van N., III. "Labor Arbitrator Training: The Internship." *The Arbitration Journal* 36, no. 2 (June 1981): 4-10.

>An overview of the problems experienced in arbitrator training is presented, along with responses to these problems, with an emphasis on internship.

238. Zack, Arnold M. "Who Is Responsible for the Development of Arbitrators: The Parties or the Arbitrators?" *Arbitration Journal* 36, no. 2 (June 1981): 11-14.

>Most arbitration work is done by a few older and favored arbitrators. The author proposes that this situation can be remedied via internships whereby the acceptability of new arbitrators increase because they have been trained by an experienced and well-known arbitrator.

239. Cahn, Marc H. "Labor Arbitrator Training Programs: Participant Perceptions." *Arbitration Journal* 37, no. 3 (September 1982): 33-40.

>An assessment of the effectiveness of ten arbitrator training programs. The participants heard more cases after completing the program, and women fared better than men in the training program.

240. Douglas, Robert L. "Arbitrators, Apprentices, and Arbitration." *Arbitration Journal* 37, no. 3 (September 1982): 46-51.

> A discussion of the mentor-apprentice relationship in arbitration that focuses on the apprentice's responsibilities.

241. Robins, Eva, and Peter Seitz. "Not Training But Sharing: The Rewarding Experiences of Two Veteran Arbitrators." *Arbitration Journal* 37, no. 3 (September 1982): 41-45.

> A general discussion of training through informal, seminar-type meetings between experienced arbitrators and neophytes.

242. Sinicropi, Anthony V. "Arbitrator Development: Programs and Models." *Arbitration Journal* 37, no. 3 (September 1982): 24-32.

> This article argues for substantive mentor-intern programs and regionally based training efforts built on rigorous selection of candidates, classroom instruction, and meaningful field experience.

243. Zack, Arnold M. "Arbitration Training: A Matter of Institutional Survival." *Labor Law Journal* 34, no. 8 (August 1983): 488-493.

> The author explains why it is essential for arbitrators to undergo continuing education and training programs, and how designating agencies and other professional organizations can ensure participation. For further information on Zack's views, see "The Retraining of Arbitrators," *Arbitration Journal* 33, no. 1 (March 1978): 31-33.

244. Nowlin, William A. "Arbitrator Development: Career Paths, a Model Program, and Challenges." *Arbitration Journal* 43, no. 1 (March 1988): 3-13.

> An examination of arbitrator training, the need for developing minority arbitrators, and a New York state program designed to increase the number of minority group arbitrators.

245. Bickner, Mei L., Steven Briggs, and Barbara Z. Tener. "New Voices in the Academy." In 43 NAA (1991): 256-272.

> Three papers that discuss the selection of new members, how to enforce the Code of Professional Responsibility, continuing education, whether arbitration is, in fact, a profession, and member attitudes toward academy governance.

C. Development of Arbitration

The Past

246. Sharfman, I. L. "Free Enterprise, Collective Bargaining, and the Arbitration Expedient." In 4 IRRA (1951): 140-150.

Study of the historical development of collective bargaining and arbitration in the United States. Includes a comparison of voluntary and compulsory arbitration.

247. Killingsworth, Charles C. "Arbitration as an Industrial Relations Technique: The Bethlehem Experience." In 6 IRRA (1953): 124-135.

Analysis of the use of grievance arbitration in the Bethlehem Steel Company between 1942 and 1952.

248. Davey, Harold W. "The John Deere-UAW Permanent Arbitration System." In 10 NAA (1957): 161-192.

History, operation, issues, and evaluation.

249. Wolff, David A., Louis A. Crane, and Howard A. Cole. "The Chrysler-UAW Umpire System." In 11 NAA (1958): 111-148.

History, operation, and analysis of the Chrysler-UAW system. Discussions by Henry H. Platt and Nathan P. Feinsinger.

250. Alexander, Gabriel N. "Impartial Umpireships: The General Motors-UAW Experience." In 12 NAA (1959): 108-160.

The history, operation, issues, and appraisal of the GM/UAW experience, with comments by Joseph Shister and Sylvester Garrett.

251. Nolan, Dennis R., and Roger I. Abrams. "American Labor Arbitration: The Early Years." *University of Florida Law Review* 35, no. 3 (1983): 373-421.

A history of grievance and interest arbitration up to World War II.

252. Nolan, Dennis R., and Roger I. Abrams. "American Labor Arbitration: The Maturing Years." *University of Florida Law Review* 35, no. 4 (1983): 557-632.

This article examines the maturation of American labor arbitration, the War Labor Board, and the changing legal environment.

253. Plass, Stephen. "The Status of Labor Arbitration Today: A Look at the Development of Labor Arbitration in the Collective Bargaining Contract/Federal Statute Context." *Howard Law Journal* 28, no. 3 (Summer 1985): 795-807.

A generally positive review of the historical development of labor arbitration in the United States.

254. Friedman, Clara H. "Arbitrators in Oral History Interviews: Looking Back and Ahead." *Employee Relations Law Journal* 12, no. 3 (Winter 1986/1987): 424-448.

An oral history of arbitration, based on interviews with 15 highly regarded arbitrators who began work when the field was new.

255. Murphy, William P. "The Academy at Forty." In 40 NAA (1988): 1-12.

> This presidential address generally reviews the development of labor arbitration over the previous 40 years, examines key elements in the history of the National Academy of Arbitrators, and provides a few speculations on the future.

256. Aaron, Benjamin. "Catalyst: The National War Labor Board of World War II." *Case Western Reserve Law Review* 39, no. 2 (Winter 1989): 519-543.

> After giving a short history of the War Labor Board, the author describes how the board was responsible for the rapid and widespread acceptance that arbitration achieved after World War II.

257. Day, Jack G. "Prologue." *Case Western Reserve Law Review* 39, no. 2 (Winter 1989): 515-518.

> An interview with arbitrators Benjamin Aaron, Louis Gill, and Sylvester Garrett in which they discuss the origins of National War Labor Board policy on grievance procedures and arbitration.

258. Gill, Lewis M. "The Nature of Arbitration: The Blurred Line between Mediatory and Judicial Arbitration Proceedings." *Case Western Reserve Law Review* 39, no. 2 (Winter 1989): 545-555.

> Relying on personal recollection and excerpts from historical documents, the author examines whether arbitration should focus on nurturing collective bargaining or function as a judicial proceeding.

259. Sharpe, Calvin William. "Introduction." *Case Western Reserve Law Review* 39, no. 2 (Winter 1989): 505-514.

> The evolution of the National War Labor Board and its influence on modern grievance arbitration.

The Present and Future

260. Elkouri, Frank. "Informal Observations on Labor Arbitration Today." *Arbitration Journal* 35, no. 3 (September 1980): 41-45.

> A long-time scholar of arbitration offers opinions on a new "golden age" of arbitration as well as on current problems in the arbitration of labor disputes.

261. Fleming, R. W. "Reflections on Labor Arbitration." In 37 NAA (1985): 11-20.

> A review of the forces that shaped labor arbitration from 1965 through 1985, with a generally optimistic view of the future of labor arbitration.

262. Stieber, Jack. "The Future of Grievance Arbitration." *Labor Law Journal* 37, no. 6 (June 1986): 366-371.

The author identifies the factors that have led to the success of arbitration and suggests that in the future the overall grievance caseload may decline.

263. Nolan, Dennis R., and Roger I. Abrams. "The Future of Labor Arbitration." *Labor Law Journal* 37, no. 7 (July 1986): 437-443.

> The authors review recent tendencies for arbitration to become both more diversified and more legalistic, and they comment on the declining caseload that has resulted from falling union membership.

264. Kochan, Thomas A. "The Future of Collective Bargaining and Its Implications for Arbitration." In 39 NAA (1987): 44-60.

> Kochan concludes that if current trends in collective bargaining and union membership continue, there will be a slow erosion in the demand for traditional arbitration services. Followed by a commentary from Michael L. Wachter.

265. Dybeck, Alfred C. "Reflections of a Second Generation Arbitrator." In 43 NAA (1991): 1-10.

> The first generation of arbitrators was confronted with situations that forced them into being much more than "contract readers." Dybeck suggests that as the parties have constructed more specific contract language, subsequent generations have adopted the contract reading approach.

266. Mittenthal, Richard. "Whither Arbitration? Major Changes in the Last Half Century." *Arbitration Journal* 46, no. 4 (December 1991): 24-32.

> Mittenthal believes that arbitration today bears a far closer relationship to litigation than to collective bargaining. Because it has become more predictable, the parties are better able to resolve grievances short of arbitration. The result is a less important role for arbitration.

267. Brennan, William J., Jr. "Arbitration in a Changing Environment." In 44 NAA (1992): 2-11.

> Supreme Court Justice Brennan discusses the changing legal environment of arbitration, its expanded use, and the changes in public policy that have affected arbitration decisions.

268. Mittenthal, Richard. "Whither Arbitration?" In 44 NAA (1992): 35-49.

> Mittenthal concludes that the legalistic model of arbitration, pioneered by J. Noble Braden, has largely prevailed over the mediative model sponsored by George Taylor. Robert McKersie argues that the prevailing Braden model needs to be changed, and Theodore St. Antoine focuses on the future.

D. Grievances and Grievance Mediation

269. Petersen, Donald J. "Why Unions Go to Arbitration: Politics and Strategy versus Merit." *Personnel* 48 (July 1971): 44-49.

>This study of 400 awards between 1961 and 1967 discloses that one out of every four grievances goes to arbitration for strategic reasons, such as support for steward or to maintain union cohesion.

270. Gandz, Jeffrey. "Employee Grievances: Incidence and Patterns of Resolution." In 31 IRRA (1979): 167-169.

>A study of grievance rates and patterns of resolution in Canadian bargaining units where grievance arbitration is required.

271. Zirkel, Perry A. "A Profile of Grievance Arbitration Cases." *Arbitration Journal* 38, no. 1 (March 1983): 35-38.

>A sample of almost 400 AAA labor arbitration cases reveals the typical duration (257 days total), sector (67 percent private), issues (discharge and discipline), and outcomes (25 percent upheld, 54 percent denied).

272. Katz, Marsha, and Helen LaVan. "Arbitrated Public Sector Employees Grievances: Analysis and Implications." *Journal of Collective Negotiations in the Public Sector* 20, no. 4 (1991): 293-305.

>A study of 1,318 public sector grievance arbitration cases, the factors that influence outcome, and methods of presenting cases effectively.

273. Davy, Jeanette A., and George W. Bohlander. "Recent Findings and Practices in Grievance-Arbitration Procedures." *Labor Law Journal* 43, no. 3 (March 1992): 184-189.

>A review of characteristics of grievance procedures such as number of steps, the parties involved, time limits, etc.

Grievance Mediation

274. O'Grady, James P., Jr. "Grievance Mediation Activities by State Agencies." *Arbitration Journal* 31, no. 2 (June 1976): 125-130.

>Results of a survey of the activities of 18 state mediation agencies regarding the mediation of grievances.

275. Gregory, Gordon A., and Robert E. Rooney, Jr. "Grievance Mediation: A Trend in the Cost-Conscious Eighties." *Labor Law Journal* 31, no. 8 (August 1980): 502-508.

>The authors contend that much of the interest in grievance mediation is the result of its effectiveness in achieving settlements and the savings in cost and time that it produces.

276. Bowers, Mollie H., Ronald L. Seeber, and Lamont E. Stallworth. "Grievance Mediation: A Route to Resolution for the Cost-Conscious 1980s." *Labor Law Journal* 33, no. 8 (August 1982): 459-464.

> The opinions expressed in a survey of federal and state mediators regarding grievance mediation.

277. Goldberg, Stephen B. "The Mediation of Grievances under a Collective Bargaining Contract: An Alternative to Arbitration." *Northwestern University Law Review* 77, no. 3 (October 1982): 270-315.

> An examination of the merits of grievance mediation: the authors argue that it resolves grievances quickly, inexpensively, and in ways that improve the parties' problem-solving ability.

278. Goldberg, Stephen B., and Jeanne M. Brett. "An Experiment in the Mediation of Grievances." *Monthly Labor Review* 106, no. 3 (March 1983): 23-30.

> In this report of a 1980 experiment in the Appalachian coal mines, mediation resolved 32 of the 37 grievances quickly and inexpensively and favorably impressed participants.

279. Brett, Jeanne M., and Stephen B. Goldberg. "Grievance Mediation in the Coal Industry: A Field Experiment." *Industrial and Labor Relations Review* 37, no. 1 (October 1983): 49-69.

> Describes an experimental program of mediation of coal miner grievances. Eighty percent of grievances taken to mediation were settled.

280. Schmedemann, Deborah A. "Reconciling Differences: The Theory and Law of Mediating Labor Grievances." *Industrial Relations Law Journal* 9, no. 4 (1987): 523-595.

> The article analyzes the law and the strengths and weaknesses of grievance mediation.

281. Skratek, Sylvia P. "Grievance Mediation of Contractual Disputes in Washington State Public Education." *Labor Law Journal* 38, no. 6 (June 1987): 370-376.

> Of the 15 grievances described, 73 percent were resolved without resort to arbitration at one-third the cost, two months faster, and with most of the participants reporting satisfaction. See also "Grievance Mediation of Contractual Disputes in Public Education," in *Missouri Journal of Dispute Resolution* (1987), 43-75, by the same author.

282. Sigler, John C. "Mediation of Grievances: An Alternative to Arbitration?" *Employee Relations Law Journal* 13, no. 2 (Autumn 1987): 266-286.

> Concludes that the mediation of grievances has been quite successful and that some attempt at mediation should precede arbitration.

283. Kolb, Deborah M. "How Existing Procedures Shape Alternatives: The Case of Grievance Mediation." *Journal of Dispute Resolution* (1989): 159-187.

> A review of research on grievance mediation and a discussion of its impact on the industrial relations system.

284. Caraway, John M. "Grievance Mediation: Is It Worth Using?" *Journal of Law and Education* 18, no. 4 (Fall 1989): 495-502.

> This article reviews the experiences of the California State Mediation and Conciliation Service, which reported a 92 percent success rate in mediating grievances. Responses to this article by Gordon A. Gregory, Mark Heinen, and Perry Zirkel are found in vol. 20, no. 1 of the journal.

285. Silberman, Allan D. "Breaking the Mold of Grievance Resolution: A Pilot Program in Mediation." *Arbitration Journal* 44, no. 4 (December 1989): 40-45.

> A description of the grievance mediation project at Southwestern Bell.

286. Roberts, Matthew T., Roger S. Wolters, William H. Holley, Jr., and Hubert S. Feild. "Grievance Mediation: A Management Perspective." *Arbitration Journal* 45, no. 3 (September 1990): 15-23.

> A study of managers at the Bell South Corporation indicates that grievance mediation is a satisfactory mechanism for dispute resolution.

287. Quinn, Thomas J., Mark Rosenbaum, and Donald S. McPherson. "Grievance Mediation and Grievance Negotiation Skills: Building Collaborative Relationships." *Labor Law Journal* 41, no. 11 (November 1990): 762-772.

> This article focuses on the grievance mediation process in Pennsylvania and discusses labor-management cooperation, negotiation skills, and other programs.

E. Practice and Procedure

General Administration Topics

288. Jones, Dallas L., and Russell A. Smith. "Management and Labor Appraisals and Criticisms of the Arbitration Process: A Report with Comments." *Michigan Law Review* 62, no. 7 (May 1964): 1115-1156.

> One of the earliest and most comprehensive studies of the "how-the-parties-see-us" variety. Issues include finality of the award, procedural matters, the development of new arbitrators, delays in awards, costs, and arbitrators' qualifications.

289. "Problems of the Ad Hoc Arbitrator." In 20 NAA (1967): 313-340.

> Brief essays by Adolph M. Koven, Frederic Meyers, Carl A. Warns, Jr., and William J. Fallon. Topics range from ethical problems to bill collecting.

290. Glasser, Joseph. "An Analysis of the Arbitration Procedure." *Personnel Journal* 52, no. 11 (November 1973): 970-976.

> Questionnaire results from companies and union locals in Connecticut. Subjects covered include source of arbitration, single arbitrator versus panel, costs, delays, and expedited arbitration.

291. Petersen, Donald J., and Julius Rezler. "Fee Setting and Other Administrative Practices of Labor Arbitrators." *Labor Arbitration Reports* 68 (1977): 1383-1395.

> Fee setting, record retention, and other administrative practices.

292. Bloch, Richard I. "Arbitrator Advertising." *Arbitration Journal* 35, no. 2 (June 1980): 21-26.

> The author argues that commercialism, through advertising, could compromise the arbitrator's role.

293. Graham, Harry, and Brian P. Heshizer. "The Experience of Wisconsin with State-Provided Labor Arbitration Service." *Journal of Collective Negotiations in the Public Sector* 11, no. 4 (1982): 337-349.

> Analysis of over 30 years of experience with free grievance arbitration by Wisconsin Employee Relations Commission discloses low level of use by the parties in both the public and private sectors.

294. Rothschild, Donald P. "Legal Requirements Affecting an Arbitrator's File Retention." *Labor Law Journal* 35, no. 9 (September 1984): 579-586.

> Discusses the issues and implications of file retention by an arbitrator. Recommends a one-year retention period from date of award and for financial rewards, at least a three-year period, for tax purposes.

295. Doering, Barbara W., C. Chester Briscoe, I. B. Helburn, and Alexander MacMillan. "Microcomputer Use in Arbitration." In 37 NAA (1985): 204-226.

> Doering discusses record-keeping software; Briscoe writes about purchase and use considerations; and Helburn and MacMillan examine word processing programs.

296. Benjamin, Edward B., Jr., and Edward F. Martin. "The Impact of the 1986 Tax Law Changes on Solo Practitioners." In 40 NAA (1988): 120-148.

> These two papers examine topics such as the deductibility of interest, losses, "kiddie" taxes, business expenses, tax planning, and benefits.

297. Jennings, Daniel F., and A. Dale Allen, Jr. "Labor Arbitration Costs and Case Loads: A Longitudinal Analysis." *Labor Law Journal* 41, no. 2 (February 1990): 80-88.

> Concludes that between 1976 and 1990, annual arbitration caseloads did

not change significantly; the proportion of public sector cases grew; the number of cases that involved racial, gender, and handicapped employees increased; and costs relative to the Consumer Price Index did not increase.

298. Berkeley, Arthur Eliot. "The Mendicant Neutral: Getting Paid after the Award." *Arbitration Journal* 45, no. 2 (June 1990): 52-55.

> The author examines problems arbitrators encounter in receiving payment, methods for dealing with this problem, interim billing, and advance payment.

Arbitral Immunity

299. Rubins, Alvin B. "Arbitrator's Immunity from Damage Claims." In 39 NAA (1987): 19-26.

> Rubins writes, "Arbitrators may act with impunity/ For theirs is a favored community/ Though losers may whine/ And even malign/ Judges will guard your immunity."

300. Nolan, Dennis R., and Roger I. Abrams. "The Arbitrator's Immunity from Suits and Subpoena." In 40 NAA (1988): 149-180.

> The general rule is that neutral arbitrators are absolutely immune from liability in their arbitral acts. This article examines exceptions to the rule and options when faced with a suit; it recommends an aggressive defense.

301. Nolan, Dennis R., and Roger I. Abrams. "Arbitral Immunity." *Industrial Relations Law Journal* 11, no. 2 (1989): 228-266.

> The authors argue that the courts should continue to reinforce arbitral immunity; they discuss charges of nonfeasance where the arbitrator has failed to render an award, and they recommend that arbitrators respond aggressively when confronted with a suit or a subpoena.

Problems in the Practice and Recommendations for Change

Problems

302. Sembower, John F. "Halting the Trend toward Technicalities in Arbitrations." In 10 NAA (1957): 98-111.

> Suggestions for simplifying the arbitration process. Discussion by G. Allan Dash, Jr.

303. Ross, Arthur M. "The Well-Aged Arbitration Case." Industrial and Labor Relations Review 11, no. 2 (January 1958): 262-271.

> Discussion of causes of time lag between filing and arbitration of a grievance.

304. Dunne, James T. "The UAW Board of Review on Umpire Appeals at General Motors." *Arbitration Journal* 17, no. 3 (1962): 162-174.

>   Experience of an internal board to screen grievances before submitting them to an umpire. The author concludes that results are generally favorable.

305. Ben Scheiber, Israel. "An Experiment in Cutting Labor Arbitration Costs and Delays." *Arbitration Journal* 18, no. 3 (1963): 148-153.

>   How Ingersoll-Rand and the Steelworkers solved an acute backlog problem. A form of expedited arbitration.

306. Fleming, R. W. "The Labor Arbitration Process." In 17 NAA (1964): 33-55.

>   Explores criticisms of arbitration relating to cost, time lag, and formality, along with the management rights issue.

307. Jaffee, Samuel H. "It's Your Money! Cutting the Cost of Labor Arbitration." *Arbitration Journal* 26, no. 3 (1971): 161-178.

>   Suggestions on cost saving from an experienced arbitrator.

308. Kilberg, William J. "The FMCS and Arbitration: Problems and Prospects." *Monthly Labor Review* 94, no. 4 (April 1971): 40-45.

>   Author proposes remedial action for excessive delays, rising costs, and need for new arbitrators.

309. Power, James F. "Improving Arbitration: Roles of Parties and Agencies." *Monthly Labor Review* 95, no. 11 (November 1972): 15-22.

>   Argues that parties themselves have prime responsibility for improving the effectiveness of arbitration procedures.

310. Usery, W. J. "Some Attempts to Reduce Arbitration Costs and Delays." *Monthly Labor Review* 95, no. 11 (November 1972): 3-6.

>   Discusses arbitrator training programs and ways to reduce delays and costs.

311. Davey, Harold W. "What's Right and Wrong with Grievance Arbitration: The Practitioners Air Their Views." *Arbitration Journal* 28, no. 4 (December 1973): 209-231.

>   The author presents the views of 26 management and 15 union practitioners. They blame the arbitrators for the process "malfunctioning."

312. Werther, William B., Jr., and Harold C. White. "Cost Effective Arbitration." *MSU Business Topics* 26, no. 3 (Summer 1978): 57-64.

>   The time of labor arbitration can be reduced and the cost effectiveness in-

creased by using less experienced arbitrators to resolve less complicated cases.

313. Skelton, B. R., and Pamela C. Marett. "Loser-Pays Arbitration." *Labor Law Journal* 30, no. 5 (May 1979): 302-309.

> Examines the thesis that a loser-pays-all arbitration clause in the collective bargaining agreement will result in more efficient utilization of the grievance procedure.

314. Coulson, Robert. "New Views of Arbitration: Satisfying the Demands of the Employee." *Labor Law Journal* 31, no. 8 (August 1980): 495-497.

> Discusses what the parties and the arbitrators must do to satisfy the demands of increasingly litigious employees.

315. Seitz, Peter. "Delay: The Asp in the Bosom of Arbitration." *Arbitration Journal* 36, no. 3 (September 1981): 29-35.

> The author criticizes delay in the grievance arbitration process and proposes procedures for combating this problem.

316. Mittenthal, Richard. "Making Arbitration Work: Alternatives in Designing the Machinery." *Arbitration Journal* 36, no. 3 (September 1981): 35-39.

> Discusses ways of avoiding delay and reducing costs.

317. Robinson, James W. "Some Modest Proposals for Reducing the Costs and Delays in Grievance Arbitration." *Personnel Administrator* 27, no. 2 (February 1982): 25-28.

> Suggests using less experienced arbitrators and no transcript or brief in appropriate cases to speed decisions and lower costs.

318. Kagel, John, Kathy Kelly, and Patrick J. Szymanski. "Labor Arbitration: Cutting Cost and Time without Cutting Quality." *Arbitration Journal* 39, no. 3 (September 1984): 34-41.

> This report reviews two successful experiences with a reform effort centered on joint fact-finding.

319. Shearer, John C. "Reducing Costs of Arbitration through Increasing the Parties' Options." *Arbitration Journal* 40, no. 2 (June 1985): 74-76.

> The author recommends that the arbitrator offer the parties a choice between settling and continuing with the hearing and between a full opinion and shorter award.

320. Nicolau, George. "Can the Labor Arbitration Process Be Simplified? If So, in What Manner and at What Expense?" In 39 NAA (1987): 69-87.

Nicolau discusses a number of methods that have been employed to settle grievances short of arbitration or to handle them more quickly or economically. Thomas W. Jennings and James H. Jordan comment, with a rejoinder by Nicolau.

321. Lewis, Daniel E. "The Declaratory Award in Arbitration Proceedings." *Labor Law Journal* 38, no. 7 (July 1987): 433-439.

Analysis of the process associated with declaratory awards in which the parties draft a statement of the issue and send a statement of agreed-upon facts to the arbitrator.

322. Berkeley, Arthur Eliot. "The Most Serious Faults in Labor- Management Arbitration Today and What Can Be Done to Remedy Them." *Labor Law Journal* 40, no. 11 (November 1989): 728-733.

The faults include the poor quality of the awards, delays in issuing awards, lack of acceptable arbitrators, and the overlegalistic nature of the process.

323. Stieber, Jack, Richard N. Block, and Victor Nichol. "Elapsed Time in Grievance Arbitration." In 43 NAA (1991): 128-141.

An examination of AAA and Federal Mediation and Conciliation Service data on the length of time taken to render arbitration awards.

Lawyers and Legalisms

324. Tobias, Paul H. "In Defense of Creeping Legalism in Arbitration." *Industrial and Labor Relations Review* 13, no. 4 (July 1960): 596-607.

Argues that legalism brings order and consistency and is in the long-run interests of labor arbitration.

325. Garrett, Sylvester. "The Role of Lawyers in Arbitration." In 14 NAA (1961): 102-134.

Lawyers as advocates and as arbitrators. Discussions by Albert Brundage and Robert H. Canan.

326. Raffaele, Joseph Antonio. "Lawyers in Labor Arbitration." *Arbitration Journal* 37, no. 3 (September 1982): 14-23.

Argues that an escalation in the number of attorney-arbitrators will pose grave obstacles to the development of mutual trust between the parties.

327. Bartlett, Anthony F. "Labor Arbitration: The Problem of Legalism." *Oregon Law Review* 62, no. 2 (1983): 195-230.

Examines both the internal and external forces that give rise to legalism in labor arbitration.

328. Kagel, Sam, and J. David Andrews. "Legalism in Arbitration." In 38 NAA (1986): 180-200.

> In the first paper, Kagel sees many of the shortcuts (e.g., elimination of transcripts) as threats to the integrity of arbitration. Andrews argues that the reasons for informality in arbitration are not supportable.

329. Deitsch, Clarence R., and David A. Dilts. "Factors Affecting Pre-Arbitral Settlement of Rights Disputes: Predicting the Method of Rights Dispute Resolution." *Journal of Labor Research* 7, no. 1 (Winter 1986): 69-78.

> The authors show that cases where neither party was represented by an attorney were more likely to be settled prior to arbitration. Attorneys will have a greater tendency to push a case through arbitration.

330. Block, Richard N., and Jack Stieber. "The Impact of Attorneys and Arbitrators on Arbitration Awards." *Industrial and Labor Relations Review* 40, no. 4 (July 1987): 543-555.

> An analysis of 1,213 discharge decisions to discover if representation by an attorney, or the identity of the arbitrator, has significant effects. Parties represented by attorneys when the other party is not represented appeared to gain more favorable outcomes.

331. Alleyne, Reginald. "Delawyerizing Labor Arbitration." *Ohio State Law Journal* 50, no. 1 (February 1989): 93-107.

> This article makes several proposals for shortening hearings, encouraging settlements, and rendering the process more accessible to nonattorney advocates.

Expedited Arbitration

332. Hoellering, Michael F. "Expedited Grievance Arbitration: The First Steps." In 27 IRRA (1974): 324-331.

> Analysis of AAA-administered expedited arbitration programs and those adopted in General Electric, the International Paper Company, the Long Island Railroad, the steel industry, the State of New York, and the United States postal industry. A later version appears in the same author's "Expedited Arbitration" in the *Proceedings of NYU Twenty-eighth Annual Conference on Labor*, pp. 319-336.

333. Cohen, Hyman. "The Search for Innovative Procedures in Labor Arbitration." *Arbitration Journal* 29, no. 2 (June 1974): 104-114.

> Discusses the problems of identifying the kind of case that might be appropriate for expedited arbitration.

334. Hoellering, Michael F. "Expedited Arbitration of Labor Grievances." *Monthly Labor Review* 98, no. 4 (April 1975): 51-52.

Reports on AAA experience with expedited grievance arbitration.

335. Seitz, Peter. "Some Thoughts on the Vogue for Instant Arbitration." *Arbitration Journal* 30, no. 2 (June 1975): 124-128.

> Seitz argues that expedited arbitration has become popular, but he feels that the short time limits given to arbitrators to render their decisions and the restricted length of awards can affect quality.

336. Murray, Matthew E., and Charles J. Griffin, Jr. "Expedited Arbitration of Discharge Cases." *Arbitration Journal* 31, no. 4 (December 1976): 263-268.

> Discusses how expedited labor arbitration has achieved its basic objectives but problems have developed as a result of legal challenges.

337. Stessin, Lawrence. "Expedited Arbitration: Less Grief over Grievances." *Harvard Business Review* 55, no. 1 (January 1977): 128-134.

> Discussion of the causes and promise of expedited arbitration procedures.

338. Sandver, Marcus H., Harry R. Blaine, and Mark N. Woyar. "Time and Cost Savings through Expedited Arbitration Procedures." *Arbitration Journal* 36, no. 4 (December 1981): 11-21.

> Reviews the experiences of labor and management in administering five different expedited arbitration systems.

339. Weatherill, J. F. W., Robert Colosimo, Sherry Barber, and William Burris. "Expedited Arbitration." In 36 NAA (1984): 236-260.

> Discussions of expedited arbitration in Canada by Weatherill and Colosimo and in the United States Postal Service by Barber and Burris.

340. Rose, Joseph B. "Statutory Expedited Grievance Arbitration: The Case of Ontario." *Arbitration Journal* 41, no. 4 (December 1986): 30-45.

> This article examines the Ontario statutory expedited grievance arbitration procedure which was adopted in response to complaints about the cost, formality, and elapsed time associated with traditional arbitration.

341. Kauffman, Nancy L. "The Idea of Expedited Arbitration Two Decades Later." *Arbitration Journal* 46, no. 3 (September 1991): 34-38.

> A general review of the advantages of expedited arbitration procedures and the conditions that favor its use.

Boards and Permanent Umpireships

342. Davey, Harold W. "The Uses and Misuses of Tripartite Boards in Grievance Arbitration." In 21 NAA (1968): 152-179.

Generally unsympathetic view of tripartite arbitration, followed by summaries of workshop sessions (pp. 180-197).

343. "Tripartite Interest and Grievance Arbitration." In 34 NAA (1982): 273-301.

Papers by Arnold M. Zack and Charles M. Rehmus. Comments by I. J. Gromfine and Roger H. Schnepp.

344. Feller, David E., Gerry M. Miller, Clyde W. Summers, Stuart Bernstein, and Robert H. Nichols. "Arbitration without Neutrals: Joint Committees and Boards." In 37 NAA (1985): 106-169.

Feller examines the underlying legal issues. Miller and Summers describe Teamster joint committees, and Bernstein and Nichols look at airline system boards.

345. Veglahn, Peter A. "Grievance Arbitration by Arbitration Boards: A Survey of the Parties." *Arbitration Journal* 42, no. 2 (June 1987): 47-54.

Interviews with parties to discover reasons for preferring arbitration boards over single arbitrators.

346. Zack, Arnold M., Elliott H. Goldstein, and James J. Sherman. "Unique Problems and Opportunities of Permanent Umpireships: A Panel Discussion." In 42 NAA (1990): 176-188.

All three authors describe their experiences with permanent umpireships and discuss topics such as reasons for losing an umpireship and the differences from standard arbitration practice.

F. The Arbitration Hearing

Conduct, Procedures, and Administration

347. Jennings, Thomas W. "New Views of Arbitration: Crossroads of the Future." *Labor Law Journal* 31, no. 8 (August 1980): 495-502.

Arbitration is doomed unless it fosters more acceptance on the part of individual employee grievants. The grievants must be allowed to participate in the process meaningfully and believe that they receive meaningful protection.

348. "Procedural Rulings during the Hearing." In 35 NAA (1983): 138-171.

Workshop discussions of third-party participation; self-incrimination subpoenas; absence of grievant or key witness; witnesses from opposing sides; medical affidavits; closing arguments, briefs, and remedies; and token presentations, agreed awards, and disqualification of the arbitrator.

349. Aaron, Benjamin, Andrea S. Christensen, and Judith P. Vladeck. "The Role of the Arbitrator in Ensuring a Fair Hearing." In 35 NAA (1983): 30-67.

> Aaron deals with a variety of procedural and evidentiary situations that arise in arbitration, including ethical dilemmas faced by the arbitrator and the issue of fairness. Comments by Christensen and Vladeck.

350. Blutrich, Michael D., and Andrew M. Cuomo. "The Discretion of Arbitrators to Grant or Deny Adjournments." *Arbitration Journal* 38, no. 4 (December 1983): 36-41.

> Reviews case law on the subject and concludes that arbitrators have substantial discretion in this area.

351. Kahn, Mark L. "Labor Arbitration: A Plea to the Parties." In 37 NAA (1985): 1-10.

> Presents the thesis that the parties should exert more control on the arbitration process: control over the arbitrator, over the design of the machinery, and over the conduct of the hearing.

352. Bloch, Richard I. "Objections at the Hearing." In 41 NAA (1989): 305-313.

> A discussion of handling objections, the admissibility of the transcripts of courtroom proceedings, documents removed without authorization from the opposing side's files, calling the grievant as management's witness, and the introduction of prior settlements.

353. Gentile, Joseph F., Richard L. Marcus, and George Nicolau. "Building the Evidence Record: The Bounds of 'Arbitral Advocacy'." In 42 NAA (1990): 100-126.

> These three papers explore control of the hearing, the boundaries of arbitral discretion, assisting either party in presenting its proofs or defending them, unequal representation, and witness sequestration.

354. Flagler, John J., Stuart Cohen, and Charles A. Werner. "Practices at the Hearing." In 43 NAA (1991): 53-72.

> These three papers touch on criticism of superactive arbitrators and overly passive ones; admitting evidence without signifying its worth; witness sequestration; calling the grievant as an adverse witness; the use of transcripts, oral summations, shorter arbitration decisions, and retention of jurisdiction.

355. Jones, James E., Jr. "Conducting the Hearing." In 44 NAA (1992): 243-253.

> Some practical advice on working with tripartite arbitration panels and on the inefficiencies caused by many of the rules of evidence.

Discovery, Disclosure, and Arbitral Ethics

Discovery

356. Jacobs, Roger B. "The 'Chilling Effect' of Discovery in Labor Proceedings: Employee Interrogation and the Right to Representation." *Employee Relations Law Journal* 6, no. 1 (Summer 1980): 62-76.

> This paper highlights the basic legal principles governing prehearing interrogation of employees and the right of an employee to union representation during questioning by an employer.

357. Downey, Laurie Eiler. "Pre-Hearing Procedures in Labor Arbitration: A Proposal for Reform." *University of Pittsburgh Law Review* 43, no. 4 (Summer 1982): 1109-1141.

> The author argues for the assignment of expanded powers of discovery to the arbitrator.

358. Decker, Kurt H. "The Public Sector Employer's and Union's Right to Conduct Prearbitration Interviews." *Journal of Collective Negotiations in the Public Sector* 14, no. 1 (1985): 13-23.

> Pennsylvania law supports the use of prearbitration interviews if the union and the employer have the right to representation, and if the topics are related to the grievance.

359. Cooper, Laura J. "Discovery in Labor Arbitration." *Minnesota Law Review* 72, no. 6 (June 1988): 1281-1329.

> This article discusses the potential use for discovery in labor arbitration, the ability of the NLRB to oversee discovery, and the role that the NLRB, the courts, and the arbitrator might play.

Disclosure

360. Sherman, Herbert L., Jr. "The Duty of Disclosure in Labor Arbitration." *Arbitration Journal* 25, no. 2 (1970): 73-100.

> Reports results of surveys sent to arbitrators, union representatives, and company representatives to determine the amount of disclosure considered proper.

361. Caraway, John F. "The Duty to Disclose." In 43 NAA (1991): 215-220.

> A discussion of the arbitrator's responsibility to disclose any past or current relationship with the company or the union.

362. Gershenfeld, Walter J. "Disclosure and Recusement: When to Tell and When to Leave." In 44 NAA (1992): 218-230.

> If a question of conflict of interest arises, arbitrators should choose to dis-

close information or recuse themselves from the case rather than the reverse. The Code of Professional Responsibility should be reexamined in terms of the disclosure of stock and bond holdings.

363. Porter, Alexander B. "Arbitral Neutrality and Accounts Receivable." In 44 NAA (1992): 230-242.

Arbitrators should disclose the existence of "accounts receivable" with one or both of the selecting parties. The article also examines the impact of employer-pays-all systems, impecunious employee cases, interim bills, and bad debts.

Arbitral Ethics

364. Epstein, Lee. "The 'Agreed' Case: A Problem in Ethics." *Arbitration Journal* 20, no. 1 (1965): 41-48.

Most arbitrators feel that they may properly issue an award in a rigged case, provided they are convinced that the purpose of the arbitration is not malevolent.

365. Glick, Leslie Alan. "Bias, Fraud, Misconduct, and Partiality of the Arbitrator." *Arbitration Journal* 22, no. 1 (1967): 161-172.

"The unique nature of the arbitration process necessitates a liberalization of even the standards applied to judges, because the arbitrator's job is often more difficult than that of a judge." Courts should "only intervene in cases of gross misconduct and blatant fraud."

366. Elson, Alex, and Herbert L. Sherman, Jr. "Ethical Responsibilities of the Arbitrator." In 24 NAA (1971): 194-234.

Elson on the case for a Code of Professional Responsibility and Sherman on the arbitrator's duty of disclosure.

367. Dilts, David A. "Award Clarification: An Ethical Dilemma?" *Labor Law Journal* 33, no. 6 (June 1982): 366-369.

If an award is ambiguous and both parties agree to clarification, the arbitrator should clarify the award.

368. Marx, Herbert L., Jr. "Arbitration as an Ethical Institution in Our Society." *Arbitration Journal* 37, no 3 (September 1982): 52-55.

Discusses the ethical dimension of the arbitration process.

369. Dilts, David A. "Timeliness of Arbitration Awards: Some Ethical Considerations." *Arbitration Journal* 43, no. 4 (December 1988): 62-64.

The author recommends active enforcement of the ethical code for labor arbitrators with regard to timely awards and the liability implications of the Bowen decision.

370. Zack, Arnold M., Robert Coulson, Jewell L. Myers, and Richard Mittenthal. "Dissemination and Enforcement of the Code of Ethics." In 41 NAA (1989): 216-246.

>Zack provides background material on the Code of Ethics and calls for strengthening it. Coulson and Myers provide commentaries from the AAA and FMCS, and Mittenthal focuses on the code's prescriptions concerning the conduct of the hearing.

371. Giacalone, Robert A., Martha L. Reiner, and James C. Goodwin. "Ethical Concerns in Grievance Arbitration." *Journal of Business Ethics* 11, no. 4 (April 1992): 267-272.

>A review of ethical issues, the impact of ethical concerns on arbitral decision-making, and the forces that may induce bias.

G. Advocacy

General Studies

372. Ashcraft, William O. "Trying Your First Labor Arbitration: What You Should Know." *Air Force Law Review* 25, no. 4 (Fall 1985): 275-301.

>An introduction to arbitration advocacy designed for members of the Judge Advocates Corps. The article focuses on the decision to arbitrate and preparation.

373. Alexander, Gabriel N., George H. Cohen, and George J. Zalas. "The Professional Responsibility of the Advocates." In 38 NAA (1986): 95-120.

>Three papers on the behavior of advocates in arbitration, the nature of potential rules for advocates, and how they might be enforced.

374. Steen, Jack E. "How to Win Arbitration Decisions." *Personnel* 63, no. 3 (March 1986): 66-69.

>A brief overview written for the practitioner.

375. Hill, Marvin F., Jr., and Anthony V. Sinicropi. "Improving the Arbitration Process: A Primer for Advocates." *Willamette Law Review* 27, no. 3 (Summer 1991): 463-511.

>At a minimum, the advocate must understand the theory of the case and the aspects of the specific grievance that make it unique.

Preparation and Prehearing Matters

376. "Prehearing Arbitration Problems." In 20 NAA (1967): 341-376.

>Brief essays by John F. O'Hara, Charles M. Heath, Richard Liebes, and Albert Brundage on topics such as deciding when to settle, framing the issue, preparing the case, and others.

377. Garrett, Robert F. "Preparation and Presentation in Arbitration." *Personnel Administrator* 22, no. 7 (September 1977): 62-67.

> Defining the issues, selecting the arbitrator, and preparing and presenting the case.

378. Abrams, Roger I. "Negotiating in Anticipation of Arbitration: Some Guideposts for the Initiated." *Case Western Reserve Law Review* 29, no. 2 (Winter 1979): 428-449.

> Offers guideposts for negotiators to ensure that the agreements they reach are complete, embody the intent of the parties, and serve as an adequate reference for resolving future disputes.

379. Shawe, Earle K. "Preparation for the Arbitration Hearing." *Labor Law Journal* 31, no. 1 (January 1980): 46-53.

> A practitioner-oriented piece on preparing for arbitration.

380. Bloom, David E., and Christopher L. Cavanagh. "Negotiator Behavior under Arbitration." *American Economic Review* 77, no. 2 (May 1987): 353-358.

> This article focuses on three problems confronting the negotiator: whether to settle or to arbitrate, selecting an arbitrator, and formulating final positions.

381. Fox, M. J., Jr., and Donna Cooner. "Arbitration: Preparing for Success." *Journal of Collective Negotiations in the Public Sector* 19, no. 4 (1990): 253-260.

> Focuses on preparation, ordering witnesses, and reasons for filing a brief.

Subpoenas

382. Heinsz, Timothy J., et al. "The Subpoena Power of Labor Arbitrators." *Utah Law Review* 1979, no. 1 (1979): 29-55.

> Argues for granting of subpoena power to arbitrators, contrary to the situation in most jurisdictions.

383. Bedikian, Mary A. "Use of Subpoenas in Labor Arbitration: Statutory Interpretations and Perspectives." *Detroit College of Law Review* 1979, no. 4 (Winter 1979): 575-601.

> Under the United States Arbitration Act, the arbitrator's subpoena powers are quite limited. If people or records are to be subpoenaed, the parties usually do so rather than the arbitrator.

384. Furlong, Gary. "Fear and Loathing in Labor Arbitration: How Can There Possibly Be a Full and Fair Hearing Unless the Arbitrator Can Subpoena Evidence?" *Willamette Law Review* 20, no. 3 (Summer 1984): 535-566.

> The author claims that a duty to exchange exists under the Labor Manage-

ment Relations Act section 301, which can provide the arbitrator with broad subpoena power.

385. Heinsz, Timothy J. "An Arbitrator's Authority to Subpoena: A Power in Need of Clarification." In 38 NAA (1986): 201-224.

> The author examines the need for arbitral subpoena power, the legal basis, and the technical processes and requirements.

Opening and Closing Statements

386. Bornstein, Tim. "The Opening Statement in Arbitration Advocacy: An Arbitrator's Perspective." *Arbitration Journal* 38, no. 1 (March 1983): 49-51.

> The author presents the opening statement as the method by which the parties educate the arbitrator. All defenses, special terminology, technological facts, or disputed clauses should be discussed in opening statements.

387. Bornstein, Tim. "To Argue, to Brief, Neither or Both: Strategic Choices in Arbitration Advocacy." *Arbitration Journal* 41, no. 1 (March 1986): 77-81.

> The author argues that oral arguments are best in short, noncomplex cases and briefs are best where the stakes are high or the decision may be subject to judicial review.

Witnesses and Examination

388. Friedman, Milton. "Problems of Cross-Examination in Labor Arbitration." *Arbitration Journal* 34, no. 4 (December 1979): 6-11.

> A critical appraisal of common but ineffective and time-wasting tendencies in cross-examination.

389. Sacks, Howard R., and Lewis S. Kurlantzick. "The Problem of the Missing Witness: Toward an Educator-Facilitator Role for Labor Arbitrators." *Industrial Relations Law Journal* 5, no. 1 (1982): 87-127.

> Examines in detail the considerations that should be made when an arbitrator is faced with the problem of a missing witness. Concludes that the arbitrator should assume an "educator-facilitator" role in such instances.

390. Tidwell, Gary L. "The Effects of Perjury Committed at an Arbitration Hearing." *Arbitration Journal* 38, no. 3 (September 1983): 44-52.

> The author argues that perjury at an arbitration hearing may lead to criminal prosecution, vacation of the arbitration award, and civil liability.

391. Emerson, Catharine. "Reluctant Witnesses in Discharge and Discipline Arbitration." *Employee Relations Law Journal* 11, no. 4 (Spring 1986): 716-722.

> A discussion of the difficulty in persuading employees to testify, hearsay, and due process considerations.

392. Gosline, Ann. "Witnesses in Labor Arbitration: Spotters, Informers, and the Code of Silence." *Arbitration Journal* 43, no. 1 (March 1988): 44-54.

>   The author describes arbitrators' attitudes toward the identification of co-worker informers or undercover investigators and draws negative inference from a grievant's failure to testify.

393. Hill, Marvin F., Jr., and James A. Wright. "Employee Refusals to Cooperate in Internal Investigations: 'Into the Woods' with Employers, Courts, and Labor Arbitrators." *Missouri Law Review* 56, no. 4 (Fall 1991): 869-929.

>   This article focuses on the right of the employee to refuse to answer questions, take a drug or polygraph test, and be a witness, and Fifth Amendment rights.

394. Bloch, Richard I. "Arbitrators as Expert Witnesses." In 44 NAA (1992): 207-217.

>   The author contends that the arbitrator's expertise should be restricted to matters of procedure.

Evidence and Proof

395. Benewitz, Maurice C. "Discharge, Arbitration, and the Quantum of Proof." *Arbitration Journal* 28, no. 2 (June 1973): 95-104.

>   The author expresses concern about the lack of consensus on the degree of proof required to sustain discipline in arbitration proceedings.

396. Clarke, Jack. "Substantial Evidence and Labor Arbitration in the Federal Sector." *Labor Law Journal* 31, no. 6 (June 1980): 368-374.

>   This article reviews the use of substantial evidence in deciding a federal sector grievance.

397. "Admissibility of Evidence." In 35 NAA (1983): 107-137.

>   Workshop discussions of admissibility of grievant's prior employment record, spotter's reports, decisions of other tribunals, new evidence at hearing, grievant's postdischarge conduct, stolen documents, and lie detector tests.

398. Farley, Larry D., and Joseph J. Allotta. "Standards of Proof in Discharge Arbitration: A Practitioner's View." *Labor Law Journal* 35, no. 7 (July 1984): 424-434.

>   The authors call for all arbitrators in discharge-for-theft cases to utilize the proof beyond a reasonable doubt standard.

399. Allotta, Joseph J., and Larry D. Farley. "Application of the Exclusionary Rule to Arbitration Proceedings." *Labor Law Journal* 37, no. 6 (June 1986): 323-331.

>   The purpose of the exclusionary rule is to prevent evidence that has been

obtained illegally from being used against a person. This article reviews the development of this rule and its application to arbitration.

400. Roberts, Thomas T. "Evidence: Taking It for What It's Worth." In 40 NAA (1988): 112-119.

This article discourages the belief that all evidence that is offered must be received.

401. Goldstein, Elliott H. "Searches in the Workplace." In 43 NAA (1991): 220-227.

This paper examines whether the admissibility of evidence depends on the propriety of a search and how arbitrators have dealt with searches on company premises or of the person, surreptitious surveillance, the use of undercover personnel, and employee interrogation.

402. Nicolau, George, and Jesse Simons. "The Arbitrator's Remedial Powers." In 43 NAA (1991): 73-127.

A mistitled NAA session. Nicolau focuses on arbitral treatment of evidence found after an employee has been discharged and argues for greater admission of such evidence. Simons argues for awarding remedies beyond those normally awarded, including, for example, payments for medical expenses and pension contributions. Kenneth B. Cooper and George J. Matkov examine whether arbitrators should consider evidence of rehabilitation in drug and alcohol cases.

403. Rahnama-Moghadam, Mashalah, David A. Dilts, and Ahmad Karim. "The Arbitration of Disciplinary Matters in the Public Sector: Does Objective Evidence Make a Difference?" *Journal of Collective Negotiations in the Public Sector* 21, no. 2 (1992): 151-158.

In the public sector, unions win most insubordination cases (where the evidence is generally less objective), and the employer wins more frequently when the issue is absenteeism (where the evidence tends to be more objective).

Medical Evidence

404. Lafferty, Linda. "Conflict in Medical Evidence in Labor Arbitration." *Arbitration Journal* 23, no. 3 (1968): 175-183.

Lafferty contends that arbitrators deal with conflict in medical testimony, "assisted by a working rule which presumptively favors the company's decision."

405. Miller, David P., Thomas T. Roberts, and Don W. Sears. "The Use of Experts in Arbitration." In 22 NAA (1969): 135-162.

Miller on medical evidence, Roberts on employment testing, and Sears on psychiatric testimony.

406. Wilson, Andrea. "Medical Evidence in Arbitration: Aspects and Dilemmas." *Arbitration Journal* 39, no. 3 (September 1984): 11-18.

> Deals with problems such as an employer's right to request a doctor's examination, the need for scrutiny of a medical witness's background, conflicting medical evidence, and psychological and emotional factors.

407. Zack, Arnold M., and Norma W. Zack. "Arbitrators and Medical Evidence." *Arbitration Journal* 39, no. 3 (September 1984): 6-10.

> According to the Zacks, because arbitrators are increasingly involved in cases that raise medical issues where the testimony is often difficult to understand, they should seek help by consulting basic medical texts.

408. Markowitz, James R., and Marlene Barken. "The Use of Physicians in Grievances and Arbitration." *Personnel* 63, no. 9 (September 1986): 11-17.

> A review of the use of physicians in grievance and arbitration proceedings.

Privacy, Lie Detectors, and Surveillance

409. Burkey, Lee M. "Lie Detectors in Labor Relations." *Arbitration Journal* 18, no. 4 (1963): 193-205.

> In their use by courts and arbitrators, prevailing thought is against relying on lie detectors.

410. Spelfogel, Evan J. "Surveillance and Interrogation in Plant Theft and Discipline Cases." *Proceedings of NYU Twenty-first Annual Conference on Labor*, edited by Thomas G. S. Christensen, 171-198. New York: Matthew Bender, 1969.

> Describes how arbitrators have tried to balance rights of property and rights of privacy. See also Lee M. Burkey, "Employee Surveillance: Are There Civil Rights for the Man on the Job?" (pp. 199-216).

411. Black, Hugo L., Jr. "Surveillance and the Labor Arbitration Process." In 23 NAA (1970): 1-28.

> Black deals with psychological testing, electronic surveillance and the right of privacy. Discussions by A. J. Smith, Jr., and Richard Lipsitz.

412. Craver, Charles B. "The Inquisitorial Process in Private Employment." *Cornell Law Review* 63, no. 1 (November 1977): 1-64.

> Analyzes arbitration, NLRB, and court decisions on topics such as interrogation, lie detectors, searches, and surveillance.

413. Dennehy, Daniel T. "The Status of Lie Detector Tests in Labor Arbitration." *Labor Law Journal* 31, no. 7 (July 1980): 430-440.

> The author argues that polygraph evidence should be admitted in arbitration and the arbitrator can then determine how much weight to give it.

Discharge is appropriate for employees who refuse to take a polygraph test when they are suspected of having committed a criminal act at the workplace.

414. Barreca, Christopher A. "Privacy Issues in Labor Arbitration." *Proceedings of NYU Thirty-fourth Annual Conference on Labor*, edited by Richard Adelman, 127-138. New York: Matthew Bender, 1982.

>Discussion of the right to privacy, including access to information about employees, polygraph tests, and other issues.

415. Carr, David J. "Employer Use of the 'Lie Detector': The Arbitration Experience." *Labor Law Journal* 35, no. 11 (November 1984): 701-713.

>Examines evidentiary problems of the polygraph and its impact on labor arbitration. Recommends a ban on discharge for failure to pass a polygraph unless there is corroborating evidence.

416. Dworkin, James B., and Michael M. Harris. "Polygraph Tests: What Labor Arbitrators Need to Know." *Arbitration Journal* 41, no. 1 (March 1986): 23-33.

>While admitting that polygraph tests can detect deception, the authors argue that they are not completely reliable and decisions based on them should undergo thorough examination.

417. Janisch-Ramsey, Kimberly. "Polygraphs: The Search for Truth in Arbitration Proceedings." *Arbitration Journal* 41, no. 1 (March 1986): 34-41.

>The article reports that lie detector results have been admitted more in recent years because of a desire to include all relevant evidence but not because of greater confidence in the results.

418. Flagler, John J. "Modern Shamanism and Other Folderol: The Search for Certainty." In 39 NAA (1987): 187-204.

>The author describes the polygraph, the voice stress analyzer, the facial ticometer, and "sundry other fidgetometers," and he questions the value of their use in arbitration.

419. Liden, Robert C., and Gene M. Kromm. "Testing Standards in Grievance Arbitration: A Case Review and Critique." *Employee Relations Law Journal* 13, no. 2 (Autumn 1987): 287-303.

>Based on published awards in BNA, a study of how much unions, management, and arbitrators understand about psychological testing.

420. Theeke, Herman A., and Tina M. Theeke. "The Truth about Arbitrators' Treatment of Polygraph Tests." *Arbitration Journal* 42, no. 4 (December 1987): 23-32.

>According to the authors, arbitrators, like courts, are generally resistant to admitting polygraph evidence.

421. Greenbaum, Marcia L., Alan F. Westin, Karen Nussbaum, and James S. Petrie. "Employee Privacy, Monitoring, and New Technology." In 41 NAA (1989): 163-196.

>After discussing the use of video display terminals in workplace monitoring, existing law, and arbitration decisions, Westin examines the privacy issue. Nussbaum views electronic monitoring negatively, and Petrie contends that such programs are warranted.

Cultural Diversity

422. Malin, Martin H., and Lamont E. Stallworth. "Grievance Arbitration: Accommodating an Increasingly Diversified Work Force." *Labor Law Journal* 42, no. 8 (August 1991): 551-556.

>This article reviews the relationship between the new work force, the legal environment, the collective bargaining agreement, and the arbitral process.

423. Fraser, Bruce, Richard B. Bird, and Michael H. Gottesman. "A New Diversity in the Workplace: The Challenge to Arbitration." In 44 NAA (1992): 143-170.

>Fraser concludes that U.S. arbitrators will have to develop a new kind of sensitivity toward people from other cultures. Bird describes the Canadian experience, and Gottesman questions the ambitious problem-solving role for arbitrators that Fraser proposes.

424. Fraser, Bruce. "New Diversity in the American Workplace: A Challenge to Arbitration." *Arbitration Journal* 47, no. 1 (March 1992): 5-15.

>This article discusses changes in the American workplace. It argues that the new diversity calls for new ways to collect and interpret evidence and that it raises new questions of social responsibility.

Due Process

425. Wirtz, W. Willard. "Due Process of Arbitration." In 11 NAA (1958): 1-46.

>Explores a variety of difficult due process issues that may arise in arbitration. Discussion by Abram H. Stockman.

426. Fleming, R. W. "Due Process and Fair Procedure in Labor Arbitration." In 14 NAA (1961): 69-101.

>Covers such topics as notice and appearance, surprises, confrontation of witnesses, and the agreed case. Discussions by David Ziskind and Irvin Sobel.

427. Williams, Jerre S. "Intervention: Rights and Policies." In 16 NAA (1963): 266-284.

>The paper's reference is to intervention by an interested employee who is

not a party to the grievance (as in promotion cases). Discussions by Leo Kotin and Abram H. Stockman.

428. Edwards, Harry T. "Due Process Considerations in Labor Arbitration." *Arbitration Journal* 25, no. 3 (1970): 141-169.

Covers topics such as admissions and confessions, self-incrimination, illegally obtained evidence, and interrogation without representation.

429. Stone, Morris. "Due Process in Labor Arbitration." *Proceedings of NYU Twenty-fourth Annual Conference on Labor,* 11-26. New York: Matthew Bender, 1972.

Stone argues that arbitrators handle due process issues pragmatically.

430. Getman, Julius G. "What Price Employment? Arbitration, the Constitution, and Personal Freedom." In 29 NAA (1976): 61-96.

Constitutional rights in arbitration. Comments by John E. Dunsford and James E. Jones, Jr.

431. Pegnetter, Richard, and Stephen L. Hayford. "State Employee Grievances and Due Process: An Analysis of Contract Arbitration and Civil Service Review Systems." *South Carolina Law Review* 29, no. 2 (1978): 305-342.

This multistate study compares arbitration and civil service adjudication. Focus is on finality.

432. Gross, James A. "Reflections on the Arbitrator's Responsibility to Provide a Full and Fair Hearing: How to Bite the Hand That Feeds You." *Syracuse Law Review* 29, no. 3 (Summer 1978): 877-899.

Argues against the traditional view of the arbitrator as a "creature of the parties." Propounds the view that arbitrators have responsibility to ensure due process.

433. Youngdahl, James E. "Uneasy Second Thoughts on the Independent Participation of Employees in Labor Arbitration Proceedings." *Arkansas Law Review* 33, no. 1 (Spring 1971): 51-58.

Discusses how independent participation by employees is inconsistent with traditional law and policy.

434. Hayford, Stephen L., and Richard Pegnetter. "Grievance Adjudication for Public Employees: A Comparison of Rights Arbitration and Civil Service Appeals Procedures." *Arbitration Journal* 35, no. 3 (September 1980): 22-29.

A study of the status of public employee grievance procedures and grievance arbitration in 1980.

435. Hogler, Raymond L. "Industrial Due Process and Judicial Review of Arbitration Awards." *Labor Law Journal* 31, no. 9 (September 1980): 570-576.

>The author presents a contrast between the due process rights of public and private sector employees. Constitutional considerations usually assure greater due process protection in the public sector.

436. Hogler, Raymond L. "Employee Discipline and Due Process Rights: Is There an Appropriate Remedy?" *Labor Law Journal* 33, no. 12 (December 1982): 783-794.

>The author proposes that a make-whole remedy be provided if information that led to discipline is obtained through an unlawful interview, or if the employer failed to interview the accused and the accused's testimony would reasonably and materially affect the disciplinary decision.

437. Dunsford, John E. "The Adversary System in Arbitration." In 38 NAA (1986): 1-21.

>Examines the rights of the grievant and the obligation of the arbitrator to secure a full record, protect the integrity of the hearing, and assure due process.

438. Sherman, Herbert L., Jr. "The Role and Rights of the Individual in Labor Arbitration." *William Mitchell Law Review* 15, no. 2 (Spring 1989): 379-432.

>This article focuses on the right of a grievant to have a grievance arbitrated, to be present at the hearing, and to be represented by personal counsel.

Fair Representation

439. Leahy, William H. "Arbitration of Disputes over Grievance Processing by Union Representatives." *Arbitration Journal* 26, no. 2 (1971): 103-114.

>Study of arbitration awards, addressing issues such as self-help, procedural requirements, baseless grievances, leaving work without permission, and excessive absenteeism.

440. Summers, Clyde W. "The Individual Employee's Rights under the Collective Agreement: What Constitutes Fair Representation." In 27 NAA (1975): 14-58.

>Focuses on the question of what standard to apply in determining whether a grievant has been fairly represented. Comments by Lester Asher, Bernard Dunau, Robert H. Kleeb, and Leo Kotin (pp. 31-58).

441. Waldman, Seymour M. "The Duty of Fair Representation in Arbitration." *Proceedings of the NYU Twenty-ninth Annual Conference on Labor*, edited by Richard Adelman, 279-295. New York: Matthew Bender, 1976.

Discussion of the legal issue and the impact on the parties and on the grievance procedures.

442. "Public Sector Grievance Procedures, Due Process, and the Duty of Fair Representation." *Harvard Law Review* 89, no. 4 (February 1976): 752-792.

Considers whether determination of the rights of public employees through contractual procedures will meet the requirement of the 14th Amendment due process clause.

443. Marchione, Anthony R. "A Case for Individual Rights under Collective Agreements." *Labor Law Journal* 27, no. 12 (December 1976): 738-747.

Argues that decisions on the duty of fair representation give the union too much power over individual rights.

444. Employee Challenges to Arbitral Awards: A Model for Protecting Individual Rights under the Collective Bargaining Agreement." *University of Pennsylvania Law Review* 125, no. 6 (June 1977): 1310-1338.

Suggests that a fair representation suit is an unsatisfactory method for challenging arbitration awards. Proposes an appeal procedure that would limit relief to vacating the award and remanding for rearbitration.

445. Murphy, William P. "Due Process and Fair Representation in Grievance Handling in the Public Sector." In 30 NAA (1978): 121- 172.

Reviews constitutional rights, government employment, and arbitration. Comments by Bernard F. Ashe, Donald H. Wollett, and Herbert Prashker.

446. Smith, N. Gregory. "Finality and Fairness in Grievance Arbitration: Whether Allegations of Unfair Representation Justify Termination of Arbitration." *Brigham Young University Law Review* 1978, no. 2 (1978): 132-154.

The author argues that termination of arbitration should be the exception rather than the rule when the grievant asserts that union-management conspiracy is in violation of the duty of fair representation.

447. "Labor Arbitration, the Duty of Fair Representation, and Union Negligence." *St. John's Law Review* 54, no. 2 (Winter 1980): 357-381.

Explores the duty of fair representation and the current status of a union's substantive duty. Concludes that an intentional or conscious harm interpretation is the most logical.

448. Levin, William. "Duty of Fair Representation: The Role of the Arbitrator." In 33 NAA (1981): 309-330.

Describes situations raising duty of fair representation questions from the arbitrator's perspective. Comments by James H. Webster.

449. Hoellering, Michael F. "Duty of Fair Representation: Bowen, Del Costello, and Beyond." In Office of the General Counsel, American Arbitration Association. *Arbitration and the Law: AAA General Counsel's Annual Report: 1983*, 72-77. New York: AAA, 1983.

> The author argues that the duty of fair representation cases have brought a share of judicial intervention into the arbitration process. The article also discusses the American Bar Association proposals to modify Sec. 9 of the NLRA, which would direct the resolution of duty of fair representation cases through arbitration.

450. Jacobs, Roger B. "Time Limitations and Section 301: A New Direction from the Supreme Court." *Labor Law Journal* 34, no. 1 (January 1983): 20-33.

> Examines possible effects of recent court decisions in breach of contract and fair representation actions and their potential implication of greater liability for employers and unions beyond the remedy contained in an arbitral award.

451. McKelvey, Jean T. "The Duty of Fair Representation: Has the Arbitrator a Responsibility?" *Arbitration Journal* 41, no. 2 (June 1986): 51-58.

> This article reviews the thinking expressed at NAA meetings between 1959 and 1974 on whether the arbitrator, the courts, or some new forum should handle duty of fair representation questions.

Fair Representation in the Public Sector

452. Francis, Thomas S. "The New Appointment Rule under *Bowen v. U.S. Postal Service*." *Labor Law Journal* 35, no. 2 (February 1984): 71-91.

> Argues that *Bowen* will impede the development of cooperative labor-management relations, threaten the financial stability of unions, and restrict unions' discretion in the grievance process.

453. Diekemper, Jerome A. *"Bowen v. United States Postal Service*: A Challenge to Labor Arbitration as It Currently Exists." *Public Law Forum* 4, no. 1 (Fall 1984): 283-295.

> In *Bowen*, back pay was provided to discharged grievants when the union was found to have failed in its duty of fair representation. The article traces the implications of this decision on arbitration.

454. Levitt, Mark E., and Wayne L. Helsby. "Arbitrability of Individual Grievances in the Public Sector: Florida's Unique Approach." *Florida Bar Journal* 58, no. 11 (December 1984): 693-696.

> Under Florida's Public Employment Relations Act, an employee may process a grievance to arbitration individually only if the union refuses to process the grievance because the employee is not a member of the union.

455. Coulson, Robert. "*Bowen v. Postal Service*: Boom or Bust for Arbitration." In Office of the General Counsel, American Arbitration Association. *Arbitration and the Law: AAA General Counsel's Annual Report: 1983*, 66-71. New York: AAA, 1986.

> An examination of the policy questions raised by *Bowen*, and its impact on grievance processing and on union (the harm may be "substantial").

456. Deitsch, Clarence R., and David A. Dilts. "Arbitrability in a Post-*Bowen* World: A Minefield for All Parties." *Arbitration Journal* 45, no. 2 (June 1990): 45-51.

> The author reviews the impact of *Bowen v. United States Postal Service* and argues that when there is some procedural error that bars arbitration on the merits, the union may ultimately become liable.

Fair Share Proceedings

457. Malin, Martin H. "The Legal Status of Union Security Fee Arbitration after *Chicago Teachers Union v. Hudson*." *Boston College Law Review* 29, no. 4-5 (September 1988): 857-898.

> An examination of the case in which the courts expressly approved arbitration as an appropriate procedure for resolving disputes over the way the union spends nonmember dues.

458. Florey, Peter. "Fair Share Proceedings: A Case for Common Sense." *Arbitration Journal* 44, no. 1 (March 1989): 35-44.

> An examination of American Arbitration Association rules in arbitrating for public sector agency shop cases.

H. Decision-Making and Decision-Writing

How Arbitrators Make Decisions

459. Teele, John W. "The Thought Processes of the Arbitrator." *Arbitration Journal* 17, no. 2 (1962): 85-96.

> A classification scheme on arbitral thinking applied to 295 discharge cases.

460. Davey, Harold W. "How Arbitrators Decide Cases." *Arbitration Journal* 27, no. 4 (December 1972): 274-287.

> In-depth interviews with 13 "competent," "experienced," and "acceptable" arbitrators and partial interviews with about 30 other arbitrators.

461. Gullett, C. Ray, and Wayne H. Goff. "The Arbitral Decision-Making Process: A Computerized Simulation." *Personnel Journal* 59, no. 8 (August 1980): 663-667.

> This article provides a review of fundamental ideas on arbitration decision-

making and a model designed to show how arbitration decisions are made.

462. Jones, Edgar A., Jr. "The Decisional Thinking of Judges and Arbitrator as Triers of Fact." In 33 NAA (1981): 45-61.

>An examination of decision-making criteria and processes followed by reports of regional study groups on perceptions and criteria of decision-making, the follow-up studies are reported on pages 62-239.

463. Greenbaum, Marcia L. "The 'Disciplinatrator', the 'Arbichiatrist', and the 'Social Psychotrator.'" *Arbitration Journal* 37, no. 4 (December 1982): 51-64.

>Inquires into how arbitrators deal with a grievant's personal problems and the extent to which they affect the award.

464. Cain, Joseph P., and Michael J. Stahl. "Modeling the Policies of Several Labor Arbitrators." *Academy of Management Journal* 26, no. 1 (March 1983): 140-147.

>Modeling of three arbitrators' decision rules led to a finding that all were quite consistent in rule application to fact patterns.

465. Rodgers, Robert C., and I. B. Helburn. "The Arbitrariness of Arbitrators' Decisions." In 37 IRRA (1984): 234-241.

>Provides a systematic view of arbitrator's decision-making processes and factors associated with reinstatement.

466. Drotning, John E., and Bruce Fortado. "The Science of Discharge Arbitration." *Labor Law Journal* 35, no. 8 (August 1984): 505-511.

>The authors apply decision tree analysis to discharge cases.

467. Garrett, Sylvester. "The Interpretive Process: Myths and Reality." In 38 NAA (1986): 121-148.

>The author challenges misconceptions about the rules arbitrators follow and concludes that arbitrators are to rely on their background and knowledge to provide as practical and realistic an interpretation as possible.

468. Dilts, David A., and Edwin C. Leonard, Jr. "Win-Loss Rates in Public Sector Grievance Arbitration Cases: Implications for the Selection of Arbitrators." *Journal of Collective Negotiations in the Public Sector* 18, no. 4 (1989): 337-344.

>The party with the burden of proof lost more than half the cases and the authors suggest that a 50-50 split of arbitration decisions may imply that the arbitrator is not impartial.

469. Dilts, David A., and Clarence R. Deitsch. "Arbitration Win/ Loss Rates as a Measure of Arbitrator Neutrality." *Arbitration Journal* 44, no. 3 (September 1989): 42-47.

To determine whether an arbitrator is truly neutral, a number of factors must be considered other than the win/loss record. The authors argue that these factors include the issue involved, the burden of proof, and the political or legal environment.

470. Thornton, Robert J., and Perry A. Zirkel. "The Consistency and Predictability of Grievance Arbitration Awards." *Industrial and Labor Relations Review* 43, no. 2 (January 1990): 294-307.

> An examination of the consistency of arbitrators, management representatives, and union representatives in six hypothetical cases. The decisions of the representatives were consistent, but arbitrators had less agreement.

471. Coulson, Robert. "The Decisionmaking Process in Arbitration." *Arbitration Journal* 45, no. 3 (September 1990): 37-41.

> Arbitrators are more apt to base decisions on their own learned strategies of decision-making than on the theory presented by the attorneys.

Factors That Influence Arbitration Decisions

472. Gross, James A. "Value Judgments in the Decisions of Labor Arbitrators." *Industrial and Labor Relations Review* 21, no. 1 (October 1967): 55-72.

> The author concludes that arbitrators' reasoning discloses a deference to the value of economic efficiency and awards are based more on this value than on other evidence. See also comments by Peter Seitz in *Industrial and Labor Relations Review* 21, no. 3 (April 1968): 427-430 and the reply by James A. Gross, pp. 431-432.

473. Barkston, Eddie W. "Value Differences between Attorney and Economist Labor Arbitrators." In 29 IRRA (1976): 151-160.

> Empirical analysis of the theory that the decisions of labor arbitrators may be expected to vary based on their educational backgrounds.

474. Woolf, Donald A. "Arbitration in One Easy Lesson: A Review of Criteria Used in Arbitration Awards." *Personnel* 55, no. 5 (September 1978): 70-78.

> Author produces list of criteria applied by arbitrators and discusses practical steps that flow from these criteria.

475. Nelson, Nels E., and Earl M. Curry, Jr. "Arbitrator Characteristics and Arbitral Decisions." *Industrial Relations* 20, no. 3 (Fall 1981): 312-317.

> This study of 74 AAA panel arbitrators' decisions in a hypothetical discharge case concludes that age and experience do affect decision-making.

476. Greenberg, Murray, and Philip Harris. "The Arbitrator's Employment Status as a Factor in the Decision-Making Process." *Human Resource Management* 20, no. 4 (Winter 1981): 26-29.

A comparison of the awards of 100 part-time arbitrators with those of 50 full-time arbitrators. Full-timers produced a higher proportion of split decisions and fewer denials of the grievance.

477. Bigoness, William J., and Philip B. DuBose. "Effects of Gender on Arbitrators' Decisions." *Academy of Management Journal* 28, no. 2 (June 1985): 485-491.

An experimental study in which male and female college students were asked to make a decision from the transcript of a grievance case where the grievant was described as male in some transcripts and female in others. No differences in the treatment of male and female grievants was found.

478. Ashenfelter, Orley. "Arbitrator Behavior." *American Economic Review* 77, no. 2 (May 1987): 342-346.

This research indicates that arbitrator behavior is statistically exchangeable, and the only systematic strategy for a successful arbitrator is to try to make decisions such as other arbitrators would make.

479. Deitsch, Clarence R., and David A. Dilts. "An Analysis of Arbitrator Characteristics and Their Effect on Decision-Making in Discharge Cases." *Labor Law Journal* 40, no. 2 (February 1989): 112-116.

From 430 disciplinary cases, the authors conclude that arbitrators were not biased by educational background or experience.

480. Zirkel, Perry A., and Robert J. Thornton. "The Predictability of Grievance Arbitration Awards: Does Arbitrator Experience Matter?" In 42 NAA (1990): 147-160.

The study is based on data provided by labor and management advocates, who predict how experienced and inexperienced arbitrators would decide certain cases.

481. Bemmels, Brian. "Arbitrator Characteristics and Arbitrator Decisions." *Journal of Labor Research* 11, no. 2 (Spring 1990): 181-192.

The authors show that there is a minimal relationship between arbitrator age, occupation, or gender, and arbitration decisions. Choosing arbitrators based on these characteristics has questionable value.

482. Gold, Charlotte. "Opinions and Awards: Inadvertent Results." In 43 NAA (1991): 227-234.

An examination of several sources of error in arbitration awards including faulty inferences, lack of familiarity with the agreement, being too familiar or unfamiliar with the parties, providing advice, and shifting the balance of power.

483. Bemmels, Brian. "Gender Effects in Grievance Arbitration." *Industrial Relations* 30, no. 1 (Winter 1991): 150-162.

This analysis reveals that male arbitrators were more likely to sustain the grievances of female grievants than of male grievants, but there was no evidence that female arbitrators treated male and female grievants differently. Gender effects are less important than the offense, the grievants' prior disciplinary record, and other mitigating factors. Bemmels develops this theme in several other articles including "Arbitrator Characteristics and Arbitrator Decisions," *Journal of Labor Research* 11, no. 2 (March 1990): 181-192; "Attribution Theory and Discipline Arbitration," *Industrial and Labor Relations Review* 44, no. 3 (April 1991): 548-562; "The Effect of Grievants' Gender on Arbitrators' Decisions," *Industrial and Labor Relations Review* 41, no. 2 (January 1988): 251-262; "Gender Effects in Discipline Arbitration: Evidence from British Columbia," *Academy of Management Journal* 31, no. 3 (September 1988): 699-706; "Gender Effects in Discharge Arbitration," *Industrial and Labor Relations Review* 42, no. 1 (October 1988): 63-76; "Gender Effects in Grievance Arbitration," *Industrial Relations* 29, no. 3 (September 1990): 513-525.

Decision-Writing

484. Aaron, Benjamin. "Arbitration Decisions and the Law of the Shop." *Labor Law Journal* 29 (August 1978): 535-542.

Somewhat mistitled, deals primarily with the art of opinion writing.

485. Fraser, Bruce. "The Role of Language in Arbitration." In 33 NAA (1981): 19-44.

A professor of linguistics analyzes language used in grievances, hearings, and decisions.

486. "The Art of Opinion Writing." In 35 NAA (1983): 69-106.

Essays cover a wide-ranging treatment of what should and should not be in an opinion, to whom it should be addressed, and the functions it should serve.

487. Petersen, Donald J., and Julius Rezler. "Arbitration Decision Writing: Selected Criteria." *Arbitration Journal* 38, no. 2 (June 1983): 18-33.

A review of arbitration awards show that the length of opinions increases with the complexity of the case; that arbitrators generally address all the parties' arguments; and that awards are written for the presenters of the case rather than the grievants.

488. Stark, Steven. "Arbitration Decision Writing: Why Arbitrators Err." *Arbitration Journal* 38, no. 2 (June 1983): 30-33.

The author criticizes obtuse, verbose, and otherwise unreadable opinion writing.

489. Abrams, Roger I., and Dennis R. Nolan. "Arbitral Craftsmanship and Competence." In 41 NAA (1989): 313-330.

> An examination of the reasons why courts vacate arbitration awards with recommendations to arbitrators. Extensive comments by Alex Elson on the style of awards and the competency of arbitrators. See also Abrams and Nolan, "Final and Binding: Arbitral Craftsmanship and Opinion Writing," *Labor Lawyer* 5, no. 2 (1989), 195-222.

490. Elliott, David. "When the Hearing Is Over: Writing Arbitral Awards in Plain Language." *Arbitration Journal* 46, no. 4 (December 1991): 53-62.

> This article provides practical suggestions for improving the writing of arbitration awards and the underlying thinking.

I. Arbitrability

Procedural and Substantive Arbitrability

491. Justin, Jules J. "Arbitrability and the Arbitrator's Jurisdiction." In 9 NAA (1956): 1-40.

> Arbitrability prior to the Trilogy. Discussion by Harold W. Davey.

492. Collins, Wilbur L. "Arbitrability and Arbitrators." *Proceedings of NYU Thirteenth Annual Conference on Labor*, edited by Emanuel Stein, 449-479. New York: Matthew Bender, 1960.

> A discussion of arbitrability before the Trilogy.

493. Smith, Russell A. "Arbitrators and Arbitrability." In 16 NAA (1163): 75-103.

> An examination of problems of arbitrability as they arise in arbitration practice, with discussions by Louis A. Crane and Peter M. Kelliher.

494. McDermott, Thomas J. "Arbitrability: The Courts versus the Arbitrator." *Arbitration Journal* 23, no. 1 (1968): 18-37.

> A review of cases shows that most arbitrators try to preserve the integrity of the arbitration procedure. The author argues that the courts should rule on arbitrability.

495. Englander, William H. "The Liverpool Decision and Public Sector Arbitration: A Question of Nondelegable Responsibilities." *Arbitration Journal* 33, no. 2 (June 1978): 25-28.

> Considers the grounds established by the New York Court of Appeals in arbitrability cases. State laws prohibiting delegation of certain responsibilities of elected officials may limit the availability of arbitration for grievance resolution.

496. Calkins, Benjamin. "Waiver of the Right to Arbitrate: An Issue for the Court or the Arbitrator?" *Arbitration Journal* 37, no. 1 (March 1982): 10-16.

>Three circumstances are raised: failure to meet time limits, laches, or an action inconsistent with arbitration. The author argues that all three should be resolved by the arbitrator.

497. McDonald, Paula L. "Judicial Interpretation of Collective Bargaining Agreements: The Danger Inherent in the Determination of Arbitrability." *Duke Law Journal* 1983, no. 4 (September 1983): 848-875.

>McDonald contends that when a court is asked to decide a question of arbitrability, it has a tendency to address the merits of the case.

498. Zirkel, Perry A. "Procedural Arbitrability of Grievance Cases." *Journal of Collective Negotiations in the Public Sector* 13, no. 4 (1984): 351-360.

>This analysis of 100 published arbitration awards dealing with procedural arbitrability reveals that timeliness was the predominant issue. The duty of fair representation did not play a readily detectable role, and the courts have generally ruled in favor of arbitrability.

499. Stanton, David W. "The Roles of the Court and the Arbitrator in Grievance Arbitration. (Case Note)." *Northern Kentucky Law Review* 14, no. 1 (Spring 1987): 153-168.

>The author examines *AT&T Technologies* and suggests the need for language in the collective bargaining agreement to speed up the dispute settlement process.

500. "Arbitration after Communications Workers: A Diminished Role?" *Harvard Law Review* 100, no. 6 (April 1987): 1307-1325.

>Considers the impact of the U.S. Supreme Court decision in *AT&T Technologies* on the presumption of arbitrability.

501. Crone, Allison Stoddard. "Labor Law: The Continuing Battle over Procedural Issues; Is It a Decision for the Courts or the Arbitrator? (Case Note)." *Memphis State University Law Review* 20, no. 1 (Fall 1989): 145-158.

>A discussion of arbitrability standards based on Sixth Circuit case law.

502. Perkovich, Robert, and Mark H. Stein. "Challenges to Arbitration under Illinois Public Sector Labor Relations Statutes." *Hofstra Labor Law Journal* 7, no. 1 (Fall 1989): 191-217.

>This article examines the challenges to arbitrability that arise in the public sector, and it reviews the Illinois public employee labor relations statute.

Postcontract Arbitrability

503. Feinberg, I. Robert. "Do Contract Rights Vest?" In 16 NAA (1963): 192-237.

>A discussion of rights that survive the expiration of a collective bargaining agreement, with comments by Harold A. Katz and Lee C. Shaw.

504. Goetz, Raymond. "Arbitration after Termination of a Collective Bargaining Agreement." *Virginia Law Review* 63, no. 5 (June 1977): 693-730.

>Review of the implications of the Supreme Court's decision in Nolde.

505. Kriksciun, Curt. "Postcontract Arbitrability since *Nolde Brothers*. (Case Note)." *University of Colorado Law Review* 54, no. 1 (Fall 1982): 103-120.

>The author argues that the presumption of postcontract arbitrability should be restricted only to rights accrued during the term of the contract.

506. Leonard, Arthur S. "Postcontractual Arbitrability after *Nolde Brothers*: Problem of Conceptual Clarity." *New York Law School Law Review* 28, no. 2 (1983): 257-294.

>An analysis of the *Nolde* decision concludes that grievances that arise prior to an impasse in negotiations are arbitrable, but those that arise after the agreement expires are arbitrable only if the contract indicates that they are.

507. Geslewitz, Irving M. "Case Law Development since *Nolde Brothers:* When Must Postcontract Disputes Be Arbitrated?" *Labor Law Journal* 35, no. 4 (April 1984): 225-239.

>An examination of the *Nolde* doctrine pertaining to the survival of the duty to arbitrate beyond the expiration of an agreement. The author is critical of the ambiguity in the decision.

508. Kouf, Kim M. "Grievances Arising after Expiration of Collective Bargaining Agreements." *South Dakota Law Review* 32, no. 1 (Spring 1987): 146-155.

>This case note addresses the conflict between federal labor policy, which favors arbitration of disputes after the expiration of the contract, and the principles of strict contract interpretation.

509. Richard, Loretta Rhodes. "Arbitration of Post-Termination Grievances. (Case Note)." *Boston College Law Review* 29, no. 1 (December 1987): 146-154.

>A critical examination of a court ruling which held that a grievance submitted under an expired labor contract is not arbitrable unless the claim is based on benefits that accrued or events that occurred during the life of the agreement.

510. Zirkel, Perry A., and David E. Koff. "Grievance Arbitration after Contract Expiration." *Labor Law Journal* 39, no. 6 (June 1988): 379-384.

An examination of the use of the *Nolde* decision on post contract arbitration in the public sector. Pennsylvania follows the private sector concept closely but Michigan and Wisconsin do not.

511. Epp, Daniel L. "The Duty to Arbitrate Public Sector Employee Grievances after Expiration of the Collective Bargaining Agreement." *Labor Law Journal* 40, no. 4 (April 1989): 195-207.

> The author argues that a grievance that occurs after the expiration of the collective agreement may be arbitrable if it is associated with an event that occurred before contract expiration or is related to a period of negotiation following contract expiration.

512. Zirkel, Perry A. "Does Grievance Arbitration Survive after Contract Expiration?" *Detroit College of Law Review* 1989, no. 3 (Fall 1989): 861-862.

> The author concludes that decisions in private sector cases confuse the situation. In the public sector, the variations are wide but generally favor extending the duty to arbitrate beyond contract expiration.

513. Nuffer, Brian E. "The Post-Expiration Duty to Arbitrate: Disregarding the *Nolde* Presumption after an Impasse in Negotiations." *Brigham Young University Law Review* 1989, no. 1 (Winter 1989): 349-364.

> Argues for the adoption of legal standards which would allow employers to implement terms of employment after an impasse without being subjected to a continuing duty to arbitrate.

514. Hodapp, Paul F. "Competing Philosophies in the Circuits Regarding Post-Contract Grievances: An Employer's Perspective." *Labor Law Journal* 42, no. 1 (January 1991): 35-46.

> This article describes the conflict in the circuit courts regarding an employer's duty to arbitrate postcontract grievances. See also the author's "The U.S. Supreme Court Rules on Duty to Arbitrate Post-Contract Grievances" in *Labor Law Journal*, 42, no. 12 (December 1991): 827-829, in which he shows that the conflict has been resolved by the Supreme Court in *NLRB v. Litton Financial Printing Division*.

Successorship

515. "The Impact of *Howard Johnson* on the Labor Obligations of the Successor Employer." *Michigan Law Review* 74, no. 525 (January 1976): 555-585.

> Criticizes the Supreme Court's decision in *Howard Johnson* as eviscerating the duty of a successor employer to honor the arbitration clause in its predecessor's agreement.

516. Severson, James, and Michael Willcoxon. "Successorship under *Howard*

Johnson: Short Order Justice for Employees." *Industrial Relations Law Journal* 1, no. 1 (Spring 1976): 118-167.

> The authors criticize the Supreme Court's *Howard Johnson* ruling that a successor employer has no duty to arbitrate under the predecessor's CBA except where there is substantial continuity in the identity of the work force.

517. Breitenbach, Thomas A. "The Arbitrability and Enforceability of a Successorship Provision in a Collective Bargaining Agreement under the Railway Labor Act. (Case note)." *Ohio State Journal on Dispute Resolution* 5, no. 1 (Fall 1989): 141-157.

> The 1986 merger between Western Airlines and Delta Airlines and the problems that arose when Delta attempted to enforce its rules and regulations on Air Line Pilots Association over those negotiated with Western.

518. Landau, Jeffrey M. "Successorship Doctrine, the Courts, and Arbitrators: Common Sense of Dollars and Cents?" *University of Miami Law Review* 44, no. 2 (November 1989): 403-441.

> This article examines the evolution of the successorship doctrine and its impact on arbitration decisions.

Bankruptcy

519. Berger, Ralph S. "The Collective Bargaining Agreement in Bankruptcy: Does the Duty to Arbitrate Survive?" *Labor Law Journal* 35 (1984): 685-692.

> Concludes that the duty to arbitrate will remain where a bankruptcy has not rejected the CBA, but it is not clear what weight arbitration awards would have where the contract has been rejected.

520. Fisher, Carrie G. "Partial Repudiation and the Survivability of Labor Arbitration Agreements in the Context of Bankruptcy." *Bankruptcy Developments Journal* 1, no. 1 (January 1984): 177-206.

> This article reviews bankruptcy cases in which arbitration under the labor agreement was allowed, disallowed, or modified.

521. Haggard, Thomas R. "Labor Arbitration and Bankruptcy: A Trek into the Serbonian Bog." *Loyola University of Chicago Law Journal* 17, no. 2 (Winter 1986): 171-202.

> This article describes jurisdictional problems between district courts, bankruptcy courts and labor arbitration, and the role that labor arbitration may play.

J. Principles of Contract Interpretation

General Principles

522. Knight, Thomas R. "Arbitration and Contract Interpretation: 'Common Law' v. Strict Construction." *Labor Law Journal* 34, no. 11 (November 1983): 714-726.

> Examines the balance between strict construction and common law principles in decisions and the impact on contract administration.

523. Grenig, Jay E. "Principles of Contract Interpretation: Interpreting Collective Bargaining Agreements." *Capital University Law Review* 16, no. 1 (Fall 1986): 31-58.

> A general discussion of contract interpretation that speaks to the influence of factors such as employer handbooks, external law, and industry practices.

524. Rutledge, Ivan C. "The Other Agreement to Arbitrate a Labor Dispute." *Ohio State Journal on Dispute Resolution* 3, no. 1 (Spring 1987): 79-116.

> Most collective bargaining agreements authorize an arbitrator to decide disputes "other" than those anticipated in the agreement. This article reviews several of these awards and concludes that the awards are generally consistent with the agreement.

525. Snow, Carlton J. "Contract Interpretation: The Plain Meaning Rule in Labor Arbitration." *Fordham Law Review* 55, no. 5 (April 1987): 681-706.

> According to the author, an arbitrator who accepts the "plain meaning" rule may exclude other evidence, such as past practice, which may provide a different interpretation of the intentions of the parties.

526. Bocher, Sheri L. "Contract Interpretation in Arbitration." *Employment Relations Today* 14, no. 2 (Summer 1987): 181-186.

> A guide to help employers draft clear and enforceable contracts. Principles and evidence used by arbitrators to interpret contract language are outlined.

527. Scott, Clyde, and Trevor Bain. "How Arbitrators Interpret Ambiguous Contract Language." *Personnel* 64, no. 8 (August 1987): 10-14.

> A presentation of the kind of internal and external evidence used by arbitrators to interpret ambiguous contract language.

528. Mittenthal, Richard, and Richard I. Bloch. "Arbitral Implications: Hearing the Sounds of Silence." In 42 NAA (1990): 65-99.

> Mittenthal and Bloch focus on the interpretation and application of contract silences. They conclude that the question is not whether arbitrators have the authority to find implications, but how they are to exercise that author-

ity wisely. Commentaries are provided by Barry E. Macey (union) and Susan B. Tabler (management), along with a response from the authors.

Stare Decisis, Res Judicata, and Collateral Estoppel

529. Doyle, C. T. "Precedent Value of Labor Arbitration Awards." *Personnel Journal* 42 (February 1963): 66-69.

> This survey provides insights into when and how arbitrators give weight to prior awards.

530. Baer, Walter E. "Precedent Value of Arbitration Awards." *Personnel Journal* 45 (September 1966): 484-488.

> A review of the approaches arbitrators take to consider prior awards in their decisions.

531. Harris, Philip. "The Use of Precedent in Labor Arbitration." *Arbitration Journal* 32, no. 1 (March 1977): 26-34.

> Arbitrators are not bound by precedent, but the author argues that parties who cite published labor arbitration awards win more cases than those who do not.

532. Jennings, Ken, and Cindy Martin. "The Role of Prior Arbitration Awards in Arbitral Decisions." *Labor Law Journal* 29 (February 1978): 95-106.

> Reviews 275 published decisions to ascertain the effect of prior awards.

533. Seitz, Peter. "The Citation of Authority and Precedent in Arbitration (Its Use and Abuse)." *Arbitration Journal* 38, no. 4 (December 1983): 58-61.

> The author criticizes the trend toward use of prior arbitration awards like judicial precedents. One well-supported argument is worth more than many citations of prior awards.

534. Williams, Jerre S. "Arbitration in Court: Judging the Judges." In 38 NAA (1986): 21-36.

> The author argues for following previous arbitrator's decisions under the same bargaining agreement; for spelling out the portions of the contract that influenced the decision; and for building a truthful record.

535. Grenig, Jay E. "Stare Decisis, Res Judicata, and Collateral Estoppel and Labor Arbitration." *Labor Law Journal* 38, no. 4 (April 1987): 195-205.

> The author examines cases and shows how arbitrators determine the precedential value of a prior arbitration award and how the application of these concepts can provide stability and predictability.

K. Management Rights and Past Practice

536. Phelps, James C., and Arthur J. Goldberg. "Management's Reserved Rights." In 9 NAA (1956): 102-148.

> Management view by Phelps union view by Goldberg and discussions by Sidney A. Wolf and Neil W. Chamberlain.

537. "Reserved Rights in Labor Arbitration." *Proceedings of NYU Twelfth Annual Conference on Labor*, edited by Emanuel Stein, 211-242. New York: Matthew Bender, 1959.

> Essays by Robert J. Doolan (management) and H. Howard Ostrin (labor) on the perennial question of reserved rights.

538. Horlacher, John Perry. "Employee Job Rights versus Employer Job Control: The Arbitrator's Choice." In 15 NAA (1962): 165-196.

> Argues for a better developed conceptual framework for balancing employees' rights and managerial interests. Discussion by Benjamin C. Sigal and David L. Benetar.

539. Chamberlain, Neil, Saul Wallen, Ralph T. Seward, and Marcia L. Greenbaum. "Management Rights and Labor Arbitration: A Symposium." *Industrial and Labor Relations Review* 16, no. 2 (January 1963): 183-278.

> A series of articles and comments on the interface between arbitration and management rights, with discussions of staffing and subcontracting.

540. Chamberlain, Neil, and Ralph T. Seward. "Work Assignments and Industrial Change." In 17 NAA (1964): 224-251.

> Essays on "Job Security, Management Rights, and Arbitration" by Chamberlain and "Reexamining Traditional Concepts" by Seward.

541. Killingsworth, Charles C. "Management Rights Revisited." In 22 NAA (1969): 1-19.

> The author rejects the "pristine" reserved rights concept.

542. Stein, Bruno. "Management Rights and Productivity." *Arbitration Journal* 32 (December 1977): 270-278.

> Review of published awards on residual rights principle.

543. Davey, Harold W. "The Arbitrator Views the Industrial Engineer." *California Management Review* 7, no. 1 (Fall 1964): 23-30.

> Discussion of similarities and differences in the approaches of arbitrators and industrial engineers to various issues.

114   ARTICLES AND PROCEEDINGS

544. King, Geoffrey R. "Seniority, Technological Change and Arbitration." *Personnel Administrator* 19, no. 6 (September 1974): 23-27.

> The author discusses the impact of technological change on seniority and resultant grievances. Unions won only two of 17 cases.

545. Ornati, Oscar A. "Rights Arbitration and Technological Change." In 38 NAA (1986): 224-239.

> A survey of arbitration decisions on contractual disputes that have followed the introduction of technological change. Arbitrators are almost entirely guided by the principles that the Elkouris had identified as the dominant practice.

546. Sibbernsen, Richard D. "What Arbitrators Think about Technology Replacing Labor." *Harvard Business Review* 64, no. 2 (March/April 1986): 8-16.

> The article concludes that arbitrators tend to recognize the employer's right to eliminate job classifications and they usually support automation and modernization efforts. However, contract clauses that specify manning levels are binding.

547. Brown, Susan R. "New Technology: How Does It Affect the Workplace?" *Arbitration Journal* 44, no. 3 (September 1989): 32-41.

> This article describes some of the effects of new technology (loss of bargaining unit work, assignment of new work, changes in job classifications and wage rates, and health and safety considerations) and the implications for arbitration.

Past Practice

548. Aaron, Benjamin. "The Uses of the Past in Arbitration." In 8 NAA (1955): 1-23.

> Aaron provides a general discussion of past practice, with discussions by Pearce Davis and Lloyd Bailer.

549. Mittenthal, Richard. "Past Practice and the Administration of Collective Bargaining Agreements." In 14 NAA (1961): 30-68.

> Covers the nature and functions of past practice in arbitration and the duration and termination of a practice. Discussions by Alex Elson and John A. Hogan.

550. Block, S. Lester. "Customs and Usages as Factors in Arbitration Decisions." *Proceedings of NYU Fifteenth Annual Conference on Labor*, edited by Emanuel Stein, 311-328. New York: Matthew Bender, 1962.

> Past practice in the wake of *Warrior and Gulf.* Critical analysis of arbitration decisions.

551. Wallen, Saul. "The Silent Contract vs. Express Provisions: The Arbitration of Local Working Conditions." In 15 NAA (1962): 117-147.

> Covers past practice and reserved rights, with discussions by Lloyd H. Bailer and Harry H. Platt.

552. Doyle, C. T. "Past Practice as a Standard in Arbitration." *Personnel* 39 (May 1962): 66-69.

> A survey of arbitrators provides a basis for recommendations on past practice.

553. McLaughlin, Richard P. "Custom and Past Practice in Labor Arbitration." *Arbitration Journal* 18, no. 4 (1963): 205-228.

> Review of arbitration awards on the nature of a practice, burden of proof, relation to contract clauses, and termination of practice.

554. Cuberley, Mark David. "Labor Law: Past Practices and Express Contract Language. (Case Note)." *Wake Forest Law Review* 18, no. 5 (October 1982): 902-920.

> This article uses a decision made by the Fourth Circuit as the basis for examining the difficulties courts have in reconciling past practices with contract language.

555. Mathis, Benton J., Jr. "Labor Law: Arbitrator's Authority and the Common Law of the Phop. (Case Note)." *Washington and Lee Law Review* 40, no. 2 (Spring 1983): 790-802.

> An arbitrator may, by an application of past practice, alter the terms of a collective bargaining agreement while keeping the award immune from judicial review. The author emphasizes the need for management consistency in disciplinary actions.

556. Dobbelaere, Arthur, Jr., William H. Leahy, and Jack Reardon. "The Effect of Past Practice on the Arbitration of Labor Disputes." *Arbitration Journal* 40, no. 4 (December 1985): 27-42.

> This article discusses the criteria that enable a past practice to become binding, how past practices help the arbitrator construe contract language, and how they might create a separate, enforceable condition of employment.

L. Discipline and Discharge

General Studies

557. Porter, J. M., Jr. "The Arbitration of Industrial Disputes Arising from Disciplinary Action." In 2 IRRA (1949): 262-271.

The author discusses various types of discipline to reveal motivations, interaction, and conflict.

558. Holly, J. Fred. "The Arbitration of Discharge Cases: A Case Study." In 10 NAA (1957): 1-20.

Analysis of 1,055 published discharge cases between 1942 and 1956 with inferences about the role of precedent. Discussion by Benjamin Aaron.

559. Kadish, Sanford H. "The Criminal Law and Industrial Discipline as Sanctioning Systems: Some Comparative Observations." In 17 NAA (1964): 125-164.

This article stresses the similarity between the criminal law and the process of disciplining employees. Discussions by Arthur Ross, John Heppel, and Bertram Diamond.

560. Fischer, Robert W. "Arbitration of Discharges for Marginal Reasons." *Monthly Labor Review* 91, no. 10 (October 1968): 1-5.

Discussion of cases where employers have tried to expand their disciplinary discretion.

561. Wheeler, Hoyt N. "Punishment Theory and Industrial Discipline." *Industrial Relations* 15, no. 2 (May 1976): 235-243.

The author suggests the use of psychological research to determine and improve the effectiveness of "corrective discipline" in the workplace.

562. Jennings, Ken, and Roger S. Wolters. "Discharge Cases Reconsidered." *Arbitration Journal* 31, no. 3 (September 1976): 164-180.

The most common reason for discharge is violation of plant rules or contract provisions.

563. Abrams, Roger I. "A Theory for the Discharge Case." *Arbitration Journal* 36, no. 3 (September 1981): 24-27.

Argues that a discharge case should be decided on the basis of a principle of prediction.

564. Wollett, Donald H. "What an Arbitrator Looks for from Management in Discharge Cases." *Employee Relations Law Journal* 9, no. 3 (Winter 1983/1984): 525-534.

Wollett argues that employers will prevail in discharge arbitrations when they give the employee adequate notice, apply the rules fairly, they investigate and allow the employee to respond to the charges, and the punishment fits the infraction.

565. Knight, Thomas R. "The Impact of Arbitration on the Administration of Disciplinary Policies." *Arbitration Journal* 39, no. 1 (March 1984): 43-56.

> This article shows how arbitration awards have increased the complexity of disciplinary policies and have enhanced employees' procedural and substantive rights.

566. Phillips, John R. "Their Own Brand of Industrial Justice: Arbitrators' Excesses in Discharge Cases." *Employee Relations Law Journal* 10, no. 1 (Summer 1984): 48-60.

> The author expresses strong displeasure with several awards in which he feels arbitrators improperly overturned discharges despite contractually incorporated work rules and proven offenses. Rejoinder by Robert Coulson, pp. 61-63.

567. Jennings, Ken, Barbara Sheffield, and Roger S. Wolters. "The Arbitration of Discharge Cases: A Forty-Year Perspective." *Labor Law Journal* 38, no. 1 (January 1987): 33-47.

> This article discusses the trends in discharge cases from 1942 to 1984, mitigating circumstances, the decline in insubordination and union activity cases, and the increase in discrimination cases.

Just Cause and Progressive Discipline

568. Irving, John S., Jr., and Carl L. Taylor. "Pre-Disciplinary Hearings: An Unbargained Procedural Trap in Arbitration." *Employee Relations Law Journal* 6, no. 2 (Autumn 1980): 195-206.

> The interpretation of just cause as requiring a hearing before discipline can be implemented is considered extreme.

569. Abrams, Roger I., and Dennis R. Nolan. "Toward a Theory of Just Cause in Employee Discipline Cases." *Duke Law Journal* 1985, no. 3-4 (June-September 1985): 594-623.

> The concept of just cause has led to inconsistent results that fail to serve the purposes of labor or management. This article develops a theory of just cause built around the nature of the employment relationship and the objectives of management and the union.

570. Zirkel, Perry A. "Labor Arbitrators' Inference of 'Progressive Discipline' in Just Cause Clauses: The Courts' View." *Journal of Collective Negotiations in the Public Sector* 17, no. 1 (1988): 27-34.

> A review of judicial decisions shows that the courts are split as to whether labor arbitrators have the authority to read a progressive discipline requirement into a just-cause clause.

571. Carter, Donald D. "Grievance Arbitration and the Charter: The Emerging Issues." *Industrial Relations (Canada)* 44, no. 2 (Spring 1989): 337-351.

> The author argues that Canadian Charter arguments could challenge almost every aspect of arbitral jurisprudence defining just cause for discipline or discharge.

572. Dunsford, John E. "Arbitral Discretion: The Tests of Just Cause." In 42 NAA (1990): 23-64.

> Dunsford reviews the classic tests of just cause and points out their limitations, with commentaries from Donald W. Cohen (union) and Robert J. Mignin (management).

Specific Disciplinary Topics

Absenteeism

573. Rosenthal, Rhoda. "Arbitral Standards for Absentee Discharges." *Labor Law Journal* 30, no. 12 (December 1979): 732-740.

> The author contends that in disputes over absentee discharges, arbitrators consider whether the rules are publicized and reasonable, and they consider concepts of progressive discipline, consistency, and due process.

574. Scott, K. Dow, and G. Stephen Taylor. "An Analysis of Absenteeism Cases Taken to Arbitration: 1975-1981." *Arbitration Journal* 38, no. 3 (September 1983): 61-70.

> Content analysis of 146 absentee discharges taken to arbitration to determine the likelihood that an attendance control policy will be upheld.

575. Block, Howard S., and Richard Mittenthal. "Arbitration and the Absent Employee." In 37 NAA (1985): 77-105.

> The conceptual issues that influence arbitrators in cases involving employee absence, elements that enter into absence cases, absences due to injury or illness, and no-fault absence plans.

AIDS

576. Dilauro, Thomas J. "Relieving the Fear of Contagion." *Personnel Administrator* 34, no. 2 (February 1989): 52-58.

> The author reviews arbitration awards relating to AIDS in the workplace and recommends involving labor in formulating special policies and programs.

577. Hauck, Vern E. "AIDS and Arbitration." *Labor Law Journal* 41, no. 5 (May 1990): 293-300.

> The article examines remedies that employers, unions, and employees are

testing; the reasonable accommodation criterion; and several employee discharge arbitrations where AIDS was an issue.

578. Abrams, Roger I., and Dennis R. Nolan. "AIDS in Labor Arbitration." *University of San Francisco Law Review* 25, no. 1 (Fall 1990): 67-91.

> The authors explain issues likely to arise in AIDS-related grievances, and the surrounding laws, and they provide guidelines for arbitrators.

Alcohol and Drugs

579. Somers, Gerald G. "Alcohol and Just Cause for Discharge." In 28 NAA (1976): 103-117.

> Describes dilemmas encountered by arbitrators dealing with this issue.

580. Levin, Edward, and Tia Schneider Denenberg. "How Arbitrators View Drug Abuse." *Arbitration Journal* 31, no. 2 (June 1976): 97-108.

> The authors conclude that because the use of drugs, unlike the consumption of alcohol, is illegal, arbitrators tend to require different levels of proof.

581. Provost, Glendel J., Richard C. Stephens, Yvonne F. Freedman, et al. "Alcohol in the Workplace: A Review of Recent Arbitration Cases." *Employee Relations Law Journal* 4, no. 3 (Winter 1978-1979): 400-414.

> According to the authors, in alcohol cases, arbitrators are influenced by the company's rules, burden of proof, and whether the offense occurred on or off the premises and on or off duty.

582. Andrewson, Dale E. "Arbitral Views of Alcoholism Cases." *Personnel Journal* 58, no. 5 (May 1979): 318-322.

> Andrewson argues that arbitrators are beginning to treat alcohol as a disease, forcing unions and management to treat alcoholism according to principles of progressive discipline.

583. Spencer, Janet Maleson. "The Developing Notion of Employer Responsibility for the Alcoholic, Drugaddicted, or Mentally Ill Employee: An Examination under Federal and State Employment Statutes and Arbitration Decisions." *St. John's Law Review* 53, no. 4 (Summer 1979): 659-720.

> Charts the evolution of the idea that the employer bears some responsibility for the troubled employee.

584. Wynns, Pat. "Arbitration Standards in Drug Discharge Cases." *Arbitration Journal* 34, no. 2 (June 1979): 19-27.

> The author discusses the different arbitral standards of proof for discharges for drug-related misconduct on and off company premises.

585. Provost, Glendel J., William R. Smolensky, Richard C. Stephens, and Yvonne F. Freedman. "Alcohol or Drug Use on the Job: A Study of Arbitration Cases." *Employee Relations Law Journal* 5, no. 2 (Autumn 1979): 245-257.

> Because alcoholism is viewed as a disease and drug abuse as a crime, the authors argue that the alcoholic employee is often offered treatment as an alternative to discipline, but the drug abuser is not.

586. Denenberg, Tia Schneider. "The Arbitration of Alcohol and Drug Abuse Cases." *Arbitration Journal* 35, no. 4 (December 1980): 16-21.

> Arbitrators show wide variation in approaches to alcohol and drug abuse related issues.

587. Marmo, Michael. "Alcoholism, Drug Addiction, and Mental Illness: The Use of Rehabilitative Remedies in Arbitration." *Labor Law Journal* 32, no. 8 (August 1981): 491-497.

> Examines the use of rehabilitative remedies in published arbitration decisions in discipline of problems caused by mental illness, alcohol, or drugs. See also Michael Marmo, "Arbitrators View Problem Employees: Discipline or Rehabilitation?" *Journal of Contemporary Law* 9 (1983): 41-79.

588. Abramson, Elliott M., and Carlton J. Snow. "Alcoholism and Kleptomania: Looking at the Legal Inconsistencies." *Employee Relations Law Journal* 7, no. 4 (Spring 1982): 619-642.

> An examination of the disease of kleptomania as a cause of theft of company property.

589. "The Arbitration of Employee Drug Abuse Cases." In 36 NAA (1984): 90-127.

> Tia Schneider Denenberg compares arbitral treatment of cases involving alcohol and drug abuse; Dr. Richard L. Masters and Kenneth B. Cooper examine the issue in the context of airline pilots; John D. Williamson comments from a management perspective.

590. Bornstein, Tim. "Drug and Alcohol Issues in the Workplace: An Arbitrator's Perspective." *Arbitration Journal* 39, no. 3 (September 1984): 19-24.

> The author proposes five "universal principles" to be applied to these and other discipline cases. He suggests that arbitrators avoid the temptation to become therapists or psychiatrists.

591. Marmo, Michael. "Arbitrators Consider Employee Drug Abuse: An Illness?" *Mid-Atlantic Journal of Business* 23, no. 1 (Winter 1984/1985): 21-33.

> This review of published cases suggests that rehabilitative remedies are considered in the arbitration of mental illness and alcohol abuse cases, but rarely in drug cases.

592. Loomis, Lloyd. "Employee Assistance Programs: Their Impact on Arbitration and Litigation of Termination Cases." *Employee Relations Law Journal* 12, no. 2 (Autumn 1986): 275-288.

> Loomis contends that arbitrators generally hold that job performance should be a deciding factor in decisions concerning employee discipline in drug and alcohol cases. The crucial issue is usually whether the grievant should have been allowed to continue to work after enrolling in an employee assistance program.

593. McHugh, William A., Jr., Willis J. Goldsmith, and Leroy D. Clark. "Substance Abuse: A Problem That Won't Go Away." In 40 NAA (1988): 67-106.

> McHugh focuses on testing, discipline, off-duty possession, and the use or sale of drugs. Goldsmith argues that drug testing can benefit employees and unions as well as management. Clark focuses on the related public policy issues.

594. Collins, Daniel G., Thomas R. Miller, Susan M. Oliver, and Linda Lampkin. "Just Cause and the Troubled Employee." In 41 NAA (1989): 21-75.

> Collins concludes that when a condition is disabling and chronic, arbitrators tend to give employees a chance to put their lives together. Miller and Oliver argue for the application of the traditional just-cause standard. Lampkin argues for a rehabilitation opportunity.

595. Thornicroft, Kenneth William. "Arbitrators, Social Values, and the Burden of Proof in Substance Abuse Discharge Cases." *Labor Law Journal* 40, no. 9 (September 1989): 582-593.

> The author discusses the level of proof in drug and alcohol cases and how an arbitrator's requirements may be influenced by social values and the gender of the grievant.

596. Bornstein, Tim. "Getting to the Bottom of the Issue: How Arbitrators View Alcohol Abuse." *Arbitration Journal* 44, no. 4 (December 1989): 46-50.

> Bornstein contends that arbitrators may not be sufficiently informed about the medical and scientific issues relating to alcohol abuse and alcoholism. They should consider seeking information from mental health professionals.

597. Hill, Marvin F., Jr., and Anthony V. Sinicropi. "Remedies, Troubled Employees, and the Arbitrator's Role." In 42 NAA (1990): 160-170.

> This paper concludes that arbitrators take many different approaches to problems in this area. The authors argue for conservatism.

598. Allen, A. Dale, Jr. "What Constitutes Drug Possession: Arbitration Case Histories and Guidelines." *Employee Relations Law Journal* 16, no. 3 (Winter 1990/1991): 359-367.

>Contains a set of guidelines for use in analyzing drug possession cases.

599. Klaas, Brian S., and Gregory G. Dell'Omo. "The Determinants of Disciplinary Decisions: The Case of Employee Drug Use." *Personnel Psychology* 44 (1991): 813-935.

>This study examines the disciplinary decision rules that managers employ when responding to substance abuse violations. It reports that substantial inconsistency is likely to exist across managers in how they respond to violations and that the decision rule a manager employs is influenced by his/her attitude toward punishment and toward drug use.

600. Denenberg, Tia Schneider, and Richard V. Denenberg. "The Arbitration of Employee Substance Abuse Rehabilitation Issues." *Arbitration Journal* 46, no. 1 (March 1991): 17-33.

>An examination of agreements that provide recovery opportunities for chemically dependent employees, focusing on topics such as the extent to which normal disciplinary sanctions are held in abeyance and last chance agreements.

Testing for Alcohol and Drugs

601. Denenberg, Tia Schneider, and Richard V. Denenberg. "Employee Drug Testing and the Arbitrator: What Are the Issues?" *Arbitration Journal* 42, no. 2 (June 1987): 19-31.

>A review of issues faced by arbitrators relating to drug testing.

602. Denenberg, Tia Schneider, and Richard V. Denenberg. "Drug Testing from the Arbitrator's Perspective." *Nova Law Review* 11, no. 2 (Winter 1987): 371-413.

>This article discusses topics such as determining the reasonableness of drug testing, just cause, chain of custody, off-duty conduct, and treatment.

603. Davidoff, Philip K., and Christopher C. Martin. "The Drug War in the Workplace: Employee Drug Testing under Collective Bargaining Agreements." *St. John's Journal of Legal Commentary* 5, no. 1 (1989): 1-28.

>A review of public policy toward drug testing with a brief discussion of the arbitration issues involved.

604. Veglahn, Peter A. "Drug Testing That Clears the Arbitration Hurdle." *Personnel Administrator* 34, no. 2 (February 1989): 62-64.

>The author concludes that employers tend to win drug-testing cases when there is reasonable suspicion or unacceptable job performance or when there have been tests prior to disciplinary action.

605. Bell, Cathleen G. "Drug Testing Issues in Arbitration." *Detroit College of Law Review* 1989, no. 3 (Fall 1989): 899-930.

> This article discusses management's right to require testing, standards, contract language, confirmation procedures, privacy concerns, and other issues.

606. Kirk, Geoffrey T. "Employee Drug Testing: Federal Courts Are Redefining Individual Rights of Privacy, Will Labor Arbitrators Follow Suit?" *University of Miami Law Review* 44, no. 2 (November 1989): 489-538.

> This article examines the competing rights of employers and employees and shows how arbitrators and the courts tend to take positions between the two extremes.

607. Tobias, Robert M., and Rick R. Doering. "Drug Testing Disputes." In 43 NAA (1991): 235-255.

> After a brief introduction by Tia Schneider Denenberg, Tobias discusses the court criteria in federal sector cases involving random testing and reasonable cause. Doering examines the regulations of the Nuclear Regulatory Commission and the Department of Transportation.

Hair and Beards

608. Valtin, Rolf, and Thomas J. McDermott. "Changing Life Styles and Problems of Authority in the Plant." In 25 NAA (1973): 235-282.

> Discussions by Valtin on "Hair and Beards in Arbitration" and McDermott on "Drugs, Bombs, and Bomb Scares," with a discussion by Martin A. Cohen.

609. Tucker, Mark M. "Arbitration of Labor Disputes Involving Hair." *Willamette Law Journal* 10 (Spring 1974): 258-271.

> Survey of reported decisions on employer regulation of hairstyles.

610. McGuckin, John J., Jr. "Employee Hairstyles: Recent Judicial and Arbitral Decisions." *Labor Law Journal* 26 (March 1975): 174-189.

> Review of decisions regarding employer's control over hairstyle and right to discipline for violation of grooming rules.

611. Marmo, Michael. "Employees' Pursuit of Hirsute: The Arbitration of Hair and Beard Cases." *Labor Law Journal* 30 (July 1979): 416-426.

> Marmo reviews 47 hair and beard cases arbitrated between 1967 and 1977. He concludes that constitutional and discrimination arguments lost while health and safety arguments won.

Insubordination

612. Graham, Joseph C., III. "Arbitration of Insubordination Disputes in the Public Sector." *Arbitration Journal* 31, no. 3 (September 1976): 191-207.

> A comparison between the arbitral treatment of insubordination cases in the public sector and in private employment.

613. Nelson, W. B. "Insubordination: Arbitral 'Law' in the Reconciliation of Conflicting Employer/Employee Interests." *Labor Law Journal* 35, no. 2 (February 1984): 112-122.

> An examination of arbitral standards for insubordination and the penalties.

Off-Duty Conduct

614. Leonard, John W. "Discipline for Off-the-Job Activities." *Monthly Labor Review* 91, no. 10 (October 1968): 5-11.

> Study of cases shows most arbitrators draw a functional rather than a physical line regarding off-job activities.

615. Hill, Marvin F., Jr., and Donald Dawson. "Discharge for Off-Duty Misconduct in the Private and Public Sectors." *Arbitration Journal* 40, no. 2 (June 1985): 24-37.

> Review of the criteria applied by arbitrators in cases of discharge or discipline for off-duty misconduct.

616. Marmo, Michael. "Public Employees: On-the-Job Discipline for Off-the-Job Behavior." *Arbitration Journal* 40, no. 2 (June 1985): 3-23.

> The author argues that a link between off-duty conduct and on-the-job activities must exist for an arbitrator to uphold disciplinary actions. Higher standards are used in public sector cases.

617. Marmo, Michael. "Off-Duty Misbehavior by Educational Employees: Arbitrators Consider On-the-Job Discipline." *Journal of Collective Negotiations in the Public Sector* 15, no. 4 (1986): 327-345.

> A survey of awards on discipline for off-duty behavior of employees of educational institutions, elementary through college.

618. Hill, Marvin F., Jr., and Mark L. Kahn. "Discipline and Discharge for Off-Duty Misconduct: What Are the Arbitral Standards?" In 39 NAA (1987): 121-154.

> This paper reviews the criteria normally employed in determining just cause in cases involving off-duty misconduct or where criminal charges are involved, and whether the problems are different in the public sector.

Other Off-the-Job Considerations

619. Roberts, Benjamin C. "The Arbitration of Alleged Security Risks." In 8 NAA (1955): 63-91.

Review of cases processed under the government industrial security program and just-cause discharges. Discussions by Israel Ben Scheiber and Lawrence J. Ackerman.

620. Stein, Bruno. "Loyalty and Security Cases in Arbitration." *Industrial and Labor Relations Review* 17, no. 1 (October 1963): 96-113.

Study of published awards between 1945 and 1961 dealing with issues such as lack of employee clearance for classified work as a cause for discharge.

621. Foster, Howard G. "Disloyalty to the Employer: A Study of Arbitration Awards." *Arbitration Journal* 20, no. 3 (1965): 157-167.

Covers dual job holding.

622. Fisher, Robert W. "How Garnisheed Workers Fare under Arbitration." *Monthly Labor Review* 90, no. 5 (May 1967): 1-6.

The article shows that arbitrators treat garnishment as on-duty behavior and sustain discharge for garnishment if correct procedures are followed and there are no mitigating factors.

623. Marmo, Michael. "Work versus Family Obligations: An Arbitral Perspective." *Arbitration Journal* 46, no. 3 (September 1991): 14-28.

Marmo argues that when ambiguous language is present, an arbitrator's personal views on the balance between work and family obligations become critical to a decision.

Sexual Harassment

624. Marmo, Michael. "Arbitrating Sex Harassment Cases." *Arbitration Journal* 35, no. 1 (March 1980): 35-40.

A study of sexual harassment arbitration cases involving grievances filed by male employees who felt that management violated their contracts by disciplining them for harassing women co-workers, and the related problems of unions and of the harassed women.

625. Murphy, William P. "Arbitration of Discrimination Grievances." In 33 NAA (1981): 285-308.

An examination of arbitration in the wake of *Gardner-Denver*, with attention to the emerging issue of sexual harassment. Comments by J. Leon Adair and Robert W. Ashmore.

626. Greenbaum, Marcia L., and Bruce Fraser. "Sexual Harassment in the Workplace." *Arbitration Journal* 36, no. 4 (December 1981): 30-41.

Focuses on reasoning used by courts in coming to the position that sexual harassment falls under Title VII and the nature of sexual harassment claims that have reached arbitration.

627. Greenbaum, Marcia L. "Sexual Harassment and Arbitration." *Proceedings of NYU Thirty-fifth Annual Conference on Labor*, edited by Richard Adelman, 379-400. New York: Matthew Bender, 1983.

Treatment of sexual harassment charges by courts and arbitrators. Suggestions for unions and employees.

628. Nelson, W. B. "Sexual Harassment, Title VII, and Labor Arbitration." *Arbitration Journal* 40, no. 4 (December 1985): 55-65.

This article reviews the case law on sexual harassment and asserts that arbitration may assume a greater role in these cases in the future.

629. Monat, Jonathan S., and Angel Gomez. "Decisional Standards Used by Arbitrators in Sexual Harassment Cases." *Labor Law Journal* 37, no. 10 (October 1986): 712-718.

This review of the decisions of arbitrators in sexual harassment cases focuses on evidence, proof, just cause, and external law.

630. Monat, Jonathan S., and Angel Gomez. "Sexual Harassment: The Impact of *Meritor Savings Bank v. Vinson* on Grievances and Arbitration Decisions." *Arbitration Journal* 41, no. 4 (December 1986): 24-29.

This article reviews the emerging legal standards in sexual harassment cases and considers the implications for arbitration.

631. Rule, William S. "Arbitral Standards in Sexual Harassment Cases." *Industrial Relations Law Journal* 10, no. 1 (1988): 12-18.

The author identifies problems of determining credibility, applicability of external law, adequacy of employer warning, and relevance of accuser's sexual activities.

632. Nowlin, William A. "Sexual Harassment in the Workplace: How Arbitrators Rule." *Arbitration Journal* 43, no. 4 (December 1988): 31-40.

Nowlin, in this review of awards, concludes that arbitrators tend to deny the grievances of employees who are disciplined for sexual harassment.

633. Fitzgibbon, Susan A. "Sexual Harassment and Labor Arbitration." *Georgia Journal of International and Comparative Law* 20, no. 1 (Spring 1990): 71-87.

The author cites a number of reasons why arbitration is an appropriate forum for sexual harassment issues.

634. Aggarwal, Arjun P. "Arbitral Review of Sexual Harassment in the Canadian Workplace." *Arbitration Journal* 46, no. 1 (March 1991): 4-16.

> Canadian arbitrators generally recognize sexual harassment as serious misconduct. They have found the testimony of the victims to be credible, but they differ on some of the key characteristics, such as whether a single incident constitutes sexual harassment. Included are four suggestions for arbitrators.

635. Costello, Edward J. "The Mediation Alternative in Sex Harassment Cases." *Arbitration Journal* 47, no. 1 (March 1991): 16-23.

> This article suggests that mediation is a simple, cheap, and quick way to deal with sexual harassment charges in the workplace and that it produces fair and just resolutions.

636. Bornstein, Tim, Helen R. Neuborne, and R. Gaull Silerman. "The Arbitration of Sexual Harassment." In 44 NAA (1992): 109-119.

> Bornstein reviews legal developments and the need for arbitral sensitivity, and he concludes that arbitration may be the only forum where both the victim and the harasser can receive due process. Neuborne focuses on the shortcomings some arbitrators have shown in this area, and Silberman describes the EEOC Guidelines.

637. Hauck, Vern E., and Thomas G. Pearce. "Sexual Harassment and Arbitration." *Labor Law Journal* 43, no. 1 (January 1992): 31-39.

> A general discussion of sexual harassment cases. The data show that most of these cases involve coworkers rather than supervisors, and are based on hostile environment considerations or unwelcome advances. Discharges occur only when the harassment is excessive, without remorse, and affects the work environment or the company's public image.

638. Crow, Stephen M., and Clifford M. Koen. "Sexual Harassment: New Challenge for Labor Arbitrators." *Arbitration Journal* 47, no. 2 (June 1992): 6-18.

> The authors propose standards for determining sexual harassment and seven tests that an arbitrator might employ.

Strike-Related Discipline

639. Leahy, William H. "Arbitration, Union Stewards, and Wildcat Strikes." *Arbitration Journal* 24, no. 1 (1969): 50-58.

> Published awards show that arbitrators impose a special duty on stewards not to participate in a wildcat strike.

640. Warns, Carl A., Jr. "Right of Management to Discipline for Refusal to Cross a Picket Line." In 26 NAA (1974): 138-161.

Discussions by Fred W. Elarbee, Jr., and Jerome R. Cooper based on a review of arbitration awards.

641. Watkins, John L. "Enforcement of No-Strike Clauses through Disparate Discipline of Union Officials: Another Dilemma in National Labor Policy?" *American Business Law Journal* 21, no. 2 (Summer 1983): 185-212.

> An examination of the discipline of union officials who contribute to the violation of a no-strike clause.

642. Levin, Edward, and Candace Reid. "Arbitration of Strike Misconduct Cases Arising Out of Legal Strikes." *Arbitration Journal* 39, no. 3 (September 1984): 42-48.

> The authors review the various categories of strike misconduct and discuss arbitrators' reasoning in reaching decisions.

643. Brotman, Billie Ann. "A Comparative Analysis of Arbitration and National Labor Relations Board Decisions Involving Wildcat Strikes." *Labor Law Journal* 36, no. 7 (July 1985): 434-441.

> A review of the positions taken by the NLRB and arbitrators on wildcat strikes caused by dangerous working conditions and by violations of a collective agreement.

644. Keim, James A., and David L. Quigg. "The Sickout: Using and Evaluating Statistical Evidence in a Prima Facie Case." *Employee Relations Law Journal* 13, no. 3 (Winter 1987/1988): 445-464.

> The author illustrates techniques of statistical analysis of attendance data for use in arbitration.

645. Bosch, Frederick J., and Paul A. Tufano. "Establishing a Uniform Standard for Striker Misconduct in Arbitration Cases." *Labor Law Journal* 39, no. 9 (September 1988): 629-633.

> An examination of the standards employed by arbitrators and the NLRB in cases of strike-related misconduct. Arbitrators tend to take a more lenient view.

646. Lovo, Mario M. "Sympathy Strikes and Employee Rights: Arbitrators 'Shopping' for Public Law Precedent in the Unclear Waiver of Section 7 Rights Market." *Detroit College of Law Review* 1989, no. 3 (Fall 1989): 1175-1211.

> This article explores the ways in which stranger picket line (a picket line formed by members of another union) issues have been treated by the NLRB and the courts and the impact of these legal decisions on arbitration.

647. Stutin, Cathy M. "Arbitration and Selective Discipline of Union Officials after

Metropolitan Edison." University of Miami Law Review 44, no. 2 (November 1989): 443-466.

> An examination of *Metropolitan Edison* in which the Supreme Court decided that it was unlawful to impose more severe penalties on union representatives for taking part in unlawful work stoppages.

648. Alexander, Gabriel N., Jerrold A. Glass, and Seth D. Rosen. "Strike Related Discipline." In 44 NAA (1992): 253-272.

> Three papers on the arbitration of discharges for misconduct by striking employees. The papers focus on whether there is a common law of arbitration in such cases, decisional criteria for them, and procedural standards.

Union-Related Discipline

649. Baer, Walter E. "Discharge and Discipline of Union Representatives." *Monthly Labor Review* 92, no. 9 (September 1969): 39-45.

> Baer concludes that, except when on union business, union representatives are treated like other employees.

650. Leahy, William H. "Arbitration and Insubordination of Union Stewards." *Arbitration Journal* 275, no. 1 (1972): 18-28.

> A review of arbitration decisions on the rights and status of stewards.

651. Leahy, William H. "Grievances over Union Business on Company Time and Premises." *Arbitration Journal* 30, no. 3 (September 1975): 191-198.

> Review of published cases finds consistency in this area.

652. Seidman, Joel. "Discipline of Union Officers by Public Management." *Arbitration Journal* 32, no. 4 (December 1977): 256-269.

> Seidman concludes that arbitration awards have limited the ability of union officials to leave the job for union business without permission, to engage in inappropriate speech and conduct, and to refuse to obey a superior's order.

Violence and Horseplay

653. Jennings, Ken. "Verbal and Physical Abuse toward Supervision." *Arbitration Journal* 28, no. 4 (December 1974): 258-271.

> Review of 70 published decisions, with focus on decisional standards.

654. Adams, Meryl, Lisa Davis, and Ken Jennings. "Employee Fighting: Will It Mean Discharge?" *Arbitration Journal* 43, no. 2 (June 1988): 37-43.

> Termination for employee fighting has not been upheld in a majority of the published awards unless there is a clear antifighting rule and a thorough in-

vestigation. Mitigating factors include location, timing, provocation, and self-defense.

655. Davis, Lisa, and Ken Jennings. "Employee Horseplay and Likely Managerial Overreaction." *Labor Law Journal* 40, no. 4 (April 1989): 248-256.

Arbitrators appear to be influenced by the extent of injury, whether reconciliation took place, and the nature of the program for discouraging horseplay.

Other Disciplinary Issues

656. Fischback, Charles P. "Past Misconduct in Discharge Cases." *Arbitration Journal* 24, no. 3 (1969): 175-183.

Review of published awards on use of past misconduct to prove present guilt and the propriety of the penalty.

657. Jennings, Ken. "Arbitrators, Blacks, and Discipline." *Personnel Journal* 54, no. 1 (January 1975): 32-37, 64.

This article examines disciplinary problems with minority group members.

658. Holley, William H., Jr. "Performance Ratings in Arbitration." *Arbitration Journal* 32, no. 1 (March 1977): 8-25.

Reviews decisions involving performance ratings and offers guidelines for establishing systems that will withstand arbitral scrutiny.

659. Mills, Miriam K. "The Energy Crisis and Labor Relations." *Arbitration Journal* 35, no. 4 (December 1980): 3-8.

The article focuses on discipline of employees who have left the work site because the employer failed to maintain a steady workplace temperature. Arbitrators have consistently found for the employers.

660. Dobranski, Bernard. "A Memo on the Falsification of Employment Applications: An Arbitral Perspective." *Chicago-Kent Law Review* 59 (1983): 997-1005.

Examines the standards established by arbitrators in these cases and several pertinent decisions made by arbitrators.

661. Helburn, I. B., and John R. Hill. "The Arbitration of Religious Practice Grievances." *Arbitration Journal* 39, no. 2 (June 1984): 3-13.

Arbitrators once were consistent in upholding management in cases involving refusals to work for religious reasons. They have come to apply a "reasonable accommodation" standard.

662. Coulson, Robert. "When God Says No to Work Rules." In Office of the General Counsel, American Arbitration Association. *Arbitration and the Law: AAA*

General Counsel's Annual Report: 1987-1988, 132-139. New York: AAA, 1988.

> This article examines the conflict between employer work rules and the religious obligations of employees and the implications for arbitration.

663. Couser, Ann, Joan Hoffman, and Ken Jennings. "Discharges for Customer Discourtesy: How Arbitrators Settle Disputes." *Employee Relations Law Journal* 13, no. 4 (Spring 1988): 667-680.

> Discharge was upheld in only 12 of 50 arbitration awards involving employee discourtesy. The article explores how employer policies, evidence, and mitigating factors affect the outcome.

664. Garbutt, Cynthia Horvath, and Lamont E. Stallworth. "Theft in the Workplace: An Arbitrator's Perspective on Employee Discipline." *Arbitration Journal* 44, no. 3 (September 1989): 21-31.

> In theft cases the arbitrator should be alert to whether conduct took place off-duty or is related to drug or alcohol abuse and to privacy and due process rights of the employee.

665. Dell'Omo, Gregory G., and James E. Jones, Jr. "Disparate Treatment in Labor Arbitration: An Empirical Analysis." *Labor Law Journal* 41, no. 11 (November 1990): 739-750.

> This study determines how arbitrators deal with disparate treatment issues, focusing on cases where rules are applied differentially and where there are differences in the penalties imposed.

666. Berkeley, Arthur Eliot. "Asleep at the Wheel: How Arbitrators View Sleeping on the Job." *Arbitration Journal* 46, no. 2 (June 1991): 48-51.

> In this discussion of sleeping on the job, arbitrators focus on the nature of the work, whether the work was getting done, threats to the health or safety of other workers or property, and the equity of the discipline.

667. Juliussen, James H. "Compulsive Gambling and Mitigation of Work Place Discipline: A Step Too Far?" *Willamette Law Review* 27, no. 3 (Summer 1991): 711-730.

> This article discusses the tendency to temper discipline to compulsive gamblers and, by implication, other troubled employees.

Performance of Reinstated Workers

668. Ross, Arthur M. "The Arbitration of Discharge Cases: What Happens after Reinstatement." In 10 NAA (1957): 21-60.

> Empirical study of 123 reinstated employees: whether they return, how long they stay, progress on the job, perceptions of employer and union. Discussion by Sidney A. Wolff.

669. Gold, Charlotte, Rodney E. Dennis, and Joseph C. Graham, III. "Reinstatement after Termination: Public School Teachers." *Industrial and Labor Relations Review* 31, no. 3 (April 1978): 310- 321.

>An examination of the performance of teachers reinstated by arbitrators. Inadequate teachers tended to remain inadequate after reinstatement.

670. Malinowski, Arthur Anthony. "An Empirical Analysis of Discharge Cases and the Work History of Employees Reinstated by Labor Arbitrators." *Arbitration Journal* 36, no. 1 (March 1981): 31-46.

>The data show that, despite the generally positive performance of reinstated employees, most employers view an order to reinstate as unacceptable.

671. Labig, Challer E., Jr., I. B. Helburn, and Robert C. Rodgers. "Discipline History, Seniority, and Reason for Discharge as Predictors of Post-Reinstatement Job Performance." *Arbitration Journal* 40, no. 3 (September 1985): 44-52.

>Study concludes that predischarge performance record is a reliable predictor of postreinstatement job performance and that employees discharged for absenteeism are more likely to be discharged a second time.

672. Rodgers, Robert C., I. B. Helburn, and John E. Hunter. "The Relationship of Seniority to Job Performance Following Reinstatement." *Academy of Management Journal* 29, no. 1 (March 1986): 101-114.

>The data show that reinstated workers with high seniority who have been exonerated by arbitrators perform significantly better than reinstated and exonerated workers with low seniority. But if they were not exonerated, those with high seniority perform more poorly than those with low seniority.

673. Simkin, William E. "Some Results of Reinstatement by Arbitration." *Arbitration Journal* 41, no. 3 (September 1986): 53- 58.

>Contrary to other studies, this article concludes that except for grievants discharged for taking part in "wildcat" strikes, reinstated employees made poor recoveries.

674. Ponak, Allen. "Discharge Arbitration and Reinstatement in the Province of Alberta." *Arbitration Journal* 42, no. 2 (June 1987): 39-46.

>A comparison of discharge arbitration and reinstatement in Alberta with other Canadian provinces and the United States. Male grievants were twice as likely to have their discharges upheld as were female grievants.

675. Helburn, I. B. "Seniority and Postreinstatement Performance." In 43 NAA (1991): 141-149.

Author finds a positive relationship between postdischarge performance and seniority among employees who were exonerated.

M. Seniority Rights, Compensation, Work Rules, and Remedies

Seniority Rights, Ability, and Testing Issues

676. Healy, James J. "The Factor of Ability in Labor Relations." In 8 NAA (1955): 45-61.

> Reports on research into "the waning role of the ability factor" and the experiences of senior employees bypassed for promotion. Discussions by Jean T. McKelvey and Gabriel N. Alexander.

677. Howard, Wayne E. "Seniority Rights and Trial Periods." *Arbitration Journal* 15, no. 2 (1960): 51-64.

> A study of published arbitration awards on the use of trial periods to assess ability under modified seniority clauses.

678. Kennedy, Thomas. "Merging Seniority Lists." In 16 NAA (1963): 1-44.

> In-depth analysis of how arbitrators have dealt with bargaining unit mergers. Author concludes that there is "no pat formula." Discussions by Vernon H. Jensen and Mark L. Kahn.

679. Metzler, John H., and El Dean V. Kohrs. "Tests and 'the Requirements of the Job.'" *Arbitration Journal* 20, no. 2 (1965): 103-111.

> Discussion of psychological issues involved in employment testing and their place in arbitration.

680. McDermott, Thomas J. "Types of Seniority Provisions and the Measurement of Ability." *Arbitration Journal* 25, no. 2 (1970): 101-124.

> Arbitral treatment of modified seniority clauses, including criteria for measuring ability (tests, experience, schooling, output data, performance ratings, etc.).

681. Gallagher, Daniel G., and Peter A. Veglahn. "Arbitral Standards in Cases Involving Testing Issues." *Labor Law Journal* 37, no. 10 (October 1986): 719-730.

> The author reviews testing in the selection and promotion process and how test determinations of employee qualifications are treated in arbitration.

682. Abrams, Roger I., and Dennis R. Nolan. "Seniority Rights under the Collective Agreement." *Labor Lawyer* 2, no. 1 (Winter 1986): 99-146.

This article describes the sources and nature of seniority rights, the administration of seniority systems, the interplay between seniority and ability, superseniority, and the civil rights statutes.

683. Cerbone, Richard R., and Joseph Walsh. "Management Judgment vs. Seniority: Grist for the Arbitration Mill." *Employee Relations Law Journal* 14, no. 3 (Winter 1988/1989): 429-437.

Arbitrators in "relative ability" seniority cases tend to focus on measurable criteria, such as demonstrated performance, education, and experience.

Compensation Issues

Wage Rates and Pay Guarantees

684. Salter, Robert. "Principles of Arbitration in Wage Rate Disputes." *Industrial and Labor Relations Review* 1, no. 3 (April 1948): 363-385.

Analysis of factors considered by arbitrators in settling wage issues.

685. Miller, Richard U. "The Arbitration of Disputes over Reopened Wages." *Arbitration Journal* 22, no. 1 (1967): 24-30.

The aims of this study were to determine the extent to which reopener clauses limit the arbitrator's authority and whether reopener disputes are decided differently from new contract wage disputes.

686. Holly, J. Fred, and Gary A. Hall. "Dispelling the Myths of Wage Arbitration." *Labor Law Journal* 28, no. 6 (June 1976): 344-354.

Attempts to dispel certain misconceptions about wage arbitration, that, e.g., it is on the decline, it entails risk and expensive tripartite panels, awards typically just split the difference, and it promotes industrial unrest.

687. Abrams, Roger I., and Dennis R. Nolan. "Buying Employees' Time: Guaranteed Pay under Collective Agreements." *Syracuse Law Review* 35, no. 3 (1984): 867-897.

Reviews principles utilized by arbitrators in deciding cases involving call-in pay and reporting pay clauses.

688. Abrams, Roger I., and Dennis R. Nolan. "Time at a Premium: The Arbitration of Overtime and Premium Pay Disputes." *Ohio State Law Journal* 45, no. 4 (1984): 837-862.

Reviews decisional criteria arbitrators utilize in resolving disputes about overtime and premium pay issues.

689. Brotman, Billie Ann, and Thomas J. McDonagh. "A Comparative Analysis of NLRB and Arbitration Decisions Involving Unilateral Wage Changes." *Labor Law Journal* 36, no. 10 (October 1985): 762-772.

The authors conclude that arbitrators and the NLRB analyze cases involving unilateral wage changes in a similar manner. Arbitrators, holding to the bargaining agreement, generally reject employer attempts to reduce or to cancel contractual wage increases.

Incentives

690. Waite, William W. "Problems in the Arbitration of Wage Incentives." In 8 NAA (1955): 25-44.

> Includes discussion by John W. Seybold and S. Herbert Unterberger.

691. Fairweather, Owen, and William Gomberg. "Arbitration of Disputes Involving Incentive Problems." In 10 NAA (1957): 61-97.

> Industry view by Fairweather; labor view by Gomberg; with discussion by Pearce Davis and Ronald W. Haughton.

692. Unterberger, S. Herbert. "The Arbitration of Wage Incentive Cases." *Arbitration Journal* 23, no. 4 (1968): 236-249.

> Discussion of the issues involved.

Job Classification, Job Evaluation, and Comparable Worth

693. Murphy, Frank J. "Job Classification Arbitrations under Bethlehem Steel Agreements." *Arbitration Journal* 16, no. 1 (1961): 8-25.

> Follow-up of a BLS study on this topic, based on a sample of awards. Stresses need for technical knowledge of job and industry in wage administration.

694. Unterberger, S. Herbert. "Arbitration of Job Evaluation Cases." *Arbitration Journal* 17, no. 4 (1962): 219-226.

> Discussion of the issues involved.

695. Unterberger, S. Herbert. "Automation and Job Evaluation Techniques." In 16 NAA (1963): 238-265.

> How arbitrators handle disputes over the evaluation of jobs changed or created by technological change. Comments by Charles C. Killingsworth and Paul N. Lehoczky.

696. Wisniewski, Stanley C. "Achieving Equal Pay for Comparable Worth through Arbitration." *Employee Relations Law Journal* 8, no. 2 (Autumn 1982): 236-255.

> Explores possible remedies for pay inequities based on comparable worth.

697. McKenna, Ian B. "Pay Equity and Arbitral Restrictions under the Public Service Employee Relations Act." *Alberta Law Review* 28, no. 3 (Spring 1990): 690-692.

The Canadian Public Service Employee Relations Act establishes arbitration procedures for compensation disputes, but it exempts job evaluation and classification. This article discusses a case which established that pay equity was compensation.

698. Ver Ploeg, Christine D., and Phyllis Marion. "Comparable Worth in Arbitration." *William Mitchell Law Review* 16, no. 5 (Winter 1990): 1223-1238.

Using Minnesota law as an example, the authors examine challenges in the arbitration of comparable worth cases.

Vacations and Holidays

699. Daykin, Walter L. "Vacation Rights under Collective Bargaining Agreements." *Arbitration Journal* 17, no. 1 (1962): 34-45.

Concludes that vacations are seen as earned rights in the nature of deferred compensation.

700. Abrams, Roger I., and Dennis R. Nolan. "The Common Law of the Labor Agreement: Vacations." *Industrial Relations Journal* 5 (1983): 603-622.

Critically examines the principles employed by arbitrators in resolving vacation disputes. In most but not all instances, these principles correctly measure the parties' intentions.

701. Abrams, Roger I., and Dennis R. Nolan. "Resolving Holiday Pay Disputes in Labor Arbitration." *Case Western Reserve Law Review* 33 (1983): 380-403.

Reviews and criticizes the principles used by arbitrators in addressing claims for holiday pay. Also suggests guidelines for resolving recurring holiday pay disputes.

Work Rules

702. Davis, Pearce. "Arbitration of Work Rules Disputes." *Arbitration Journal* 16, no. 2 (1961): 51-60.

Discussion of the kinds of issues arising out of the establishment or revocation of work rules.

703. Daykin, Walter L. "Arbitration of Work Rules Disputes." *Arbitration Journal* 18, no. 1 (1963): 36-45.

While arbitrators rely on subjective reasoning in deciding work rule grievances, Daykin shows that they also are concerned with ethical codes and justice.

704. Gruenberg, Gladys W. "Smoking in the Workplace: The Issues Heat Up." *Arbitration Journal* 43, no. 3 (September 1988): 8-14.

Gruenberg concludes that the spread of no smoking rules will increase the demand for arbitration. The most common questions will involve arbitrability, past practice, and just cause.

705. Bowers, Mollie H. "What Labor and Management Need to Know about Workplace Smoking Cases." *Labor Law Journal* 43, no. 1 (January 1992): 40-49.

Bowers contends that the courts have been reluctant to restrict smoking in the workplace. However, arbitrators have been more willing to impose smoking control policies.

Health and Safety

706. Summa, Joseph B. "Criteria for Health and Safety Arbitration." *Labor Law Journal* 26 (June 1975): 368-374.

Analyzes 200 health and safety cases.

707. Wolfson, Beth Anne. "Arbitration and OSHA." *Arbitration Journal* 38, no. 3 (September 1978): 12-21.

Explores the judiciary's treatment of arbitration awards incorporating external law on workplace safety.

708. Britton, Raymond L. "Courts, Arbitrators, and OSHA Problems: An Overview." In 33 NAA (1981): 260-284.

Britton discusses scientific and legal issues and how arbitrators might handle them, and Adolph E. Schwartz comments.

709. Smith, J. Martin. "Arbitrating Safety Grievances: Contract or Congress?" *Labor Law Journal* 33, no. 4 (April 1982): 238-246.

Reviews three approaches arbitrators have taken regarding the duty of employers to provide a safe workplace for employees.

710. Gellens, Kathryn A. "Resolving Industrial Safety Disputes: To Arbitrate or Not to Arbitrate." *Labor Law Journal* 34, no. 3 (March 1983): 149-159.

Reviews and evaluates the evolution of law and arbitrators' rulings on right of employees to refuse to work for safety reasons.

711. Duran, Rowena M. "The Employer's Dilemma: The Implications of Occupational Safety and Health in the Arbitral Process-Conflicting Contractual and Statutory Commands." *Syracuse Law Review* 34, no. 4 (Fall 1983): 1067-1105.

In cases involving occupational safety and health, employees who lose in arbitration may still bring an action under OSHA. But if an employer loses in arbitration, judicial review may be obtained only by showing fraud, prejudice, lack of jurisdiction, or violation of the law.

712. Gross, James A., and Patricia A. Greenfield. "Arbitral Value Judgments in Health and Safety Disputes: Management Rights over Worker's Rights." *Buffalo Law Review* 34, no. 3 (Fall 1985): 645-691.

> Health and safety issues are divided into refusal to work, safety rules, crew size reductions, and disease and disability cases. The authors examine the impact of personal values upon arbitral thinking.

Refusal to Perform Hazardous Work

713. Allen, Robert E., and Patricia Linenberger. "The Employee's Right to Refuse Hazardous Work." *Employee Relations Law Journal* 9, no. 2 (Autumn 1983): 251-275.

> An individual's right to refuse to do hazardous work without discipline is reviewed. The standard is viewed as unclear and dependent on the forum.

714. Rabin, Robert J. "Some Comments on Obscenities, Health and Safety, and Workplace Values." *Buffalo Law Review* 34, no. 3 (Fall 1985): 725-734.

> An examination of the "obey now, grieve later" rule, the health and safety exception, and whether the rule should be treated as binding.

715. Widenor, Marcus R., and Allison Hassler. "Refusal of Hazardous Work Assignments: The Search for Arbitral Standards." *Arbitration Quarterly of the Northwest* 12, no. 2 (Fall 1991): 17-24.

> A review of the standards adopted by arbitrators to deal with discipline that is imposed after a worker invokes the "safety exception" in refusing to perform an assigned task.

ERISA and Pension Disputes

Legal Disputes

716. Seifman, Donald H. "Arbitration of Pension Disputes: Judicial Rights under ERISA." *Pension and Profit Sharing Tax Journal* 2, no. 3 (Summer 1976): 232-239.

> A review of issues concerning arbitration of pension disputes under ERISA.

717. Murphy, Michael E. "The Impact of ERISA on Arbitration." *Arbitration Journal* 32, no. 2 (June 1977): 123-132.

> The article shows that ERISA claims cannot be treated as pure and simple contract matters, and employees may not be required to exhaust arbitral remedies before filing an action in court.

718. Tilove, Robert. "The Arbitration of Pension Disputes." *Arbitration Journal* 34, no. 4 (December 1979): 28-30.

> Tilove argues that legislation should be amended to reduce or remove legal

problems related to the finality of the arbitration award and fiduciary liability.

719. Schneider, Randy J. "Surviving ERISA Preemption: Pension Arbitration in the 1980s." *Columbia Journal of Law and Social Problems* 16, no. 2 (1980): 269-326.

> Considers individual grievances and trustee deadlock cases.

720. Dobranski, Bernard. "The Arbitrator as a Fiduciary under the Employee Retirement Income Security Act of 1974: A Misguided Approach." *American University Law Review* 32, no. 1 (Fall 1982): 65-88.

> Arbitrators who resolve disputes involving pension and welfare plans may be deemed fiduciaries and incur personal liability. The author contends that the fiduciary responsibility should remain with the trustees.

721. Driver, Claudia L. "Arbitration and Collectively Bargained Benefit Funds: Trustee Collection Choices. (Case Note)." *Arkansas Law Review* 37, no. 2 (Spring 1984): 440-456.

> An examination of an Eighth Circuit Court decision that found a dispute between an employer and a Teamster welfare and pension fund over the trustees' right to audit employer records to be nonarbitrable.

722. Tideman, Curtis. "The Eighth Circuit Allows Pension Trustees to Bypass Arbitration. (Case Note)." *Creighton Law Review* 17, no. 4 (Fall 1984): 1209-1225.

> A review of an Eighth Circuit Court decision which runs contrary to the normal presumption of arbitrability.

723. Lister, Phyllis. "Labor Law: Arbitration Is Mandatory Only When Predicted by an Agreement. (Case Note)." *Thurgood Marshall Law Review* 10, no. 2 (Spring 1985): 656-665.

> An analysis of *Schneider v. Robbins*, in which the Supreme Court held that the courts take precedence in disputes over contribution to employee health and welfare plans unless the collective bargaining agreement expressly provides for arbitration.

724. Bendixsen, Glen M. "Contributions to Collectively Bargained Pension Funds Regulated by ERISA: The Employer's Right to Arbitration of Delinquency Claims." *Santa Clara Law Review* 27, no. 1 (Winter 1987): 61-90.

> This article provides a general examination of the arbitration of delinquency claims.

725. Brice, Amy L. "Statutory Claims under ERISA: Is Arbitration the Appropriate Forum? (Case Note)." *Journal of Dispute Resolution* 1991, no. 1 (1991): 171-181.

> A discussion of a case that held that statutory claims under ERISA may be

heard in arbitration. The author predicts that ERISA claims will be held to be completely arbitrable.

Multi-Employer Amendments

726. Smith, Barry F. "Arbitration and the Multi-Employer Pension Plan Amendments: From the Golden Age to the Age of Reason." *Capital University Law Review* 12, no. 1 (Fall 1982): 17-44.

>This article discusses the incorporation of mandatory arbitration into the Multi-Employer Pension Plan Amendments Act of 1980.

727. Pritzker, Malcolm L. "Arbitration of Employer Withdrawal Liability." *Employee Benefits Journal* 7, no. 4 (December 1982): 22-24, 31.

>This article reviews the rules that have been adopted between the AAA and the International Foundation of Employee Benefit Plans on withdrawal from multi-employer pension plans.

728. Raposa, John Francis. "The Use of Arbitration to Determine Liability: the Multiemployer Pension Plan Amendments Act of 1980." *Ohio State Journal on Dispute Resolution* 2, no. 1 (Fall 1986): 169-184.

>This article discusses the Employment Retirement Security Act of 1974, the expansion of multi-employer pension plans, and the 1980 amendment which empowered arbitrators to decide the liability of single employers who withdraw from multi-employer plans.

729. Grossman, Mark M. "Dispute Resolution and Multiemployer Pension Plan Withdrawal Liability." *Arbitration Journal* 46, no. 2 (June 1991): 41-47.

>This article examines the employer's liability for interim payments under the Multiemployer Pension Plan Amendments Act, and the use of arbitration to resolve disputes.

Subcontracting

730. Crawford, Donald A. "The Arbitration of Disputes over Subcontracting." In 13 NAA (1960): 51-77.

>Study of arbitral awards, with comments by Mark L. Kahn.

731. Bernhardt, Herbert N. "Subcontracting during the Term of a Contract: A Clash between the NLRB and Arbitral Principle." *Arbitration Journal* 37, no. 1 (March 1982): 45-49.

>An examination of the relationship between the requirement that an employer have sound business reasons for subcontracting and the requirement that the employer bargain about subcontracting.

732. Abrams, Roger I., and Dennis R. Nolan. "Subcontracting Disputes in Labor

Arbitration: Productive Efficiency vs. Job Security." *University of Toledo Law Review* 15, no. 1 (Fall 1983): 7-34.

> Examines the body of principles developed and applied by arbitrators in resolving subcontracting disputes and fashioning remedies.

733. Clark, R. Theodore, Jr., Sheldon Friedman, John Fryer, and Roy L. Heenan. "Privatization, Outsourcing, and Subcontracting." In 41 NAA (1989): 101-162.

> Clark defines basic terms, how arbitrators handle the issues, and the differences between public and private sector. Friedman focuses on the hidden costs of outsourcing. Fryer, speaking from a Canadian union perspective, treats privatization as the "single, most common threat" to job security. Heenan, representing management, discusses the Canadian court cases.

734. Kirsner, Kenneth M. "Arbitral Treatment of Subcontracting after Milwaukee Spring II: Much Ado about Nothing?" *University of Miami Law Review* 44, no. 2 (November 1989): 371-402.

> The author argues that arbitrators should enforce the collective agreement rather than the precedents of the NLRB or the courts in deciding subcontracting issues.

735. McCammon, Marlise, and John L. Cotton. "Arbitration Decisions in Subcontracting Disputes." *Industrial Relations* 29, no. 1 (Winter 1990): 135-144.

> The factors that influenced arbitration decisions on subcontracting were the severity of threats to the existence of the union and to overtime benefits, attempted contract evasion, and the reserved rights of management.

Other Forms of Work Removal

736. Krotseng, Richard Van M. "Judicial and Arbitral Resolution of Contractual Plant Closing Issues." *Labor Law Journal* 35, no. 7 (July 1984): 393-406.

> The article addresses the right to terminate operations, severance pay, vacation pay, and benefits for retired employees.

737. Burroughs, John. "The Bases and Limits of Arbitral Decision-making in Plant Relocation and Transfer of Work Disputes." *Industrial Relations Law Journal* 7, no. 3 (1985): 362-400.

> The author argues that the NLRB should prohibit plant relocations during the life of a contract when the relocation is motivated by factors that grow out of the collective agreement. Arbitrators should apply standards of reasonableness and good faith in assessing the rationale offered by the business for its move.

738. Fleischli, George R. "The Arbitration of Plant Closing Disputes." In 43 NAA (1991): 149-170.

> This paper discusses arbitration cases involving plant closings and focuses on disputes over severance pay, vacation and holiday pay, insurance benefits, restrictions on the employer's right to close a plant, and the impact of the Worker Adjustment and Retraining Notification Act (WARN).

739. Grenig, Jay E. "The Removal of Work from Bargaining Unit Employees: The Supreme Court, the Board, and Arbitrators." *Willamette Law Review* 27, no. 3 (Summer 1991): 595-611.

> The article examines the case law and arbitration decisions on whether an employer may remove work from a bargaining unit, either by transferring it to another unit or by subcontracting.

Remedies

740. Stein, Emanuel. "Remedies in Labor Arbitration." In 13 NAA (1960): 39-50.

> This general discussion of remedial power advocates arbitral restraint. Comment by Irving Bernstein.

741. Sirefman, Joseph. "Rights without Remedies in Labor Arbitration." *Arbitration Journal* 18, no. 1 (1963): 17-35.

> This inquiry examines the idea of de minimis in labor arbitration and the rationale for awards without remedies.

742. Stutz, Robert L. "Arbitrators and the Remedy Power." In 16 NAA (1963): 54-74.

> Focuses on compensatory damages and injunctions. Discussions by M. S. Ryder and Dudley E. Whiting.

743. Seitz, Peter, and Sidney A. Wolff. "Remedies in Arbitration." In 17 NAA (1964): 165-207.

> Discussions by David E. Feller and Jesse Freiden. Focus is on monetary awards. See also: "Remedies: New and Old Problems," 34 NAA 109-177 (1981).

744. Teele, John W. "But No Back Pay Is Awarded." *Arbitration Journal* 19, no. 2 (1964): 103-112.

> Study of arbitral decisions in discharge cases involving reinstatement without back pay. Shows that rationale for such outcomes is often obscure.

745. Jones, Dallas L., and Patrick J. Fisher. "Ramifications of Back-Pay Awards in Suspension and Discharge Cases." In 22 NAA (1969): 163-182.

> Jones examines the nature of discharge cases and the effects of reinstatement, while Fisher discusses back pay awards.

746. Stone, Morris. "Why Arbitrators Reinstate Discharged Employees." *Monthly Labor Review* 92, no. 10 (October 1969): 47- 50.

> Study of 10 years of American Arbitration Association cases reveals uneven application of rules pertaining to the reasons for reinstatement.

747. "Protecting Intangible Expectations under Collective Bargaining Agreements: Overcoming the Proscription of Arbitral Penalties." *Minnesota Law Review* 61 (November 1976): 127-150.

> The article discusses whether monetary awards should be made when deliberate breach of the contract injures intangible interests.

748. Seitz, Peter. "Substitution of Disciplinary Suspension for Discharge (A Proposed 'Guide to the Perplexed' in Arbitration)." *Arbitration Journal* 35, no. 2 (June 1980): 27-31.

> Seitz puts forth the idea that, in cases where neither party budges from its position on a discharge case, the arbitrator should consider issuing an interim award, typically reinstatement with no determination on the issues. The parties should be ordered to continue their search for a solution, and if they fail the arbitrator should make the final award.

749. Staudohar, Paul D. "Exhaustion of Remedies in Private Industry Grievance Procedures." *Employee Relations Law Journal* 7, no. 3 (Winter 1981/1982): 454-465.

> Examines the principle of exhaustion of remedies as it applies to labor arbitration.

750. Feller, David E. "The Remedy Power in Grievance Arbitration." *Industrial Relations Law Journal* 5, no. 1 (1982): 128-155.

> Argues that an arbitrator is implicitly granted the authority to award only specific performance of the provisions of the agreement and not damages.

751. Feller, David E., and Anthony V. Sinicropi. "Remedies: New and Old Problems." In 34 NAA (1982): 109-177.

> Feller deals primarily with an overarching conception of the remedy power; Sinicropi addresses remedies in practice. Comment by Robert S. Katz.

752. Howan, Lillian T. "The Prospective Effect of Arbitration." *Industrial Relations Law Journal* 7, no. 1 (1985): 60-87.

> The article proposes that the best way to discourage one party to a collective bargaining agreement from repeating the same violation and forcing the other to spend its resources on ineffectual arbitration is a clause that allows for progressive damages for repeated violations.

753. Shearer, John C. "Reinstatement without Back Pay: An Appropriate Remedy?" *Arbitration Journal* 42, no. 4 (December 1987): 47-52.

> The author argues that reinstatement without back pay is an inappropriate arbitral remedy under the typical just-cause clause.

754. King, Otis H. "How Whole Is Whole?: Remedies in Labor Arbitration." *Journal of Contemporary Legal Issues* 3, no. 1 (Fall-Spring 1989): 167-181.

> This article focuses on whether arbitrators should award damages in addition to typical make-whole remedies. The author advocates that the traditional approach be continued.

Miscellaneous Issues

755. Harris, Philip. "Supervisory Performance of Bargaining Unit Work." *Arbitration Journal* 20, no. 3 (1965): 129-142.

> Based on content analysis of 324 published decisions.

756. Krislov, Joseph, and John Mead. "Arbitrating Union Conflicts: An Analysis of the AFL-CIO Internal Disputes Plan." *Arbitration Journal* 36, no. 2 (June 1981): 21-29.

> A study of rulings under Internal Disputes Plan between 1962 and 1978.

757. Mangum, David G. "Arbitration of Representational Issues: A Critique of Carey." *Brigham Young University Law Review* 1983, no. 2 (1983): 349-375.

> The author argues that the arbitration of jurisdictional/representational disputes violates employee rights of self-determination and causes arbitrators to work outside their areas of competence.

758. Hubek, Philip J., and Donald J. Petersen. "Arbitration and the Shortened Work Week: No Easy Answer." *Personnel* 62, no. 3 (March 1985): 8-10.

> Shortened work weeks have been both approved and denied by arbitrators, without any consistent pattern.

759. Rehmus, Charles M. "The Code and Postaward Arbitral Discretion." In 42 NAA (1990): 127-146.

> The topic in these papers concerns the retention of jurisdiction; Rehmus presents the lead paper, and arbitrators Dennis R. Nolan and Francis X. Quinn provide commentaries.

N. Arbitration and the Courts

General Studies

760. Kagel, Sam. "Recent Supreme Court Decisions and the Arbitration Process." In 14 NAA (1961): 1-29.

Reflections on the Trilogy. Discussions by Jesse Freidin and David E. Feller.

761. Meltzer, Bernard D. "Ruminations about Ideology, Law, and Labor Arbitration." In 20 NAA (1967): 1-19.

> Discussion of the compatibility of arbitration with public policy and judicial review, followed by a panel discussion.

762. Mittenthal, Richard. "The Role of Law in Arbitration." In 21 NAA (1968): 42-58.

> Papers by Bernard Meltzer and Robert Howlett, with discussion by Theodore J. St. Antoine. The issue is the extent to which arbitration should incorporate external law.

763. Gross, James A. "The Labor Arbitrator's Role: Tradition and Change." *Arbitration Journal* 25 (1970): 221-233.

> If arbitration is to prosper, arbitrators must make the process a system of justice for all. This article includes the application of public rights and obligations.

764. Sovern, Michael I. "When Should Arbitrators Follow Federal Law?" In 23 NAA (1970): 29-54.

> Another entry in the debate over the applicability of external law to arbitration. Comment by Thomas S. Adair.

765. Jones, Edgar A., Jr. "The Role of Arbitration in State and National Labor Policy." In 24 NAA (1971): 42-83.

> General discussion of arbitration and the law. Comments by Charles J. Morris and David E. Feller.

766. Feller, David E. "The Coming End of Arbitration's Golden Age." In 29 NAA (1976): 97-151.

> This paper focuses on the intrusion of substantive external law on what the author calls "industrial self-governance." Comments by Theodore Sachs and Lee C. Shaw.

767. Stanley, Douglas C. "The Statutory Framework of Grievance Arbitration in New Brunswick." *University of New Brunswick Law Journal* 29 (1980): 257-262.

> The author suggests that the statutory and private systems of arbitration in Canada are not working very well because the process is too expensive and too drawn-out.

768. Dorsey, James E. "Arbitration under the Canada Labour Code: A Neglected

Policy and an Incomplete Legislative Framework." *Dalhousie Law Journal* 6, no. 1 (July 1980): 41-70.

> The author contends that the Canadian Labour Code provides very little guidance concerning the role that arbitration is to play and the powers of the arbitrator.

769. Morris, Charles J. "Twenty Years of Trilogy: A Celebration." In 33 NAA (1981): 331-374.

> Special attention to judicial review under *Enterprise Wheel & Car*, circuit by circuit.

770. Ratner, Mozart G. "Observations on Some Current Issues in Labor Arbitration." *Labor Law Journal* 32, no. 2 (February 1981): 114-118.

> This article discusses whether arbitrators should follow external law in their decisions, deferral, and whether an arbitrator should be cast in the role of fiduciary (the author says no!).

771. Siwica, Richard P. "Defining Relationships between Judges, Arbitrators, and Employee Rights." *Labor Law Journal* 33, no. 7 (July 1982): 417-433.

> Proposes a model for the analysis of employee statutory rights, with suggestions for their proper disposition in the arbitration process.

772. Castagnera-Cain, James. "A Point of View: Using Statutory Law to Resolve Labor Contract Ambiguities." *Employee Relations Law Journal* 9, no. 2 (Autumn 1983): 194-202.

> Makes the argument that arbitrators should consider public law when a party offers it to resolve a dispute.

773. Casto, William R. "The Steelworkers Trilogy as Rules of Decision Applicable by Analogy to Public Sector Collective Bargaining Agreements: The Tennessee Valley Authority Paradigm." *Boston College Law Review* 26, no. 1 (December 1984): 1-59.

> Using the Tennessee Valley Authority as a model for the public sector, the author argues that many portions of the Steelworkers' Trilogy should apply to the public sector, but not the general presumption of arbitrability.

774. Yedwab, Janet G. "The 'Essence' of the Labor Arbitration Process: A New Focus." *Arbitration Journal* 39, no. 4 (December 1984): 28-37.

> The author proposes that arbitrators increase their familiarity with external law and make a reasoned application of it.

775. Zirkel, Perry A. "The Use of External Law in Labor Arbitration: An Analysis of Arbitral Awards." *Detroit College of Law Review* 1985 (Spring 1985): 31-46.

Concludes that external law plays very little role in the decision-making process.

776. Scheinholtz, Leonard L., and Phillip A. Miscimmara. "The Arbitrator as Judge and Jury: Another Look at Statutory Law in Arbitration." *Arbitration Journal* 40, no. 2 (June 1985): 55-66.

The authors examine the questions of whether and under what circumstances an arbitrator's consideration of statutory issues is appropriate.

777. Anderson, Arvid. "Arbitrators and the Interpretation and Application of External Law." *Stetson Law Review* 15, no. 1 (Fall 1985): 87-98.

The safe course for arbitrators is to interpret the agreement and avoid the interpretation of external law except where the parties have placed the external law in the agreement.

778. Gottesman, Michael H. "How the Courts and the NLRB View Arbitrators' Awards." In 38 NAA (1986): 168-179.

A paper on the necessity for arbitrators to explain their reasoning when they reach a conclusion contrary to the plain meaning of the contract, on whether they should interpret external laws, and on the Spielberg (deferral) doctrine.

779. Kramer, Andrew M. "External Law and the Interpretive Process." In 38 NAA (1986): 149-167.

This article proposes that the answers to the most important questions in contract interpretation lie with the negotiators. The parties want an award based on their agreement and understandings, not those of the arbitrator, the courts, or the board.

780. Reinhardt, Stephen R., Bernard D. Meltzer, and Abraham H. Raskin. "Arbitration and the Courts: Is the Honeymoon Over?" In 40 NAA (1988): 25-66.

Three papers on the enforcement of arbitration agreements and awards. Reinhardt argues that a fundamental conflict exists between arbitration and the courts, Meltzer discusses the public policy defense, and Raskin forecasts the end of the arbitrator's reign.

781. Ver Ploeg, Christine D. "Labor Arbitration: The Participants' Perspective." *Arbitration Journal* 43, no. 1 (March 1988): 36-43.

A survey of 100 experienced arbitration participants on the appropriateness of addressing statutory issues and about the characteristics of the process.

782. Anderson, Arvid. "Labor Arbitration Today." In 41 NAA (1989): 1-8.

Anderson argues that in grievance cases, arbitrators who depart from the language of the collective agreement invite legal challenges. The author also calls attention to the necessity of explaining the reasoning behind awards in interest cases.

783. Jascourt, Hugh. "When Can a Grievance Arbitrator Apply Outside Law?" *Journal of Law and Education* 18, no. 4 (Fall 1989): 503-504.

Arbitrators who omit obvious external law considerations guarantee review of their awards. But arbitrators who consider external law invite vacation of awards. For further discussion on the same issue, see articles with the same title by George R. Fleischli and Jay E. Grenig, pp. 501-513 and 515-526, respectively.

784. Garrett, Sylvester. "Resolving the Tension: Arbitration Confronts the External Legal System." *Case Western Reserve Law Review* 39, no. 2 (Winter 1989): 557-575.

An arbitrator examines the evolution of the relationship between arbitration and the courts from the pre-World War II years through the *Misco* decision.

785. "Report on the Labor Arbitrator's Role in Cases Involving External Law." In Office of the General Counsel, American Arbitration Association. *Arbitration and the Law: AAA General Counsel's Annual Report: 1989-1990*, 178-199. New York: AAA, 1990.

This article sets forth the state of statutory and decisional law affecting the arbitrator's use or nonuse of external law and focuses on the decisional standards used by the NLRB and the courts in reviewing arbitrators' decisions.

786. Easterbrook, Frank H. "Arbitration, Contract, and Public Policy." In 44 NAA (1992): 65-76.

The practice of overturning arbitration awards by the courts reduces the value of arbitration to the parties. Richard Gear calls for a deeper review of public policy by arbitrators, and David Silberman generally supports Easterbrook's view.

787. Greenfield, Patricia A. "How Do Arbitrators Treat External Law?" *Industrial and Labor Relations Review* 45, no. 4 (July 1992): 683-696.

An examination of arbitrators' treatment of external law in 106 cases decided between 1980 and 1985 in which an unfair labor practice charge had been filed. Arbitrators usually gave external law only cursory treatment.

Enforcement of Arbitration Awards

788. Snow, Carlton J. "Late Arbitration Awards." *Journal of Collective Negotiations in the Public Sector* 11, no. 3 (1982): 225-234.

Lateness may jeopardize an arbitration award as a result of the Fourth Circuit decision in *Huntington Alloys*. In that case, the contract was clear, there was no waiver of time limits, and the objection was prompt.

789. Mason, Ronald L. "Collective Bargaining Agreements without Arbitration Clauses: Does the Finality Doctrine Bar Section 301 Suits?" *University of Dayton Law Review* 7, no. 2 (Spring 1982): 387-401.

> The author contends that courts differ over the finality of a decision made in a grievance procedure that does not call for binding arbitration. Federal courts tend to bar an employee from further litigation of the merits of a grievance, but state courts have generally held that the employee is not barred.

790. Hopkins, Ronald. "Civil Rights: Federal Courts Shall Not Afford *Res Judicata* or *Collateral Estoppel* Effect to an Award in an Arbitration Proceeding Brought Pursuant to the Terms of a Collective Bargaining Agreement." *Thurgood Marshall Law Review* 10, no. 1 (Fall 1984): 249-259.

> *McDonald v. City of West Branch* dealt with a police officer whose discharge was upheld by an arbitrator, despite a claim by the officer that he was discharged for exercising freedom of speech. The Supreme Court held that the existence of an arbitration award would not bar independent statutory action in the courts.

791. Russell, Craig. "Judicial Intervention in Arbitration Enforcement Cases: The Tenth Circuit Expands upon the Limited Judicial Review Standard of *Enterprise Wheel*. (Case Note)." *Denver University Law Review* 62, no. 2 (Spring 1985): 593-614.

> This article examines the increasingly interventionist approach adopted by the lower federal courts in reviewing arbitration awards.

792. Warner, Elizabeth F. "Labor Law: Six-Month Limitation Period for Employee Hybrid Suits Enforcing Arbitration Awards. (Case Note)." *Temple Law Quarterly* 59, no. 4 (Winter 1986): 1315-1334.

> A review of law. An employee has a right to bring a Section 301 suit to enforce an arbitration award, but the suit must be filed within six months of the date of the award.

793. Gordon, John A. "Judicial Refusal to Enforce Arbitration Awards on Public Policy Grounds. (Case Note)." *Boston College Law Review* 29, no. 1 (December 1987): 138-146.

> The author concludes that the outcome of a request to vacate an arbitration award may depend on which Circuit hears the case rather than on any factual considerations.

794. Popper, Seth Michael. "Judicial Review in Section 301 Labor Arbitration Prospective Claims: The Effect of Communication Workers." *Fordham Law Review* 58, no. 6 (May 1990): 1289-1307.

>The article examines whether the court should enforce an arbitration award from a prior case if the offending party continues with the behavior.

Judicial Review

Judicial Review of Arbitration Awards

795. Christensen, Thomas G. S., William B. Gould, IV, and Benjamin C. Roberts. "Judicial Review: As Arbitrators See It." In 25 NAA (1973): 99-228.

>Discussion of judicial review by Christensen, review in discrimination cases by Gould, and arbitral misconduct by Roberts, followed by a panel discussion from the parties' viewpoint.

796. "Appealing the Procedural Decisions of Arbitrators." *Minnesota Law Review* 59 (November 1974): 109-153.

>Addresses the substantive law governing appeals, the problem of forum shopping, and the scope of review.

797. Yarowsky, Jonathan. "Judicial Deference to Arbitral Determinations: Continuing Problems of Power and Finality." *UCLA Law Review* 23 (June 1976): 936-962.

>Examines the relationship between judge and arbitrator in deciding questions of arbitrability and challenge to an award.

798. Edwards, Harry T. "Labor Arbitration at the Crossroads: The 'Common Law of the Shop' vs. External Law." *Arbitration Journal* 32, no. 2 (June 1977): 65-95.

>Comprehensive review of judicial deference to arbitration.

799. St. Antoine, Theodore J. "Judicial Review of Labor Arbitration Awards: A Second Look at *Enterprise Wheel* and Its Progeny." In 30 NAA (1978): 29-71.

>Argues that as the parties' "designated, definitive reader of their labor contract," an arbitrator should make the final interpretation of "either contract or external law."

800. Friedman, George H. "Correcting Arbitrator Error: The Limited Scope of Judicial Review." *Arbitration Journal* 33, no. 4 (December 1978): 9-16.

>An outline of procedural and fairness issues that courts consider grounds for reviewing arbitral awards.

801. Kaden, Lewis B. "Judges and Arbitrators: Observations on the Scope of Judicial Review." *Columbia Law Review* 80, no. 2 (March 1980): 267-298.

>The degree of uncertainty that surrounds judicial review has increased, and this prevents the arbitrator from fulfilling his or her duties.

802. Fogel, Walter. "Court Review of Discharge Arbitration Awards." *Arbitration Journal* 37, no. 2 (June 1982): 22-34.

> Examines court challenges of awards that have revoked or modified discharges and were challenged on the ground that the arbitrators exceeded their authority.

803. Roumell, George T., Jr. "Reversing the Arbitrator." *Michigan Bar Journal* 62, no. 7 (July 1982): 519-521.

> Reviews recent court cases that modify an arbitrator's award.

804. Jones, Edgar A., Jr. "His Own Brand of Industrial Justice: The Stalking Horse of Judicial Review of Labor Arbitration." *UCLA Law Review* 30 (1983): 881-897.

> Examines the paradox of the "essence test" laid down in *Enterprise Wheel & Car*. Argues for judicial restraint.

805. Jones, Edgar A. Jr. "A Meditation on Labor Arbitration and 'His Own Brand of Industrial Justice.' " In 35 NAA (1983): 1-15.

> An analysis of the "essence" test of *Enterprise Wheel & Car*, with a warning against excessive judicial interference.

806. Ashe, Bernard F. "Arbitration Finality: Myth or Reality?" *Arbitration Journal* 38, no. 4 (December 1983): 42-51.

> Expresses concern over the dilution of finality in arbitration awards owing to the intrusion of external law and "review-minded judges."

807. Trumka, Richard L. "Keeping Miners Out of Work: The Cost of Judicial Revision of Arbitration Awards." *West Virginia Law Review* 86, no. 3 (Spring 1984): 705-716.

> This article examines and deplores the tendency of some federal courts to retry arbitration cases and thereby aid the employer's attempt to avoid an unfavorable award.

808. Stephens, Elvis C. "Why Courts Overrule Arbitrators' Awards." *Labor Law Journal* 36, no. 2 (February 1985): 108-117.

> Finds the most common reasons for overruling to be that the arbitrator exceeded contractual authority or the award violated a law or public policy.

809. Page, Rosemary S. "A Miranda Warning in Arbitration." In Office of the General Counsel, American Arbitration Association. *Arbitration and the Law: AAA General Counsel's Annual Report: 1986*, 76-79. New York: AAA, 1986.

> A commentary on *American Postal Workers Union, AFL-CIO v. U.S. Postal Service*. Concludes that the decision provides a clear rationale for limited court review of charges that the arbitrator misapplied the law in the interpretation of evidence.

810. Grenig, Jay E. "Legal Research: The Appellate Courts and Labor Arbitration—Recent Developments 1985-1986." *Journal of Collective Negotiations in the Public Sector* 16, no. 2 (1987): 151-168.

> A review of recent appellate court decisions. Various grounds for setting aside awards are found insufficient.

811. Heinsz, Timothy J. "Judicial Review of Labor Arbitration Awards: The *Enterprise Wheel* Goes Around and Around." *Missouri Law Review* 52, no. 2 (Spring 1987): 243-298.

> A discussion of judicial scrutiny given by courts to labor arbitration awards that encompass constitutional and statutory rights. Most awards have been upheld, but the basis for attack has broadened.

812. Gottlieb, Ira. "The Vermont Labor Relations Board's Role in Grievance Proceedings: Let's Make This Process Work." *Vermont Law Review* 12, no. 2 (Fall 1987): 429-458.

> The Vermont Labor Relations Board hears grievances, but employees may appeal board decisions to the courts. This article examines the tensions that have developed between the board and the courts.

813. Hogler, Raymond L. "Just Cause, Judicial Review, and Industrial Justice: An Arbitral Critique." *Labor Law Journal* 40, no. 5 (May 1989): 281-292.

> As courts become more willing to review arbitration awards, the effectiveness of the arbitration (in terms of speed and finality) is diminished.

814. Gould, William B., IV. "Judicial Review of Labor Arbitration Awards—Thirty Years of the Steelworkers Trilogy: The Aftermath of *AT&T* and *Misco*." *Notre Dame Law Review* 64, no. 4 (Fall 1989): 464-496.

> The *AT&T Technologies* and *Misco* cases have left confusing attitudes toward judicial involvement. This article notes a need for arbitral finality.

815. Feuille, Peter, and Michael LeRoy. "Grievance Arbitration Appeals in the Federal Courts: Facts and Figures." *Arbitration Journal* 45, no. 1 (March 1990): 35-47.

> An examination of how federal courts deal with appeals of labor arbitration awards; they usually compel arbitration and sustain the award.

816. Feuille, Peter, Michael LeRoy, and Timothy Chandler. "Judicial Review of Arbitration Awards: Some Evidence." *Labor Law Journal* 41, no. 8 (August 1990): 477-484.

> From 1,216 arbitration cases appealed to federal courts, the authors conclude that most awards are never appealed; court appeals are generally initiated by the employer; and awards are vacated only if an arbitrator goes beyond the scope of the bargaining agreement.

Primarily *Alexander v. Gardner-Denver*

817. Brodie, Donald W. "Antidiscrimination Clauses and Grievance Processes." *Labor Law Journal* 25, no. 6 (June 1974): 352-379.

> Review of arbitration decisions and contract clauses dealing with employment discrimination in the immediate wake of *Gardner-Denver.*

818. Aksen, Gerald, Winn Newman, and Harry T. Edwards. "Post-*Gardner-Denver* Developments in Arbitration Laws." In 28 NAA (1976): 24-92.

> The Edwards paper includes a report on a survey of NAA members on the capacity of arbitrators to deal with legal issues arising out of Title VII.

819. Robinson, William L., Mollie W. Neal, Wendy W. Williams, and Bernard D. Meltzer. "Arbitration and Discrimination." In 29 NAA (1976): 20-60.

> Discussions of the impact and implications of the *Gardner-Denver* decision.

820. Hill, Marvin F., Jr. "Authority of a Labor Arbitrator to Decide Legal Issues Under a Collective Bargaining Contract: The Situation after *Gardner-Denver.*" *Indiana Law Review* 10 (1977): 899-930.

> Reviews post-*Gardner-Denver* court rulings and argues that courts should enforce statutory rights in addition to, and not as a substitute for, contractual rights.

821. Jacobs, Roger B. "Confusion Remains Five Years after *Alexander vs. Gardner-Denver.*" *Labor Law Journal* 30, no. 10 (October 1979): 623-636.

> Examines the court's reasoning in *Gardner-Denver* and its impact on arbitrators and the courts.

822. Owens, Stephen D. "Arbitral Reaction to *Alexander v. Gardner-Denver Co.*: Analysis of Arbitrators' Awards, 1974-1980." In 34 IRRA (1981): 60-61.

> Analysis of the extent to which arbitrators follow the guidelines of *Gardner-Denver* in resolving racial discrimination grievances.

823. Hoyman, Michele M., and Lamont E. Stallworth. "Arbitrating Discrimination Grievances in the Wake of *Gardner-Denver.*" *Monthly Labor Review* 106, no. 10 (October 1983): 3-10.

> A review of the Supreme Courts' ruling in *Alexander vs. Gardner-Denver* and the results of a follow-up survey conducted in 1981. See also "The Arbitration of Discrimination Grievances in the Aftermath of *Gardner-Denver*" by the same authors, in *Arbitration Journal* 29, no. 3 (September 1984): 49-57.

824. Elwell, Karen, and Peter Feuille. "Arbitration Awards and *Gardner-Denver* Lawsuits: One Bite or Two?" *Industrial Relations* 23, no. 2 (Spring 1984): 287-297.

> Authors examine 50 court cases decided between 1974 and 1983. The arbitrators' awards were seldom explicitly evaluated and in most cases the courts sustained the award.

825. Fowler, Aubrey R., Jr. "Arbitration, the Trilogy, and Individual Rights: Developments since *Alexander v. Gardner-Denver*." *Labor Law Journal* 36 (March 1985): 173-182.

> Fowler argues that although *Gardner-Denver* may threaten the finality of arbitration awards, the courts generally uphold the arbitrator's decision.

826. Levine, Marvin J. "Judicial Review of Arbitration Awards: Criticisms and Remedies." *Employee Relations Law Journal* 10, no. 4 (Spring 1985): 669-683.

> This article examines the Supreme Court decision in *Alexander vs. Gardner-Denver* and the reluctance of arbitrators to apply public statutes to discrimination grievances.

827. Page, Rosemary S. "Developments in 1990 in *Alexander v. Gardner-Denver*." In Office of the General Counsel, American Arbitration Association. *Arbitration and the Law: AAA General Counsel's Annual Report: 1990-1991*, 122-126. New York: AAA, 1991.

> This examination of a number of 1990 cases, with reference to those that preceded them, focuses on the weight to which courts grant arbitration awards when an individual's statutory rights are involved in the case.

Mainly *Misco*

828. Dunsford, John E. "The Judicial Doctrine of Public Policy: *Misco* Reviewed." *Labor Lawyer* 41, no. 4 (Fall 1988): 669-682.

> A review of *Misco*, concluding that the unanimous court decision "ringingly reaffirmed" the limited scope of judicial review of the merits of an arbitration award.

829. Parker, Joan. "Judicial Review of Labor Arbitration Awards: *Misco* and Its Impact on the Public Policy Exception." *Labor Lawyer* 4, no. 4 (Fall 1988): 683-714.

> A review of the doctrine of judicial deference to arbitration and an examination of *Misco* and several post-*Misco* cases. Arbitrators are urged to re-examine the principles that guide their interpretation of "just cause."

830. Ray, Douglas E. "Protecting the Parties' Bargain after *Misco*: Court Review of Labor Arbitration Awards." *Indiana Law Journal* 64, no. 1 (Winter 1988): 1-41.

> An examination of the post-*Misco* role of the court in vacating labor arbi-

tration awards, the standards under which an arbitration can be overturned, and the use of external law in contract interpretation.

831. Wayland, Robert F., Elvis C. Stephens, and Geralyn McClure Franklin. "*Misco*: Its Impact on Arbitration Awards." *Labor Law Journal* 39, no. 12 (December 1988): 813-819.

> A review of the *Misco* case and the public policy exception.

832. Kelley, Kevin W. "*United Paperworkers International Union v. Misco*. (Case Note)." *Capital University Law Review* 18, no. 1 (1989): 161-173.

> A discussion of *Misco*, the finality of arbitration awards, and reasons for overturning an award.

833. Vetter, Jan, Michael H. Gottesman, and John S. Irving, Jr. "Enforceability of Awards." In 41 NAA (1989): 75-100.

> Three articles on the enforceability of arbitration awards in the wake of the *Misco* decision. Vetter reviews the case, its antecedents, and subsequent decisions. Gottesman focuses on the conflict between the Supreme Court and the Circuits. Irving expresses a belief that *Misco* does not represent any substantial threat to the arbitration process.

834. Tremiti, Joseph F. "*Misco* and the Enforcement of Labor Arbitration Awards: No Longer a House Divided?" *University of Dayton Law Review* 14, no. 2 (Winter 1989): 279-294.

> The *Misco* case is viewed as supportive of arbitration and the finality of an arbitration award.

835. Estes, R. Wayne. "Life after *Misco*." In 44 NAA (1990): 170-176.

> This review of post-*Misco* cases concludes that judicial scrutiny of arbitration awards may, in the future, be based on theories other than the public policy exception.

836. Banta, Don A., Kevin M. McCarthy, Henry G. Stewart, and Elizabeth A. Vorro. "Labor Arbitration and the Law of Collective Bargaining Agreements." *Labor Lawyer* 7, no. 3 (Summer 1991): 747-770.

> Commenting on post-*Misco* court actions, the authors argue that judicial override occurs only when an arbitrator exceeds arbitral authority. The article also examines the duty of fair representation.

Primarily *Gilmer*

837. Burstein, James A., and Kenneth D. Schwartz. "*Gilmer v. Interstate/Johnson Lane Corporation*: The Supreme Court Endorses Arbitration of Age Discrimination Claims." *Employee Relations Law Journal* 17, no. 2 (Autumn 1991): 173-190.

The author explores the potential expansion of arbitration in discrimination claims and some practical considerations for the employer in the creation and implementation of arbitration procedures after the *Gilmer* case.

838. Weisel, Martha S. "The Tension between Statutory Rights and Binding Arbitration." *Labor Law Journal* 42, no. 11 (November 1991): 766-772.

Focusing on *Gilmer*, this article examines the tension between arbitration agreements involving individual employment contracts and statutory rights.

839. Bernstein, Michael I. "Arbitration Born Again . . . and Again? Post *Gilmer*." In Office of the General Counsel, American Arbitration Association. *Arbitration and the Law: AAA General Counsel's Annual Report: 1991-1992*, 127-143. New York: AAA, 1992.

An examination of post-*Gilmer* cases. The article asks how often the Supreme Court can express and revive its endorsement of a congressional labor policy in favor of arbitration, only to abandon, spurn, or otherwise undermine that endorsement later.

840. Sweeney, Michael T. "Employment Arbitration Age Discrimination in Employment Act Arbitrability of Claims under Age Discrimination Act Upheld Pursuant to Arbitration Agreement." *Seton Hall Law Review* 22, no. 2 (Spring 1992): 540-571.

The author argues that the court made several errors in *Gilmer* that would have been avoided had it viewed the agreement to arbitrate as part of an employment contract.

841. Weisel, Martha S. "The Effectiveness of Arbitration Clauses in Employment Contracts." *Arbitration Journal* 47, no. 2 (June 1992): 19-25.

An examination of the U.S. Supreme Court's *Gilmer* decision, which the author contends leaves many questions unanswered.

Related Cases and Issues

842. Lenz, Laurence H., Jr. "Labor Law: An Unfortunate Departure from Vigorous Enforcement of the Proarbitration Policy of the Labor Management Relations Act. (Case Note)." *Journal of Corporation Law* 6, no. 1 (Fall 1980): 195-223.

A critical examination of *Carbon Fuel v. United Mine Workers of America,* which held that a union has no obligation to try to bring an unauthorized work stoppage to an end.

843. Westerkamp, Patrick R. "Barrentine: Milestone or Detour?" *Labor Law Journal* 34, no. 1 (January 1983): 46-57.

Considers the effect on arbitration of *Barrentine v. Arkansas-Best Freight Systems, Inc.,* which held that an employee may sue under the Federal Labor Standards Act after unsuccessfully arbitrating the wage claims.

844. Eisenhofer, Jay. "Labor Law: National Labor Relations Board Must Defer to Private Arbitration Committees's Decision to Uphold Dismissal of Employees if Such Decision Plausibly Was Based on Committee's Finding That the Employees Were 'Supervisors' Unprotected by National Labor Relations Act. (Case Note)." *Villanova Law Review* 30, no. 3-4 (1985): 1040-1059.

>The article questions whether arbitrators, with limited expertise in labor law, should be permitted to determine whether certain employees are supervisors within the meaning of the NLRA.

845. Ray, Douglas E. "Court Review of Labor Arbitration Awards under the Federal Arbitration Act." *Villanova Law Review* 32, no. 1 (February 1987): 57-99.

>The author argues that the U.S. Federal Arbitration Act does not apply to arbitration arising under a collective bargaining agreement.

846. Conlon, Mark T. "Arbitration: Expanding the Scope of Judicial Review of Labor Arbitration Awards. (Case Note)." *Suffolk University Law Review* 23, no. 1 (Spring 1989): 88-95.

>A review of *S. D. Warren Co. v. United Paperworkers*, where the contract prohibited the possession, use, or sale of marijuana on company property. The arbitrator reduced a discharge to a suspension and the award was vacated.

Judicial Review: Public Sector

847. Cohen, Victor. "Compulsory Arbitration: The Scope of Judicial Review." *St. John's Law Review* 51 (Spring 1977): 604-631.

>Inquiries into judicial review of public sector arbitration in several states, emphasizing New York.

848. Toole, Judith H. "Judicial Activism in Public Sector Grievance Arbitration: A Study of Recent Developments." *Arbitration Journal* 33, no. 3 (September 1978): 6-15.

>Reviews cases that demonstrate a shift from Trilogy principles in public sector grievance arbitration.

849. Craver, Charles B. "The Judicial Enforcement of Public Sector Grievance Arbitration." *Texas Law Review* 58, no. 2 (February 1980): 329-353.

>The author argues that judicial review should be limited and doubts should be resolved in favor of arbitrability.

850. Deitsch, Clarence R., and David A. Dilts. "Arbitration Challenged: The Case of Indiana." *Journal of Collective Negotiations in the Public Sector* 10, no. 2 (1981): 173-179.

>Concludes that court review of merits of an arbitrator's decision will undercut arbitration of grievances.

851. Sigal, Benjamin C. "Public Employee Arbitration in Hawaii: A Study in Erosion." *University of Hawaii Law Review* 2, no. 2 (Winter 1981): 477-538.

> Hawaii has authorized voluntary grievance and interest arbitration for public employees. The author proposes that the Hawaii Public Employee Relations Board has reversed enough awards to threaten their finality.

852. Dilts, David A., and Clarence R. Deitsch. "Arbitration Lost: The Public Sector Assault on Arbitration." *Labor Law Journal* 35, no. 3 (March 1984): 182-188.

> A discussion of an Appellate Court decision in Indiana and of a statute in Iowa that provides for ease of judicial review of arbitration decisions. The effect is to weaken public sector grievance arbitration. See also "Indiana's Retreat from Arbitration: The Saga of Judicial Review," *Journal of Collective Negotiations in the Public Sector*, vol. 14, no. 1 (1985), pp. 45-52, by the same authors.

853. Dilts, David A., and Clarence R. Deitsch. "*Rockville Training Center v. Alvin Peschke:* Vindication of Court Rationale Underlying the Steelworkers Trilogy." *Employee Relations Law Journal* 10, no. 1 (Summer 1984): 95-105.

> Reviews the rationale and implications of a 1983 Indiana Court decision that set aside an arbitration award. Indiana has a history of efforts to discourage arbitration.

854. Snow, Carlton J. "The Steelworkers Trilogy in Oregon's Public Sector." *Willamette Law Review* 21, no. 3 (Summer 1985): 445-530.

> This article contrasts the New Jersey and Oregon public sector policies with each other and with reference to the Trilogy.

855. Sargrad, Gita D. "Arbitration Awards in Public Sector Disputes. (Case Note)." *Rutgers Law Journal* 17, no. 1 (Fall 1985): 175-188.

> The New Jersey Supreme Court misapplied the current standards of judicial review in County College of Morris and misinterpreted the role of the arbitrator. See also Babjak, Betty Ann, "Arbitrator Exceeds Authority by Reading Requirements for Progressive Discipline into Labor Agreement," *Seton Hall Law Review*, vol. 17, no. 2 (Spring 1987): 307-329.

856. Hafferty, Carole A. "Arbitration—Judicial Vacation of Arbitration Awards in Rhode Island: A Departure from Finality. (Case Note)." *Suffolk University Law Review* 23, no. 2 (Summer 1989): 433-440.

> Critical analysis of a decision made in a public sector case in which a Rhode Island state court reviewed the substance of an arbitration decision and overturned it.

857. Levin, Anne S. "Labor Law: Review of Arbitration Awards in Public Sector Disputes. (Case Note)." *Temple Law Review* 63, no. 2 (Summer 1990): 437-450.

871. Berlowe, Amanda J. "Judicial Deference to Grievance Arbitration in the Private Sector: Saving Grace in the Search for a Well-Defined Public Policy Exception." *University of Miami Law Review* 42, no. 3 (January 1988): 767-802.

>This article discusses how judges rarely reverse the arbitrator on public policy grounds, but awards have been overturned because they were contrary to explicitly stated public policies or because they violated the court's concept of common sense.

872. Murphy, Betty Southard, Wayne E. Barlow, and D. Diane Hatch. "Federal Courts' Jurisdiction on Arbitration Awards." *Personnel Journal* 67, no. 2 (February 1988): 30.

>The article interprets *Misco* as limited to cases where the challenging party demonstrates that public policy is clear, explicit, and based upon statutory or case law.

873. McGill, Linda D. "Public Policy Claims in Employee Termination Disputes." *Employment Relations Today* 15, no. 1 (Spring 1988): 43-48.

>Three questions to help resolve public policy exception questions: (1) is there a statute or other external law supporting the claim? (2) if so, does it specifically relate to the workplace? (3) did the employee actually engage in the action protected by the policy?

874. Bedikian, Mary A. "Riding on the Horns of a Dilemma: The Law of Contract v. Public Policy in the Enforcement of Labor Arbitral Awards." *Detroit College of Law Review* 1988, no. 3 (Fall 1988): 693-720.

>A general review of arbitration as it has developed since the Trilogy decisions.

875. Roebker, Maria T. "Public Policy Exception to the General Rule of Judicial Deference to Labor Arbitration Awards. (Case Note)." *University of Cincinnati Law Review* 57, no. 2 (Fall 1988): 819-846.

>Argues that in *Misco* the Supreme Court's decision was meant to encourage arbitral finality and make sure that the vagaries inherent in public policy considerations do not undermine the arbitration process.

876. Edwards, Harry T. "Judicial Review of Labor Arbitration Awards: The Clash between the Public Policy Exception and the Duty to Bargain." *Chicago-Kent Law Review* 64, no. 1 (Winter 1988): 3-34.

>Edwards claims that an expansive public policy exception could be a "mischievous weapon in the hands of a judge determined to implement his or her own brand of industrial justice."

877. Magee, James Michael. "The Public Policy Exception to Judicial Deferral of

Labor Arbitration Awards: How Far Should Expansion Go? (Case Note)." *South Carolina Law Review* 39, no. 2 (Winter 1988): 465-492.

> This article reviews the public policy exception to the finality of an arbitration award and argues that the area of exception expanded after 1983.

878. McIntosh, Kristin E. "Judicial Review of Arbitration Awards on Public Policy Grounds. (Case Note)." *Boston College Law Review* 30, no. 1 (December 1988): 130-139.

> This article emphasizes the limited nature of judicial review of arbitration decisions.

879. MacKay, Duncan Ross. "Arbitration: Reinforcement of Arbitration's Role in Maintaining Industrial Peace. (Case Note)." *Suffolk University Law Review* 23, no. 1 (Spring 1989): 78-87.

> A review of the public policy exception. This exception applies only when the policy is well-defined, dominant, and originates in statutory or case law.

880. Moran, James P. "Public Policy Exception in Judicial Review of Arbitration Awards. (Case Note)." *William Mitchell Law Review* 15, no. 3 (Summer 1989): 767-791.

> A review of cases in which the public policy exception to the finality of an arbitration award was narrowly interpreted so as not to undermine the arbitrator's role in settling disputes.

881. Fox, Carie, and Brian Gruhn. "Toward a Principled Public Policy Standard: Judicial Review of Arbitrators' Decisions." *Detroit College of Law Review* 1989, no. 3 (Fall 1989): 863-898.

> The authors contend that the public policy exception should be confined to instances where the arbitration award jeopardizes the policy; where the knowledge of the judiciary exceeds the arbitrator's special knowledge of the shop; or where the interests of persons not party to the contract are endangered.

882. Hexter, Christopher T. "Judicial Review of Labor Arbitration Awards: How the Public Policy Exception Cases Ignore the Public Policies Underlying Labor Arbitration." *Saint Louis University Law Journal* 34, no. 1 (Fall 1989): 77-109.

> The author argues for a limited review of arbitration awards under the public policy exception.

883. Mouser, Deanna J. "Analysis of the Public Policy Exception after *Paperworkers v. Misco*: A Proposal to Limit the Public Policy Exception and to Allow

Parties to Submit the Public Policy Question to the Arbitrator." *Industrial Relations Law Journal* 12, no. 1 (1990): 89-152.

> A distinction is drawn between awards sanctioning employee action that violates public policy and awards ordering employer action that violates public policy. This article argues that only in the latter case is vacatur appropriate.

884. Hamilton, Arthur, and Peter A. Veglahn. "Public Policy Exceptions to Arbitration Awards." *Labor Law Journal* 42, no. 6 (June 1991): 366-370.

> The author examines how public policy violation is the primary exception whereby the courts will review arbitration awards.

Deferral Policies

NLRB Deferral Policies

885. Waks, Jay W. "The 'Dual Jurisdiction' Problem in Labor Arbitration: A Research Report." *Arbitration Journal* 23 (1969): 201-227.

> A study of 338 AAA cases involving issues that fell within NLRB jurisdiction. In most awards there is no reference to NLRB policies.

886. Feller, David E. "Arbitration: The Days of Its Glory are Numbered." *Industrial Relations Law Journal* 2, no. 1 (Spring 1977): 97-130.

> Feller argues that the NLRB's *Collyer* Policy and increasing statutory regulation of conditions of employment are ending the virtual immunity from court review that arbitration has enjoyed since the Steelworkers Trilogy.

887. Irving, John S., Jr. "Arbitration and the National Labor Relations Board." *Arbitration Journal* 35, no. 1 (March 1980): 5-9.

> The evolution of the NLRB's deferral policies and the role played by the author (a former general counsel of the board).

888. Adams, John A. "The Assertion of Statutory Rights under FLSA and OSHA: Expand or Limit the *Gardner-Denver* Rationale." *Brigham Young University Law Review* 1981, no. 2 (1981): 361-397.

> The author argues that the nondeferral policy articulated in *Alexander v. Gardner-Denver* should be extended to claims under the Fair Labor Standards Act and the Occupational Safety and Health Act.

889. Harper, Michael C. "Union Waiver of Employee Rights under the NLRA: Part II—A Fresh Approach to Board Deferral to Arbitration." *Industrial Relations Law Journal* 4, no. 4 (1981): 680-704.

> The NLRB and the judiciary have relied too heavily on arbitration as the means of resolving labor-management disputes.

890. "Judicial Review and the Trend toward More Stringent NLRB Standards on Arbitral Referrals." *University of Pennsylvania Law Review* 129, no. 3 (January 1981): 738-773.

> A review of board deferral policies between 1955 and 1977. The board readily deferred to the arbitration decision in those years but of late it has deferred only where the arbitrator has considered all of the statutory issues and has taken an approach similar to that of the NLRB.

891. Venuti, Michael D. "Labor Law—National Labor Relations Board—Board Must Defer to an Arbitration Award Which is Arguably Consistent with Board Policy. (Case Note)." *Villanova Law Review* 26, no. 3-4 (March 1981): 827-845.

> A critical review of a Third Circuit decision in which the court supported a broad policy of deferral to arbitration by the NLRB.

892. Finston, Felicia A. "The Board's Role in the Arbitral Process." *Labor Law Journal* 32, no. 12 (December 1981): 799-807.

> A review of NLRB deferral policies with proposals to decrease the board's workload while ensuring that the contractual and statutory rights of the parties are protected.

893. Gregorich, John E. "The NLRB and Deferral to Awards of Arbitration Panels." *Washington and Lee Law Review* 38, no. 1 (Winter 1981): 124-138.

> A general review of cases dealing with NLRB deferral to arbitration.

894. Guckeen, Alice. "No Deferral to Arbitrator Awards in Section 8(a)(3) Cases." *Golden Gate University Law Review* 12, no. 1 (Spring 1982): 268-279.

> A discussion of the trend toward deferral in the Ninth Circuit Court. The trend is to uphold refusals of the board to defer to arbitration.

895. Raits, Vivian I. "Deferral to Arbitration in Individual Rights Cases: A Comparison of the NLRB and Oregon's ERB." *Willamette Law Review* 18, no. 3 (Summer 1982): 475-508.

> On individual rights issues, Oregon has generally followed the NLRB's reluctance to defer cases to arbitration. This article examines a case in which the Oregon Employee Relations Board took a different approach.

896. Castle, Robert C., and Paul Lansing. "Arbitration of Labor Grievances Brought under Contractual and Statutory Provisions: The Supreme Court Grows Less Deferential to the Arbitration Process." *American Business Law Journal* 21 (Spring 1983): 49-88.

> Reviews Supreme Court deferral doctrine from the 1960 Steelworkers Trilogy decision to the 1981 *Barrentine v. Arkansas-Best Freight Systems, Inc.*

897. Kahn, Steven C., and Andrew Sandler. "Deference to Arbitration Awards: A Proposed Policy." *Corporation Law Review* 6, no. 1 (Winter 1983): 74-81.

>The proposal is to increase deferral to arbitration, but an NLRB hearing could be obtained if certain conditions were demonstrated.

898. Moses, Mary Helen. "Deferral to Arbitration in Individual Rights Cases: A Reexamination of Spielberg." *Tennessee Law Review* 51, no. 2 (Winter 1984): 187-234.

>Reviews the limits on finality of arbitration, especially in *Gardner-Denver* and *Barrentine*, and concludes that the NLRB should reconsider its deferral policy.

899. Morris, Charles J. "NLRB Deferral to the Arbitration Process: The Arbitrator's Awesome Responsibility." *Industrial Relations Law Journal* 7, no. 3 (1985): 290-312.

>The author recommends that the NLRB carefully screen cases presented for deferral and that a more clear standard for judicial review be developed.

900. Shank, Mark A. "Deferral to Arbitration Accommodation of Competing Statutory Policies." *Hofstra Labor Law Journal* 2, no. 2 (Spring 1985): 211-263.

>Deferral requires the accommodation of the Supreme Court's preference for arbitration with the congressional interest in safeguarding the power of the NLRB.

901. Peck, Cornelius J. "A Proposal to End NLRB Deferral to the Arbitration Process." *Washington Law Review* 60, no. 2 (April 1985): 355-388.

>This article recommends that the board defer to arbitration only in cases where the interpretation of the collective bargaining agreement is mixed in with an unfair labor practice.

902. Zimmerman, Gregory E. "The Teamster Joint Grievance Committee and NLRB Deferral Policy: A Failure to Protect the Individual Employee's Statutory Rights." *University of Pennsylvania Law Review* 133, no. 6 (July 1985): 1453-1480.

>This article questions the wisdom of the NLRB in deferring to decisions made by the Joint Teamster Grievance Committee.

903. Mack, Curtis L., and Ira P. Bernstein. "NLRB Deferral to the Arbitration Process: The Arbitrator's Demanding Role." *Arbitration Journal* 40, no. 3 (September 1985): 33-43.

>Under the Reagan board, an arbitrator has adequately considered an unfair labor practice if the contractual issue is factually parallel to the unfair labor practice and the facts were presented that would enable it to be resolved.

904. Edwards, Harry T. "Deferral to Arbitration and Waiver of Duty to Bargain: A Possible Way Out of Everlasting Confusion at the NLRB." *Ohio State Law Journal* 46, no. 1 (Winter 1985): 23-40.

> Generally the parties should be required to use contractual mechanisms before resorting to NLRB processes. This article points out exceptions to the rule.

905. Fox, M. J., Jr., and Sheldon A. Wolstein. "The Current State of the NLRB's Decisions for Deferral to Arbitration." *Journal of Collective Negotiations in the Public Sector* 15, no. 2 (1986): 99-105.

> The authors conclude that the NLRB permits deferral in situations not involving 8(a)(5) violations where the arbitration clause clearly covers the circumstances.

906. Morris, Charles J. "NLRB Deferral to the Arbitration Process: The Arbitrator's Awesome Responsibility," In 37 NAA (1986): 51-76.

> This review of cases indicates that the NLRB had shifted to a position in favor of deferral to arbitration.

907. Brotman, Billie Ann. "The Existence of Shared Jurisdiction between the National Labor Relations Board and Arbitrators." *Labor Law Journal* 37, no. 7 (July 1986): 423-431.

> A discussion of the boundary between the NLRB and the arbitrator in cases involving unfair labor practices and in cases that involve both contractual violations and unfair labor practices.

908. Jeannette, Michael W. "NLRB Policies Concerning Deferral to Arbitrators." *Labor Law Journal* 38, no. 6 (June 1987): 348-359.

> This article contends that the board should base its policy on the contract waiver theory. The parties should negotiate which employee rights will be protected by the contract and which by the NLRA.

909. Sharpe, Calvin William. "NLRB Deferral to Grievance-Arbitration: A General Theory." *Ohio State Law Journal* 48, no. 3 (Summer 1987): 595-662.

> The author argues that the board should decide an issue rather than defer to an arbitrator in cases involving employee representation, domination and assistance, and unfair labor practices that may threaten the collective bargaining process.

910. St. Antoine, Theodore J. "Deferral to Arbitration and Use of External Law in Arbitration." *Industrial Relations Law Journal* 10, no. 1 (1988): 19-26.

> St. Antoine proposes that labor arbitrators may consider external law when the contract includes deferral policies that reflect the policies of the court and the NLRB.

911. Bornong, Joseph H. "Judicial Review by Sense of Smell: Practical Application of the Steelworkers Essence Test in Labor Arbitration Appeals." *University of Detroit Law Review* 65, no. 4 (Summer 1988): 643-677.

> A review of the 1960 Trilogy decisions in respect to whether a dispute should be submitted to arbitration. The author concludes that deferral to arbitration is an appropriate goal of public policy.

912. Wollett, Donald H. "NLRB Deferral: The Arbitrator's Role." *Whittier Law Review* 11, no. 3 (Fall 1989): 605-616.

> An examination of the impact of deferral on arbitration. The arbitrator's role is not changed by deferral; the arbitrator's job is to do what the parties wish.

913. Lynch, Dennis O. "Deferral, Waiver, and Arbitration under the NLRA: From Status to Contract and Back Again." *University of Miami Law Review* 44, no. 2 (November 1989): 237-339.

> The author argues that the NLRB should develop narrower deferral and waiver standards in order to protect its jurisdiction over fundamental questions of statutory policy.

914. Northrop, Michael K. "Distinguishing Arbitration and Private Settlement in NLRB Deferral Policy." *University of Miami Law Review* 44, no. 2 (November 1989): 341-370.

> The author argues that the board should continue to accord deference to private settlements.

915. Oldham, James. "Arbitration and the Relentless Legalization in the Workplace." In 43 NAA (1991): 23-40.

> Oldham focuses on how arbitrators have dealt with deferral cases and with requests for statutory interpretation. Anthony T. Oliver provides the management viewpoint and Robert M. Dohrmann the union perspective.

Primarily *Spielberg*

916. Rosenzweig, Linda E. "*Spielberg* and Deferral to Arbitration: Recent Decisions." *Employee Relations Law Journal* 6, no. 1 (Summer 1980): 173-179.

> Suggests a number of proposed standards to assist the board in determining whether to defer a given case to arbitration.

917. Robinson, Cammie R. "Limiting Deferral under the *Spielberg* Doctrine." *Virginia Law Review* 67, no. 3 (April 1981): 615-635.

> The author argues that NLRB review of arbitrator awards provides inadequate protection of employee individual statutory rights.

918. Culhane, John G. "*Spielberg* Reconsidered: Problems in Application and Content of the Deferral Doctrine." *Fordham Law Review* 49, no. 6 (May 1981): 1116-1139.

>This article reviews the NLRB's deferral doctrine and the problems, and suggests that responsibility for protecting National Labor Relations Act rights is with the board.

919. Cromwell, Cynthia A. "Mandatory Deferral under *Spielberg*: An 'Arguably Correct' Decision? (Case Note)." *Connecticut Law Review* 13, no. 2 (Winter 1981): 397-413.

>The article suggests that Congress create less rigid standards for deferral.

920. Taylor, Brian S. "NLRB Deferral to Arbitration: The Evolution of the *Spielberg* Doctrine." *William and Mary Law Review* 23, no. 2 (Winter 1981): 291-332.

>The development of the Spielberg standard for deferral to arbitration and the cases decided shortly after the doctrine was enunciated.

Primarily *Collyer* and *Suburban Motor Freight*

921. Nash, Peter G., et al. "The Development of the *Collyer* Deferral Doctrine." *Vanderbilt Law Review* 22 (January 1974): 23-80.

>Covers the rationale for the Collyer decision, its subsequent implementation, and its effect on the board.

922. Nash, Peter G. "The NLRB and Arbitration: Some Impressions of the Practical Effect of the Board's *Collyer* Policy upon Arbitrators and Arbitration." In 27 NAA (1975): 106-153.

>Comments by James E. Barden, C. Paul Barker, Edwin R. Teple, and Herbert L. Sherman, Jr.

923. Naffziger, Fred J. "All Power to the Arbitrator: Aftermath of the Steelworkers Trilogy, *Collyer Wire*, and ENA." *American Business Law Journal* 12, no. 3 (Winter 1975): 295-311.

>An examination of the impact of NLRB deferral policies on trilogy concepts. The ENA is the Experimental National Agreement negotiated in the steel industry.

924. Covington, Robert N. "Arbitrators and the Board: A Revised Relationship." *North Carolina Law Review* 57 (October 1978): 91-136.

>Examines board policy after 1977 decisions reversed earlier extension of *Collyer* and distinguished between cases that involved the hiring or tenure of employees and those cases that were concerned with good faith bargaining.

925. Alleyne, Reginald. "Arbitrators and the NLRB: The Nature of the Deferral Beast." *Industrial Relations Law Journal* 4, no. 4 (1981): 587-603.

> The author argues that *Collyer* should be abandoned and the choice of forum left to the charging party.

926. Alleyne, Reginald. "Courts, Arbitrators, and the NLRB: The Nature of the Deferral Beast." In 33 NAA (1981): 240-259.

> Updating *Collyer* and *Spielberg*.

927. Lynch, Lawrence T. "*Suburban Motor Freight* —End of the NLRB's Deferral Policy Flip-Flop? (Case Note)." *Journal of Corporation Law* 6, no. 2 (Winter 1981): 399-412.

> A review that points out that, as a result of changing board membership, the *Suburban Motor Freight* policy signaled a switch to a nondeferral attitude.

928. Fox, M. J., Jr., Glenna M. Witt, and Thomas R. Fox. "The Deferral Policy Revisited . . . From *Spielberg* to *Suburban Motor Freight*." *Journal of Collective Negotiations in the Public Sector* 11, no. 3 (1982): 235-242.

> Reviews NLRB policy on deferral from 1955 to 1980.

929. Vacura, Julie R. "Arbitration and NLRB Deferral: From *Spielberg* to *Suburban Motor Freight* and Beyond. (Case Note)." *Willamette Law Review* 20, no. 4 (Fall 1984): 785-822.

> This article traces the NLRB's deferral policy from the *Spielberg* doctrine to *Suburban Motor Freight*.

930. Wolkinson, Benjamin W. "The Impact of the *Collyer* Policy of Deferral: An Empirical Study." *Industrial and Labor Relations Review* 38, no. 3 (April 1985): 377-391.

> The author finds that deferral of duty to bargain charges frequently led to outcomes incompatible with statutory objectives, but that deferral in employee hiring and tenure cases were more likely to produce compatible results.

931. Deitsch, Clarence R., and David A. Dilts. "*Collyer* and Neutral Site Selection: Another Burden for an Already Overburdened Process." *Labor Law Journal* 41, no. 11 (November 1990): 794-798.

> The American Arbitration Association rules state that if a dispute location has not been designated in the collective bargaining agreement, the AAA shall determine the location. The Federal Mediation and Conciliation Service and most state agencies leave the decision of location to the arbitrator.

Primarily *Olin*

932. Briggs, James I., Jr. "The National Labor Relations Board's Policy of Deferring to Arbitration." *Florida State University Law Review* 13, no. 4 (Winter 1986): 1141-1169.

> An examination of the NLRB's policy on deferral to arbitration with particular emphasis on the *United Technologies* and *Olin* cases.

933. Henkel, Jan W., and Mark Kelly. "Deferral to Arbitration after *Olin* and *United Technologies*: Has the NLRB Gone Too Far?" *Washington and Lee Law Review* 43, no. 1 (Winter 1986): 37-62.

> An examination of the contradiction between the tendency of the NLRB to expand their deferral policy while the Supreme Court limits the jurisdiction of arbitrators over individual statutory rights cases.

934. Ray, Douglas E. "Individual Rights and NLRB Deferral to the Arbitration Process: A Proposal." *Boston College Law Review* 28, no. 1 (December 1986): 1-23.

> This article discusses the expansive view of both forms of deferral in *Olin* and *United Technologies*.

935. Swenson, Leanne M. "Labor Law: The Rejection of the *Olin* Standard for Deferral to an Arbitrator's Award. (Case Note)." *Journal of Corporation Law* 12, no. 4 (Summer 1987): 801-814.

> This article discusses an Eleventh Circuit decision in which the *Olin* standard for deferral to arbitration was rejected.

936. Gates, Conrad J., and Celia J. Elder. "*Olin* Must Not and Will Not Survive." *Labor Law Journal* 38, no. 11 (November 1987): 723-732.

> The authors review the deferral cases that led to *Olin* and argue that the criteria established by the decision are "badly flawed."

937. Lind, Kate H. "NLRB Standards for Deferral to Arbitration Awards. (Case Note)." *Boston College Law Review* 29, no. 1 (December 1987): 154-161.

> The author examines the NLRB standards for deferral established in the 1984 *Olin* decision and NLRB application of these standards.

938. Bush, Raymond G. "The Nature of the Deferral Problem Involving Section 8(a)(1) and 8(a)(3) charges. (Reprinted from *Perspective*, August 1987 and *Labor Lawyer*, Winter 1988)." *Labor Law Journal* 39, no. 3 (March 1988): 131-147.

> A discussion of the deferral policies of the NLRB after the *Olin* decision. The focus is on whether the board should defer to an arbitration award when interference, restraint, and coercion or employee hiring and tenure are involved.

939. Greenfield, Patricia A. "The NLRB's Deferral to Arbitration Before and after *Olin*: An Empirical Analysis." *Industrial and Labor Relations Review* 42, no. 1 (October 1988): 34-49.

> NLRB regional data reveals frequent deferral before the *Olin* decision, more frequent deferral after it, and a possible loss of statutory rights.

940. Kittle-Kamp, Thomas L. "Further Convolutions in a Convoluted Policy: *Olin, Taylor,* and NLRB Deferral to Arbitral Decisions." *Northwestern University Law Review* 82, no. 2 (Winter 1988): 443-491.

> An examination of the history of the NLRB's polices on deferral to arbitration. The author argues in favor of the broad deferral policy.

941. Patton, Craig Dow. "NLRB Deferral to Arbitration: Placing Individual Employees' Statutory Rights upon the Sacrificial Altar of *Olin* to Promote a National Labor Policy Favoring Private Dispute Resolution." *John Marshall Law Review* 21, no. 2 (Winter 1988): 323-339.

> The author generally applauds the board's deferral policies except where an individual's statutory rights could be violated.

Public Sector

942. Hayford, Stephen L., and Lynelle M. Wood. "Deferral to Grievance Arbitration on Unfair Labor Practice Matters: The Public Sector Treatment." *Labor Law Journal* 32, no. 10 (October 1981): 379-392.

> An analysis of the reluctance of public sector jurisdictions to defer to arbitration and follow private sector precedents with regard to deferral.

943. Reischl, Dennis K. "Applying *Collyer* in the Federal Sector: Past Due Remedy." *Labor Law Journal* 33, no. 6 (June 1982): 359- 365.

> This article argues that the Federal Labor Relations Authority should adopt a *Collyer*-type deferral policy for federal sector grievances that involve unfair labor practice charges.

Arbitration and the Civil Rights Laws

Role of the Arbitrator

944. Coulson, Robert. "Title Seven Arbitration in Action." *Labor Law Journal* 27 (March 1976): 141-151.

> Study of case files of the American Arbitration Association, supplemented by questionnaire returns from 260 arbitrators.

945. Edwards, Harry T. "Arbitration of Employment Discrimination Cases: A Proposal for Employer and Union Representatives." *Labor Law Journal* 27, no. 5 (May 1976): 265-277.

Parties should specify what may and may not be heard by arbitrators. Also urges special arbitral procedures and panels.

946. Youngdahl, James E. "Arbitration of Discrimination Grievances." *Arbitration Journal* 31, no. 3 (September 1976): 145-163.

The experience of the International Woodworkers of America and the Weyerhauser Company in modifying their grievance procedure to meet the objectives of civil rights legislation.

947. Owens, Stephen D. "Settling Title VII Disputes: A Role for the Arbitrator." *Employee Relations Law Journal* 2, no. 2 (Autumn 1976): 163-171.

The trend is for arbitrators to render decisions based on their interpretation of external law. The article suggests that courts give credence to such awards.

948. Hill, Marvin F., Jr. "The Union's Duty to Process Discrimination Claims." *Arbitration Journal* 32, no. 3 (September 1977): 180-194.

Hill shows that a union's refusal to process a discrimination claim because the claim may be pursued in a Title VII suit is a violation of Title VII and the Labor Management Relations Act.

949. Hill, Marvin F., Jr., and Anthony V. Sinicropi. "Excluding Discrimination Grievances from Grievance and Arbitration Procedures: A Legal Analysis." *Arbitration Journal* 33, no. 1 (March 1978): 16-20.

By excluding claims from arbitration because they could be covered under Title VII, the employer is making employment-classification decisions using criteria prohibited by the Civil Rights Act.

950. Webster, Carol. "Arbitrating Title VII Disputes: A Proposal." *Arbitration Journal* 33, no. 1 (March 1978): 25-30.

This article suggests that an independent judgment standard by the courts in reviewing arbitrators' decisions be established.

951. Edwards, Harry T. "Arbitration as an Alternative in Equal Employment Disputes." *Arbitration Journal* 33, no. 4 (December 1978): 22-27.

Concludes that arbitration is a viable means of resolving relatively simple employee discrimination cases. Proposes a two-track arbitration system and an EEOC arbitration scheme.

952. Kandel, William. "EEO Challenges Arbitration." *Employee Relations Law Journal* 4, no. 4 (Spring 1979): 577-590.

This article contends that the courts feel that arbitrators' competence is in "law of the shop" and not in "law of the land."

953. Oppenheimer, Margaret, and Helen LaVan. "Comparing Arbitration and Litigation of Employment Discrimination Cases." *Monthly Labor Review* 102, no. 5 (May 1979): 335-336.

>Arbitrators and the courts are about as likely to find a challenged policy discriminatory. See also "The Use of Arbitration and Litigation in Employment Discrimination Disputes: An Empirical Comparison," 31 IRRA (1978): 291-298 by the same authors.

954. Rubenfeld, Stephen A., and Dennis D. Strouble. "Arbitration and EEO Issues." *Labor Law Journal* 30, no. 8 (August 1979): 489-495.

>Discusses arbitration as an alternative to government enforcement procedures to achieve nondiscrimination in employment.

955. Brusch, Stephen Anthony. "The Role of Arbitration in Employment Discrimination Claims." *Industrial and Labor Relations Forum* 14, no. 1 (January 1980): 55-63.

>The author states that arbitrators are not only inconsistent in interpreting and applying statutory law in the area of employment discrimination, but they often err.

956. Wolfson, Steven R. "Social Policy in Title VII Arbitrations." *Kentucky Law Journal* 68, no. 1 (Winter 1980): 101-140.

>Wolfson concludes that arbitrators can hear Title TII grievances although courts should reserve the right to review their social policy aspects of the awards.

957. Bartlett, Anthony F. "Employment Discrimination and Labor Arbitrators: A Question of Competence." *West Virginia Law Review* 85, no. 5 (Summer 1983): 873-909.

>Examines the competence of labor arbitrators to handle employment discrimination disputes in light of the "special competence" requirement of Footnote 21 of Gardner-Denver.

958. Gregory, David L. "Conflict between Seniority and Affirmative Action Principles in Labor Arbitration, and Consequent Problems of Judicial Review." *Temple Law Quarterly* 57, no. 1 (1984): 47-75.

>Examines the nexus between labor law and employment discrimination law, with particular attention to the seniority provisions of a collective bargaining agreement.

959. Wrong, Elaine Gale. "Arbitrators' Determinations of Reverse Discrimination or Affirmative Action Cases." *Labor Law Journal* 35, no. 9 (1984): 587-593.

>For the most part, arbitrators ignore other arbitrators' awards and demon-

strate a "desire to preserve the contract and leave the examination of the law to judges." For further discussion, please see "The Social Responsibility of Arbitrators in Title VII Disputes." *Labor Law Journal* 32, no. 9 (1981): 621-626, by the same author.

960. Hauck, Vern E. "The Efficacy of Arbitrating Discrimination Complaints." *Labor Law Journal* 35, no. 3 (March 1984): 175-181.

Finds statistical support for the contention that arbitrators use traditional decision rules in cases involving seniority, discharge, and promotion. Almost all decisions comply with factors cited in *Gardner-Denver*'s Footnote 21.

961. Wrong, Elaine Gale. "Arbitrators' Decisions in Seniority-Discrimination Cases." *Arbitration Journal* 39, no. 4 (December 1984): 22-27.

A study of eight arbitration awards decided between 1975 and 1979 that involved seniority provisions and Title VII claims. In six cases arbitrators upheld plant seniority even when white males were demoted.

962. Kostyack, John F. "U.S. Supreme Court Refuses to Adopt Rule Giving Preclusive Effect to Labor Arbitration Awards in Civil Rights Suits." *Stetson Law Review* 14, no. 3 (Summer 1985): 792-794.

In reviewing a case in which an arbitrator upheld a discharge of a Michigan police officer, the Supreme Court held that an arbitration award should not prevent subsequent litigation in the courts.

963. Clark, Leroy D., and Barbara A. Bush. "Arbitration of Employment Discrimination Claims: A Need for Statutory Reform?" *Thurgood Marshall Law Review* 11, no. 1 (Fall 1985): 47-64.

This article examines ambiguities in Title VII cases, the limited ability of agencies to handle the cases, and the capacity of binding arbitration to deal with them.

964. Carmell, William A., and Patrick R. Westerkamp. "Arbitration of EEO Claims a Decade after Gardner-Denver." *Employee Relations Law Journal* 12, no. 1 (Summer 1986): 80-97.

A review of the use of arbitration in equal employment opportunity cases since the ruling in *Gardner-Denver*.

965. Fowler, Aubrey R., Jr. "Discrimination Grievances in Arbitration." *Personnel* 63, no. 12 (December 1986): 18-25.

An examination of the issues resulting from conflict between legislated individual rights and collectively bargained rights in discrimination cases.

966. Conlon, Mark T. "Employment Law: Arbitration Not a Prerequisite to a Federal Court Proceeding on a Title VII Claim. (Case Note)." *Suffolk University Law Review* 24, no. 1 (Spring 1990): 271-278.

> Conlon contends that arbitration is not the proper forum when a matter of public policy is involved. A member of a bargaining unit may bypass arbitration and take the case directly to the courts.

967. Malin, Martin H., and Lamont E. Stallworth. "Affirmative Action Issues and the Role of External Law in Labor Arbitration." *Seton Hall Law Review* 20, no. 4 (Fall 1990): 745-785.

> This is a review of arbitration awards involving grievances that are tied to affirmative action.

968. Hillock, Laura R. "Arbitration of Title VII and Parallel State Discrimination Claims: A Proposal." *California Western Law Review* 27, no. 1 (Winter 1990): 179-208.

> Because the courts are willing to review arbitration awards on their merits when a Title VII violation is involved, an increasing number of grievants elect to bypass arbitration and litigate their Title VII claims directly.

969. Layton, Robert, Glen D. Nager, and Deena B. Jenab. "Using Compulsory Arbitration to Resolve EEO Disputes." In Office of the General Counsel, American Arbitration Association. *Arbitration and the Law: AAA General Counsel's Annual Report: 1991-1992*, 118-127. New York: AAA, 1992.

> In the wake of the Gilmer case, the Civil Rights Act of 1991, and the Americans with Disabilities Act, this article discusses the need for arbitrating employment discrimination claims, legal limitations on the use of arbitration, human resource concerns, and the structure for an arbitration procedure.

Sex Discrimination

970. McKelvey, Jean T. "The Presidential Address: Sex and the Single Arbitrator." In 24 NAA (1971): 1-29.

> The courts, administrative agencies, and arbitrators on sex discrimination issues.

971. McKelvey, Jean T. "Sex and the Single Arbitrator." *Industrial and Labor Relations Review* 24, no. 3 (April 1971): 339-353.

> Argues that arbitrators too often fail to deal with external law in sex discrimination cases and look only at contractual provisions.

972. Block, Richard N. "Legal and Traditional Criteria in the Arbitration of Sex Discrimination Cases." *Arbitration Journal* 32, no. 4 (December 1977): 241-255.

Examines the criteria arbitrators have employed in deciding charges of sex discrimination.

973. Rosenberg, Sheldon. "Sex Discrimination and the Labor Arbitration Process." *Labor Law Journal* 30, no. 2 (February 1979): 102-117.

> This article examines reported cases from the end of WWII through the 1970s in which female employees charged sex discrimination, usually involving pay, promotion, or recall. In almost all cases examined, the arbitrator found against the woman.

974. Kovarsky, Irving, and Vern E. Hauck. "The No-Spouse Rule, Title VII, and Arbitration." *Labor Law Journal* 32 (1981): 366-374.

> This article deals with no-spouse rules, under which individuals who marry someone employed in the same plant, department, or company are discharged.

975. Wolkinson, Benjamin W., and Dennis H. Liberson. "The Arbitration of Sex Discrimination Grievances." *Arbitration Journal* 37, no. 2 (June 1982): 35-44.

> A study of the efficacy of arbitration for settling sex discrimination cases.

976. Wrong, Elaine Gale. "Arbitrators, the Law, and Women's Job Bids." *Labor Law Journal* 33, no. 12 (December 1982): 798-808.

> An examination of arbitration awards rendered between 1966 and 1981 in cases of job bidding involving charges of sex discrimination.

977. Willig, Deborah R. "Arbitration of Discrimination Grievances: Arbitral and Judicial Competence Compared." In 39 NAA (1987): 101-120.

> A favorable view of arbitration in gender discrimination cases.

978. Andiappan, Palaniappan, Martha Reavley, and S. Silver. "Discrimination against Pregnant Employees: An Analysis of Arbitration and Human Rights Tribunal Decisions in Canada." *Journal of Business Ethics* 9, no. 2 (February 1990): 143-149.

> A study of pregnancy related arbitrations in Canada from 1980 to 1987. Except in dealing with the right to sick leave, the employee prevailed when the discrimination claim was based on pregnancy.

Age Discrimination

979. Rodenberg, Thomas D. "To Arbitrate or Not to Arbitrate? The Protection of Rights under the Age Discrimination in Employment Act. (Case Note)." *Journal of Dispute Resolution* 1988 (1988): 199-218.

> This article reviews two cases involving whether claims under the Age Discrimination in Employment Act are to be decided by arbitration or by the courts.

980. Wrong, Elaine Gale. "Arbitrators' Awards in Cases Involving Age Discrimination." *Labor Law Journal* 39, no. 7 (July 1988): 411-417.

>The issues that are addressed include training, promotion, forced retirement, and bona fide occupational qualifications.

981. Baxter, Ralph H., Jr., and Evelyn M. Hunt. "Alternative Dispute Resolution: Arbitration of Employment Claims." *Employee Relations Law Journal* 15, no. 2 (Autumn 1989): 187-207.

>In cases involving Title VII and the Age Discrimination Act, the courts have the right to give arbitration decisions great weight.

982. Gillin, Leslie M. "A Test of Arbitrability: Does Arbitration Provide Adequate Protection for Aged Employees? (Case Note)." *Villanova Law Review* 35, no. 2 (April 1990): 389-433.

>An examination of *Nicholson v. CPA International*, in which the U.S. Court of Appeals addressed contradictions between the Age Discrimination in Employment Act and the Federal Arbitration Act.

983. Lieberman, Michael. "Overcoming the Presumption of Arbitrability of ADEA Claims: The Triumph of Substantive over Procedural Values. (Case Note)." *University of Pennsylvania Law Review* 118, no. 6 (June 1990): 1817-1855.

>The author argues against the presumption of arbitrability in age discrimination claims, contending that arbitration often fails to award equitable remedies.

984. Burstein, James A., and Lynne D. Mapes-Riordan. "The Arbitrability of Age Discrimination Claims: A Split in the Circuits." *Employee Relations Law Journal* 16, no. 2 (Autumn 1990): 139-156.

>This article discusses the split in the Circuit Courts over the arbitrability of Age Discrimination Employment Act disputes in light of *Gilmer*.

985. "Agreements to Arbitrate Claims under the Age Discrimination in Employment Act." *Harvard Law Review* 104, no. 2 (December 1990): 568-587.

>According to this article, disputes under the Age Discrimination Act should be subject to arbitration because of crowded dockets and high litigation costs.

986. Stewart, Thomas H. "Arbitrating Claims under the Age Discrimination of Employment Act of 1967. (Case Note)." *University of Cincinnati Law Review* 59, no. 4 (Spring 1991): 1415-1440.

>An examination of the arbitrability of claims under the Age Discrimination in Employment Act.

Other Forms of Discrimination

Religion

987. Wolkinson, Benjamin W. "Title VII and the Religious Employee: The Neglected Duty of Accommodation." *Arbitration Journal* 30, no. 2 (June 1975): 89-111.

> Wolkinson argues that arbitrators are insufficiently aware of EEOC guidelines requiring employers to accommodate religious preferences.

Handicap

988. Kovarsky, Irving, and Vern E. Hauck. "Arbitration and the Epileptic." *Labor Law Journal* 28 (September 1977): 597-607.

> This article examines 28 reported decisions involving discharge of epileptics. Many arbitrators seem to assume that all epileptics pose a threat to industrial safety.

989. Wolkinson, Benjamin W., and David Barton. "Arbitration and the Rights of Mentally Handicapped Workers." *Monthly Labor Review* 103, no. 4 (April 1980): 41-47.

> Concludes that arbitrators often order employers to make reasonable accommodation for mentally handicapped workers.

990. Marmo, Michael. "The Arbitration of Mental Illness Cases." *Labor Law Journal* 31 (July 1980): 403-416.

> This article reviews the circumstances under which the issue of mental illness is raised, the relationship of the illness to the job, the effect of seniority, and when a discharged employee can be considered cured.

991. Cramer, Dorothy J. "Arbitration and Mental Illness: The Issues, the Rationale, and the Remedies." *Arbitration Journal* 35, no. 3 (September 1980): 10-21.

> This article covers discharge of mentally ill employees and suggests an approach for arbitrators dealing with these issues.

992. Wolkinson, Benjamin W. "Arbitration and the Employment Rights of the Physically Disadvantaged." *Arbitration Journal* 36, no. 1 (March 1981): 23-30.

> Examines the protection afforded the physically handicapped worker from dismissal under just-cause provisions.

993. Roumell, George T., Jr. "Mental Illness, the Workplace and Grievance Arbitration." *Michigan Bar Journal* 62, no. 9 (September 1983): 758-763.

> A review of arbitration decisions in mental illness cases. In nondisciplinary matters that involve removal from the job, arbitrators focus on the nature of the illness, its effects on the employee's ability to perform the work, and

the potential risk to others. In discipline cases, the arbitrator focuses on whether the employee was actually ill at the time of the incident.

994. Leap, Terry L., Jozetta H. Srb, and Paul F. Petersen. Health and Job Safety: An Analysis of Arbitration Decisions." *Arbitration Journal* 41, no. 3 (September 1986): 41-52.

> An analysis of 65 cases in which arbitrators were called upon to evaluate whether health-impaired workers posed significant safety hazards on the job.

National Origin

995. Ornati, Oscar A. "Arbitrators and National Origin Discrimination." *Arbitration Journal* 36, no. 2 (June 1981): 30-34.

> Discusses the way in which the courts and arbitrators have dealt with the issue of national origin discrimination.

O. Interest Arbitration and Other Forms of Dispute Resolution

General Material

996. Taylor, George W. "Is Compulsory Arbitration Inevitable?" In 1 IRRA (1948): 64-77.

> Analyzes the use of compulsory arbitration and proposes three alternatives: voluntary arbitration, procedural substitutes for the strike, and plant seizures.

997. Van de Water, John B. "Involuntary Arbitration and National Defense." *Arbitration Journal* 18, no. 2 (1963): 96-104; no. 3: 147-161.

> Argues against use of compulsory arbitration even in the defense industry.

998. Phelps, Orme W. "Compulsory Arbitration: Some Perspectives." *Industrial and Labor Relations Review* 18, no. 1 (October 1964): 81-91.

> Argues that the judicial process is not appropriate to all labor-management disputes.

999. Stevens, C. M. "Analytics of Voluntary Arbitration of Contract Disputes." *Industrial Relations* 7, no. 1 (October 1967): 68-79.

> Examines voluntary interest arbitration and concludes it does not threaten effective negotiation when used on an ad hoc basis.

1000. Stieber, Jack. "Voluntary Arbitration of Contract Terms." In 23 NAA (1970): 71-124.

> The results of a questionnaire survey.

1001. Morris, Charles J. "The Role of Interest Arbitration in a Collective Bargaining System." *Industrial Relations Law Journal* 1, no. 3 (Fall 1976): 427-531.

>Interest arbitration is viewed as an adjunct to the collective bargaining process.

1002. Seitz, Peter. "The Gotterdammerung of Grievance Arbitration." *Employee Relations Law Journal* 2, no. 4 (Spring 1977): 386-395.

>The author argues that the finality of grievance arbitration is being threatened by the increasing use of interest arbitration. Arbitrators' decisions in interest cases are often appealed to the courts, thereby threatening the finality of the grievance arbitration process.

1003. Krislov, Joseph, and Raymond D. Horton. "Arbitration, Arbitrators, and the Public Interest." *Industrial and Labor Relations Review* 31, no. 1 (October 1977): 71-77.

>The authors present differing views on interest arbitration.

1004. Donn, Clifford B., and Barry T. Hirsch. "Making Interest Arbitration Costly: A Policy Proposal." *Journal of Collective Negotiations in the Public Sector* 12, no. 1 (1983): 21-32.

>Proposes charging a fee based on size of unit and magnitude of difference in party's position to provide incentive to bargain.

1005. DeCoste, F. C. "Compulsory Arbitration of Interest Disputes: Rational Model or Social Necessity." *Saskatchewan Law Review* 49, no. 2 (Summer 1984): 279-302.

>This article examines collective bargaining and compulsory arbitration as social, economic, and ethical policy.

1006. Helburn, I. B., and Robert C. Rodgers. "Hesitancy of Arbitrators to Accept Interest Arbitration Cases: A Test of Conventional Wisdom." *Public Administration Review* 45, no. 3 (May-June 1985): 398-402.

>An examination of the factors that cause some arbitrators to reject interest arbitration cases.

1007. Zack, Arnold M. "The Arbitration of Interest Disputes: A Process in Peril." *Arbitration Journal* 41, no. 2 (June 1986): 38-42.

>Zack contends that interest arbitration processes are too cumbersome, too adversarial, and they are hampered by impediments to settlement. For earlier views, see *Understanding Fact-Finding and Interest Arbitration in the Public Sector*, Washington, D.C., U.S. Dept. of Labor, 1974, 1976, 1980; "Dispute Settlement in the Public Sector," *New York Law Forum*, vol. XIV, no. 2 (Summer 1968): 249-70; and "Final Offer Selection: Panacea or Pandora's Box?" *New York Law Forum* 19, no. 3 (Winter 1974): 568-586.

1008. La Rue, Homer C. "A Historical Overview of Interest Arbitration in the United States." *Arbitration Journal* 42, no. 4 (December 1987): 13-22.

>The author traces historical development of interest arbitration in the public sector in the United States.

Private Sector

1009. Handsaker, Morrison. "Arbitration and Contract Disputes." In 13 NAA (1960): 78-100.

>Focuses on voluntary interest arbitration in the private sector. Discussions by John Waddleton and Bernard Cushman.

1010. Miller, Richard U. "Arbitration of New Contract Wage Disputes: Some Recent Trends." *Industrial and Labor Relations Review* 20, no. 2 (January 1967): 250-264.

>Analysis of private sector wage arbitration from 1953 to 1965 discloses that it rarely takes place and, when it does, mainly in cases involving low-profit firms.

1011. Feller, David E. "The Impetus to Contract Arbitration in the Private Area." *Proceedings of NYU Twenty-fourth Annual Conference on Labor*, 79-101. New York: Matthew Bender, 1972.

>Analysis of why contract arbitration is seldom adopted voluntarily and some recent proposals for its use.

1012. "Arbitration of Interest Disputes in the Local Transit and Newspaper Publishing Industries." In 26 NAA (1974): 8-61.

>A series of essays by various spokesmen for the parties.

1013. Mayo, Thomas W. "The Enforceability of Interest Arbitration Agreements under Section 301(a) of the LMRA." *Syracuse Law Review* 27 (Summer 1976): 985-1010.

>Analyzes the conflict in lower federal court decisions on this issue.

1014. "Interest Arbitration and the NLRB: A Case for the Self-Terminating Interest Arbitration Clause." *Yale Law Journal* 86, no. 4 (March 1977): 715-732.

>Challenges the wisdom of NLRB decisions that hold interest arbitration clauses as a nonmandatory subject of bargaining.

1015. Scharman, Clifford. "Interest Arbitration in the Private Sector." *Arbitration Journal* 36, no. 3 (September 1981): 14-23.

>An examination of the NLRB policy of discouraging interest arbitration as a method for determining new contracts in the private sector.

1016. Hall, Gary A. "Wage Arbitration as a Bargaining Proxy: A Test of Split the Difference." *Review of Business and Economic Research* 20, no. 1 (Fall 1984): 121-127.

>A study testing the split-the-difference model based on private sector cases in various industries between 1950 and 1980. Arbitrators do not usually split the difference.

1017. Liberson, Dennis H. "Long-Term Agreements Work at Philip Morris." *Personnel Journal* 68, no. 12 (December 1989): 36-39.

>The success of an interest arbitration agreement at the Philip Morris Company is discussed.

1018. Datz, Harold J. "Alternative Dispute Resolution: Interest Arbitration and the National Labor Relations Act." *Labor Lawyer* 6, no. 1 (Winter 1990)8 127-132.

>An overview of interest arbitration and the principle that interest arbitration is not a mandatory topic of bargaining.

Public Sector

General Studies

1019. Ross, David B. "The Arbitration of Public Employee Wage Disputes." *Industrial and Labor Relations Review* 23, no. 1 (October 1969): 3-14.

>Of historical interest. Proposes that comparisons of expenditures for given services be a primary factor in wage determination.

1020. Gilroy, T. P., and Anthony V. Sinicropi. "Impasse Resolution in Public Employment: A Current Assessment." *Industrial and Labor Relations Review* 25 (July 1972): 496-511.

>Recommends fact-finding and last-best offer arbitration where the fact finder's package is also available for the arbitration panel.

1021. Hines, R. J. "Mandatory Contract Arbitration: Is It a Viable Process?" *Industrial and Labor Relations Review* 25 (July 1972): 533-545.

>Examines experience with arbitration of hospital disputes in Ontario, Canada.

1022. McAvoy, Joan Zeldon. "Binding Arbitration of Contract Terms: A New Approach to the Resolution of Disputes in the Public Sector." *Columbia Law Review* 72, no. 7 (November 1972): 1192-1213.

>The author predicts that if present statutes succeed in deterring strikes, similar laws will be enacted in other jurisdictions.

1023. Houseman, K. A. "Compulsory Arbitration in the Public Sector: Constitutionality and Enforcement Issue." *Public Personnel Management* 2, no. 3 (May/June 1973): 194-199.

This article raises questions about what would happen if the government steadfastly refused to implement an interest arbitration award.

1024. Thompson, Mark, and James Cairnie. "Compulsory Arbitration: The Case of British Columbia Teachers." *Industrial and Labor Relations Review* 27, no. 1 (October 1973): 3-17.

> Analyzes a compulsory arbitration system that has been in effect since 1937. Bargaining has not atrophied nor have wage settlements been unreasonable.

1025. Bowers, Mollie H. "Legislated Arbitration-Legality, Enforceability, and Face-Saving." *Public Personnel Management* 3, no. 4 (July-August 1974): 270-278.

> An examination of arbitration systems mandated by legislation to resolve public employee disputes.

1026. "Lessons from Interest Arbitration in the Public Sector: The Experience of Four Jurisdictions." In 27 NAA (1975): 59-105.

> Varied reports and analyses on experiences in New York City, Pennsylvania, Michigan, and Wisconsin, by Arvid Anderson, J. Joseph Loewenberg, Charles M. Rehmus, and James L. Stern.

1027. Horton, Raymond D. "Arbitration, Arbitrators, and the Public Interest." *Industrial and Labor Relations Review* 28, no. 4 (July 1975): 497-507.

> Author questions the increased use of interest arbitration in the public sector.

1028. Bowers, Mollie H., and David M. Cohen. "Drafting Public Sector Arbitration Legislation." *Arbitration Journal* 30, no. 4 (December 1975): 253-272.

> Interest arbitration in the public sector, as an alternative to strikes, is compatible with collective bargaining so long as the arbitration system is properly designed. A workable design system is suggested.

1029. Berkowitz, Monroe. "Arbitration of Public-Sector Interest Dispute: Economics, Politics, and Equity." In 29 NAA (1976): 149-193.

> Discussion of wage comparisons, ability to pay, and the role of the neutral. Comments by Russell H. Smith and Arnold M. Zack.

1030. McCormick, Mary. "A Functional Analysis of Interest Arbitration in New York City Municipal Government, 1968-1975." In 29 IRRA (1976): 249-257.

> Study of the role of interest arbitration in resolving New York City public employee union disputes from 1968 to 1975.

1031. Bornstein, Tim. "Interest Arbitration in Public Employment: An Arbitrator Views the Process." *Labor Law Journal* 29 (February 1978): 77-86.

Discusses the difficulties faced by arbitrators in switching from the "judicial" role of grievance arbitration to the "legislative" role of interest arbitration.

1032. Mironi, Mordehai. "Arbitration as a Strike Substitute in Labor Negotiations: Public Policy Reconsidered." *Alberta Law Review* 18 (1980): 163-197.

This analysis of binding interest arbitration in Alberta focuses on delay, acceptance, ability to innovate, and the ability to maintain peace and preserve free collective bargaining.

1033. Gallagher, Daniel G. "The Use of Interest Arbitration in the Public Sector." *Labor Law Journal* 33, no. 8 (August 1982): 501-507.

Focusing on Iowa, Michigan, Minnesota, and Wisconsin, the author argues that interest arbitration protects the public from strikes and makes some pre-impasse procedural suggestions to encourage voluntary settlements.

1034. Newman, Harold, Jeffrey B. Tener, Robert Emmet Murray, Arvid Anderson, Charles R. Greer, and D. Scott Sink. "Interest Arbitration Symposium." *Arbitration Journal* 37, no. 4 (December 1982): 7-31.

A discussion of interest arbitration procedures by Public Employment Relations Board chairs and advocates in several states.

1035. Gershenfeld, Walter J., Victor Gotbaum, Marcia L. Greenbaum, and Robert Vercruysse. "Interest Arbitration." In 36 NAA (1984): 190-235.

Gershenfeld reviews the experience with compulsory interest arbitration in the public sector, and Greenbaum looks at voluntary interest arbitration in the transit industry. Comments by Vercruysse (management) and Gotbaum (unions).

1036. Craver, Charles B. "Public Sector Impasse Resolution Procedures." *Chicago-Kent Law Review* 60, no. 4 (Fall 1984): 779-814.

Methods of resolving bargaining impasses in the public sector.

1037. Howlett, Robert G. "Interest Arbitration in the Public Sector." *Chicago-Kent Law Review* 60, no. 4 (Fall 1984): 815-837.

Strikes and other job actions are important vehicles for bringing closure to public employee contract negotiations. The article reviews the arguments for and against interest arbitration.

1038. Lester, Richard Allen. "Lessons from Experience with Interest Arbitration in Nine Jurisdictions." *Arbitration Journal* 41, no. 2 (June 1986): 34-37.

The author concludes that: 1) systems of interest arbitration are increasingly accepted; 2) arbitration awards are increasingly being agreed upon;

3) such programs are more effective where parties participate equally in the process; 4) no one form is best suited for application in every state.

1039. Mukamal, Stuart S. "Unilateral Employer Action under Public-Sector Binding Interest Arbitration." *Journal of Law and Commerce* 6, no. 1 (Summer 1986): 107-153.

>An examination of the advantages and the side effects of interest arbitration and of the procedures designed to aid the bargaining process before arbitration.

1040. Dunn, John K., and Craig E. Overton. "Arbitrator's Utilization of Private Sector Criteria in Resolving Public Sector Disputes." *Journal of Collective Negotiations in the Public Sector* 17, no. 3 (1988): 197-206.

>The authors argue that interest arbitrators should have more decision-making latitude than grievance arbitrators because they have no contractual criteria to guide them.

1041. Giacobbe, Jane. "Factfinding and Arbitration: Procedural Justice for All?" *Journal of Collective Negotiations in the Public Sector* 17, no. 4 (1988): 295-308.

>A survey of school districts in three midwestern states on attitudes toward interest arbitration.

1042. Rueschhoff, M. Susan. "Public Sector Interest Arbitration: An Examination of Relevant Normative Premises and a Test of Underlying Assumptions." *Journal of Collective Negotiations in the Public Sector* 17, no. 3 (1988): 177-196.

>This survey in a Nebraska county showed that the citizenry and public employees share certain normative premises about public sector interest arbitration.

1043. McGinnis, William, Jr. "Interest Arbitration in Perspective." *Government Union Review* 10, no. 1 (Winter 1989): 36-49.

>The author describes the interest arbitration process in various state statutes for public safety personnel.

1044. Bucheit, Scott E., and Robert M, Ackerman. "Interest Arbitration." In 43 NAA (1991): 171-189.

>Bucheit describes interest arbitration experiences in Delaware, New Jersey, Pennsylvania, and major league baseball. Ackerman suggests that the arbitration system that has evolved does work.

1045. Samavati, Hedayeh, Lawrence J. Haber, and David A. Dilts. "Comparability and the Interest Arbitration of Economic Disputes in the Public Sector." *Journal of Collective Negotiations in the Public Sector* 20, no. 2 (1991): 159-166.

> The authors argue for the use of statistical information rather than inspection or witness testimony to determine comparability between public sector jurisdictions.

1046. Rueschhoff, M. Susan. "Measuring and Explaining Attitudes of Four Interest Groups toward Selected Aspects of Public Sector Interest Arbitration." *Public Personnel Management* 20, no. 4 (Winter 1991): 493-504.

> This study examines the attitudes of the general public, public sector employees, public sector employers, and the legislature toward arbitration, decision-making, collective bargaining, essentiality of work, and strikes.

Public Interest and Political Considerations

1047. Rehmus, Charles M. "Legislated Interest Arbitration." In 27 IRRA (1974): 307-314.

> Analysis of whether legislated interest arbitration serves the public interest and its impact on strikes, collective bargaining, and settlements.

1048. Grodin, Joseph R. "Political Aspects of Public Sector Interest Arbitration." *Industrial Relations Law Journal* 1, no. 1 (Spring 1976): 1-24.

> A general review of the system of public sector labor relations that existed before the emergence of collective bargaining, and an examination of public employee strikes and interest arbitration.

1049. Grodin, Joseph R. "Political Aspects of Public Sector Interest Arbitration." *California Law Review* 64 (May 1976): 678-701.

> Argues that arbitrators sometimes make social policy decisions usually reserved for elected or appointed officials.

1050. Chauhan, D. S. "The Political and Legal Issues of Binding Arbitration in Government." *Monthly Labor Review* 102, no. 9 (September 1979): 35-41.

> Compulsory arbitration as an alternative to strikes in the public sector and the constitutional issues.

1051. Feuille, Peter. "Selected Benefits and Costs of Compulsory Arbitration." *Industrial and Labor Relations Review* 33 (October 1979): 64-75.

> Focuses on political considerations that should be addressed in evaluating compulsory arbitration.

1052. Babcock, Linda C., and Craig A. Olson. "The Causes of Impasses in Labor Disputes." *Industrial Relations* 31, no. 2 (Spring 1992): 348-360.

> The study concludes that negotiators wish to avoid the political costs of a compromise settlement and prefer to blame arbitrators for the outcome. Negotiators base their judgments of fairness on consistency with their own position.

Strike Considerations

1053. Clark, R. Theodore, Jr. "Legislated Interest Arbitration: A Management Response." In 27 IRRA (1974): 319-323.

>   Argues that it is preferable for public employees to strike than submit to compulsory arbitration.

1054. Rains, Harry H. "The Right to Strike and Compulsory Arbitration as an Alternative." *Employee Relations Law Journal* 1, no. 2 (Autumn 1975): 339-342.

>   This review of the right to strike in the public sector and statutory penalties recommends last-best offer arbitration.

1055. Dunham, Robert E. "Interest Arbitration in Non-Federal Public Employment." *Arbitration Journal* 31, no. 1 (March 1976): 45-57.

>   Dunham points out that in nonfederal public employment, binding arbitration is used more often than work stoppages or fact-finding for resolving contract disputes. Strikes occur less frequently when arbitration is the final step in impasse procedures.

1056. Backhouse, Constance. "The Fleck Strike: A Case Study in the Need for First Contract Arbitration. (Canada)." *Osgoode Hall Law Journal* 18, no. 4 (December 1980): 495-553.

>   This article examines a violent Canadian strike over a first contract, and it uses the example of that strike to argue for a public policy which provides for first contract arbitration.

1057. Stern, James L., and Craig A. Olson. "The Propensity to Strike of Local Government Employees." *Journal of Collective Negotiations in the Public Sector* 11, no. 3 (1982): 201-214.

>   The authors conclude that the propensity to strike by local governmental employees is highest in states without bargaining laws, lowest in states with a mandatory interest arbitration statute, and intermediate for those with a bargaining law that does not mandate arbitration.

1058. Ichniowski, Casey. "Arbitration and Police Bargaining: Prescription for the Blue Flu." *Industrial Relations* 21, no. 2 (Spring 1982): 149-165.

>   Reviews impasse record in police negotiations and demonstrates that arbitration statutes prevent job actions.

1059. Johnson, Richard. "Interest Arbitration Examined." *Personnel Administrator* 28, no. 1 (January 1983): 53-57.

>   Argues that interest arbitrations have done more damage to the public interest than the strikes they were designed to replace.

1060. Champlin, Frederic C., and Mario F. Bognanno. "Time Spent Processing Interest Arbitration Cases: The Minnesota Experience." *Journal of Collective Negotiations in the Public Sector* 14, no. 1 (1985): 53-65.

> Data show that in disputes where there is a good chance of a strike, the parties invest more time in bargaining than in disputes where arbitration is the likely outcome.

1061. Olson, Craig A. "Strikes, Strike Penalties, and Arbitration in Six States." *Industrial and Labor Relations Review* 39, no. 4 (July 1986): 539-551.

> This comparative study concludes that legalization of strike activity increases strike frequency, poorly enforced penalties have little effect, and interest arbitration reduces strike frequency.

1062. Doherty, Robert E. "Trends in Strikes and Interest Arbitration in the Public Sector." *Labor Law Journal* 37, no. 8 (August 1986): 473-479.

> This empirical study concludes that there were fewer strikes in the public sector, a lower percentage of impasses going to arbitration, and little difference between salary increases awarded through arbitration and those reached through negotiation.

1063. Anderson, Arvid, and Loren A. Krause. "Interest Arbitration: The Alternative to the Strike." *Fordham Law Review* 56, no. 2 (November 1987): 153-179.

> Interest arbitration avoids the harm that strikes often cause while permitting labor to retain the leverage necessary to bargain effectively.

1064. DiLauro, Thomas J. "Interest Arbitration: The Best Alternative for Resolving Public-Sector Impasses." *Employee Relations Law Journal* 14, no. 4 (Spring 1989): 549-568.

> Mandatory binding interest arbitration is preferable to fact-finding for crucial public sector employees. It is a civilized substitute for strikes.

Ability to Pay and Impact on Management

1065. Holden, Lawrence T. "Final-Offer Arbitration in Massachusetts." *Arbitration Journal* 31, no. 1 (March 1976): 26-35.

> The study focuses on the relationships among arbitration, fact-finding, and mediation and the impact final offer arbitration has on community funding decisions.

1066. Fleming, R. W. "Binding Arbitration Can Put Public Employers in a Bind." *Monthly Labor Review* 102, no. 1 (January 0979): 73-75.

> Discusses special problems interest arbitration can cause for effective use of public funds.

1067. Fox, Michael. "Criteria for Public Sector Interest Arbitration in New York City: The Triumph of 'Ability to Pay' and the End of Interest Arbitration." *Albany Law Review* 46, no. 1 (Fall 1981): 97-131.

> The author examines the decisional criteria used by interest arbitrators during the New York City financial crisis from 1968 through 1979. He focuses on the change from equity to ability to pay.

1068. Minami, Wayne, R. Theodore Clark, Jr., and William J. Fallon. "Interest Arbitration: Can the Public Sector Afford It? Developing Limitations on the Process." In 34 NAA (1982): 241- 272.

> Papers by Minami, Clark (a management view), and Fallon (an arbitrator's view, with emphasis on experience in New England).

1069. Foster, Howard G. " 'Ability to Pay' in Public Sector Fact-finding and Arbitration." *Labor Law Journal* 35, no. 2 (February 1984): 123-126.

> Considers the implications of the requirements in many state statutes that a third party evaluate ability to pay in addressing economic issues of bargaining.

1070. Krinsky, Edward B., and Felicity D. Briggs. "Interest Arbitration and the Ability to Pay." In 41 NAA (1989): 197-215.

> Krinsky argues that unless the employer presents substantial documentation, arbitrators typically give ability to pay little attention. Briggs, approaching the topic from a Canadian union perspective, reports "happily" that ability to pay is not a relevant criterion.

Interest Arbitration and the Law

Conceptual Works

1071. Corcoran, Kevin J., and Diane Kutell. "Binding Arbitration Laws for State and Municipal Workers." *Monthly Labor Review* 101, no. 10 (October 1978): 36-40.

> A summary of interest arbitration laws that existed in 1977.

1072. Fleischli, George R. "Some Problems with the Administration of Compulsory Final Offer Arbitration Procedures." *Chicago-Kent Law Review* 56, no. 2 (Spring 1980): 559-587.

> Outlines the key features of compulsory final-offer arbitration laws and the problems encountered.

1073. Kruger, Daniel H., and Harry E. Jones. "Compulsory Interest Arbitration in the Public Sector: An Overview." *Journal of Collective Negotiations in the Public Sector* 10, no. 4 (1981): 335-380.

> Authors review state developments and suggest proposed changes to state system.

1074. Hyman, Warren H. "Arbitration and the Public Employee: An Alternative to the Right to Strike." *Detroit College of Law Review* 1983, no. 3 (Fall 1983): 743-756.

>A discussion of interest arbitration. Statutes of various states and the federal government are examined.

Specific State Legislation on Interest Arbitration (Alphabetized by State)

California

1075. Attia, Gilles Simon. "Public Sector Interest Arbitration: Threat to Local Representative Government?" *Pacific Law Journal* 9, no. 1 (January 1978): 165-215.

>The author asks how much will the California courts permit arbitration to intrude on the representative character of local government, and how can the legislature build political accountability into its arbitration scheme.

Connecticut

1076. Clemow, Brian, and Thomas B. Mooney. "Impasse Resolution in Local Government Labor Relations: The Connecticut Approach." *Connecticut Law Review* 9, no. 4 (Summer 1977): 579-607.

>Discusses public sector impasse resolution generally and two Connecticut statutes. See also response in vol. 10, no. 4 (Summer 1978), pp. 997-1015.

1077. Bingham, Lisa B. "Mid-Term Bargaining Disputes and Binding Interest Arbitration for Public Sector Employees." *Connecticut Law Review* 17, no. 2 (Winter 1985): 365-386.

>There is a history of midterm bargaining in the Connecticut public sector. The author concludes that the statutory requirement for binding arbitration should not be applied to midterm bargaining.

Illinois

1078. Laner, Richard W., and Julia W. Manning. "Interest Arbitration: A New Terminal Impasse Resolution Procedure for Illinois Public Sector Employees." *Chicago-Kent Law Review* 60, no. 4 (Fall 1984): 839-862.

>A description and analysis of the Illinois Public Labor Relations Act and the impact of its compulsory arbitration provision on collective bargaining.

Iowa

1079. Gallagher, Daniel G. "Interest Arbitration under the Iowa Public Employment Relations Act." *Arbitration Journal* 33, no. 3 (September 1978): 30-36.

>Examination of experience under Iowa's Public Employment Relations Act.

1080. Phillips, John R. "Impasse Resolution in Public Sector Collective Bargaining: The Need to Reevaluate Options." *Drake Law Review* 28, no. 3 (1978-1979): 547-570.

>The author concludes that Iowa's impasse resolution system has a deleterious effect on collective bargaining.

1081. Gallagher, Daniel G., and Richard Pegnetter. "Impasse Resolution under the Iowa Multistep Procedure." *Industrial and Labor Relations Review* 32, no. 3 (April 1979): 327-338.

>Examines first two years of experience under new law that allows arbitrator to choose fact finder's package as well as one of parties' in last-offer format.

Massachusetts

1082. Dempster, George D. "Final Offer Arbitration in Massachusetts." *New England Law Review* 12, no. 3 (Winter 1977): 693-717.

>Reviews constitutional and procedural issues surrounding the statute.

1083. Robitzer, William D. "Final Offer Arbitration and the Labor-Management Posse: Heading Off Municipal Disputes at Impasse." *Boston University Law Review* 59, no. 1 (January 1979): 105-128.

>Review and appraisal of Massachusetts statute after five years of experience. Concludes that consequences often run counter to intended policy.

Michigan

1084. Rehmus, Charles M. "Is a 'Final Offer' Ever Final?" *Monthly Labor Review* 97, no. 9 (September 1974): 43-45.

>Discusses the degree of discretion allowed arbitrators under the Michigan statute. This law provides for mediation/arbitration.

1085. Cattel, Thomas A. "Compulsory Arbitration for Police and Fire Fighters: Is It Here to Stay?" *Detroit College of Law Review* 1979, no. 4 (Winter 1979): 701-733.

>A generally critical discussion of the Michigan compulsory arbitration law for interest disputes involving police and fire fighters.

1086. Meiners, Roger S. "Labor Relations—Compulsory Arbitration—Michigan Public Employees Claiming Access to Compulsory Arbitration as Policemen, Firemen, or Persons Subject to the Hazards Thereof, Are Eligible Only When Their Strikes Would Cause Imminent Danger to Public Safety, Order, and Welfare. (Case Note)." *University of Detroit Journal of Urban Law* 59, no. 1 (Fall 1981): 117-126.

>Michigan's Act 312 provides for compulsory arbitration in the resolution of contract impasses involving police and fire fighters. This article examines Michigan case law, which has concluded that the legislature intended to apply the act to other employees in hazardous and critical occupations.

1087. Kruger, Daniel H. "Interest Arbitration Revisited." *Labor Law Journal* 36, no. 8 (August 1985): 497-514.

> This article discusses the history, amendments, impact, and some problems with the Michigan Compulsory Arbitration Act that affects police, fire fighters, emergency medical service technicians, and 911 operators.

Nevada

1088. Grodin, Joseph R. "Arbitration of Public Sector Labor Disputes: The Nevada Experiment." *Industrial and Labor Relations Review* 28, no. 1 (October 1974): 89-102.

> In 1971, Nevada gave its governor authority to order fact-finder's awards binding on all issues if requested by either party. This article examines some of the problems associated with the statute.

New Jersey

1089. Weitzman, Joan, and John M. Stochaj. "Attitudes of Arbitrators toward Final-Offer Arbitration in New Jersey." *Arbitration Journal* 35, no. 1 (March 1980): 25-34.

> The article concludes that New Jersey's Fire and Police Arbitration Act is working reasonably well.

1090. Bloom, David E. "Customized 'Final-Offer': New Jersey's Arbitration Law." *Monthly Labor Review* 103, no. 9 (September 1980): 30-33.

> The New Jersey Fire and Police Arbitration Act of 1977 gave the parties the choice of several forms of arbitration in settling labor disputes involving public safety employees. This article describes the act and summarizes the early experiences.

New York

1091. Anderson, Arvid, et al. "Impasse Resolution in Public Sector Collective Bargaining: An Examination of Compulsory Interest Arbitration in New York." *St. John's Law Review* 51, no. 3 (Spring 1977): 453-515.

> Examination of arguments against compulsory arbitration in light of experience of New York State, New York City, and other jurisdictions. Generally supportive of arbitration.

Oklahoma

1092. Greer, Charles R., and D. Scott Sink. "Oklahoma's Experience with a Unique Interest Arbitration Procedure for Fire Fighters and Police." *Arbitration Journal* 37, no. 4 (December 1982): 21-31.

> Oklahoma's interest arbitration statute permits municipalities to reject an arbitrator's award but allows no such option to the union. This article reports on ten years' experience with the law.

Pennsylvania

1093. Compton-Forbes, Patricia. "Interest Arbitration Hasn't Worked Well in the Public Sector." *Personnel Administrator* 29, no. 2 (February 1984): 99-104.

> A study of attitudes toward the system of voluntary arbitration in Pennsylvania to resolve teacher bargaining disputes. The study shows distrust and resentment.

1094. Doty, Ethan Allen. "Philadelphia's Compulsory Arbitration Program." *Villanova Law Review* 29, no. 6 (November 1984): 1449-1461.

> The author describes the history, the mechanics, and the logistics of the above-referenced program.

1095. Loewenberg, J. Joseph. "Act 111 of 1968 and the Pennsylvania Labor Relations Board." *Labor Law Journal* 40, no. 12 (December 1989): 765-774.

> A description of the role played by the Pennsylvania Labor Relations Board in administering the state's compulsory arbitration law for police and fire contract disputes from 1968 through 1977.

1096. Decker, Kurt H. "Approaching Pennsylvania's Police and Fire Collective Bargaining's Silver Anniversary: Is It Time to Reassess Act 111?" *Journal of Collective Negotiation in the Public Sector* 20, no. 4 (1991): 307-319.

> This article reviews the administrative problems associated with the Pennsylvania interest arbitration statute for police and fire fighters, and jurisdictional questions.

1097. Loewenberg, J. Joseph. "The Courts and Compulsory Arbitration in Pennsylvania." *Labor Law Journal* 42, no. 5 (May 1991): 296-302.

> A discussion of appeals of arbitration awards under the Pennsylvania Act 111 of 1968, generally as the result of employer noncompliance. The courts have been willing to entertain appeals.

Wisconsin

1098. Stern, James L. "Final-Offer Arbitration: Initial Experience in Wisconsin." *Monthly Labor Review* 97, no. 9 (September 1974): 39-42.

> Discusses early record of final-offer arbitration in Wisconsin.

1099. Clume, William H., III. "Final Offer Interest Arbitration in Wisconsin: Legislative History, Participant Attitudes, Future Trends." *Marquette Law Review* 64, no. 3 (Spring 1981): 455-505.

> Examines attitudes of labor and management after the first year of experience with Wisconsin's law to determine if attitudes changed after some experience with the new impasse procedures.

Final-Offer Arbitration

1100. Grodin, Joseph R. "Either-Or Arbitration for Public Employee Disputes." *Industrial Relations* 11, no. 2 (May 1972): 260-266.

> Discusses early state experimentation with final-offer interest arbitration and notes some potential pitfalls.

1101. Feuille, Peter, and Gary Long. "The Public-Administrator and Final-Offer Arbitration." *Public Administration Review* 34, no. 6 (November/December 1974): 575-583.

> Considers the differing impacts of a variety of final-offer arbitration procedures on the parties' incentives to bargain and on their incentives to arbitrate.

1102. Nelson, Nels E. "Final Offer Arbitration: Some Problems." *Arbitration Journal* 30, no. 1 (March 1975): 50-58.

> Nelson argues that final-offer arbitration works better with single issues, can be used successfully by parties with little bargaining experience, and may prove a satisfactory alternative to a strike.

1103. Staudohar, Paul D. "Results of Final-Offer Arbitration of Bargaining Disputes." *California Management Review* 18, no. 1 (Fall 1975): 57-61.

> According to Staudohar, final-offer interest arbitration appears to be worthwhile to resolve impasses for essential public services and for major league sports. It works best when the number of issues is low.

1104. Feigenbaum, Charles. "Final-Offer Arbitration: Better Theory than Practice." *Industrial Relations* 14, no. 3 (October 1975): 311-317.

> The author contends that final-offer arbitration does not excel over conventional arbitration in preventing impasse. Systems that encourage mediation will emerge as the most desirable form of final-offer arbitration.

1105. Donn, Clifford B. "Games Final-Offer Arbitrators Might Play." *Industrial Relations* 16, no. 3 (October 1977): 306-314.

> The author suggests three procedural strategies that arbitrators might use to overcome problems inherent in FOA proceedings.

1106. Wheeler, Hoyt N. "Closed-Offer: Alternative to Final-Offer Selection." *Industrial Relations* 16, no. 3 (October 1977): 298-305.

> Concludes that closed-offer interest arbitration (where arbitrator has no knowledge of previous bargaining offers) avoids unworkable awards.

1107. Crawford, Vincent P. "On Compulsory-Arbitration Schemes." *Journal of Political Economy* 87, no. 1 (February 1979): 131-159.

Under "multiple" final-offer arbitration, each side proposes several final offers, the arbitrator decides which side has made the most reasonable offers, and then the other side chooses which of the several offers to accept.

1108. Crawford, Vincent P. "Arbitration and Conflict Resolution in Labor-Management Bargaining." *American Economic Review* 71, no. 2 (May 1981): 205-210.

> A review of conventional interest arbitration, FOA, multiple FOA and issue-by-issue FOA.

1109. Rehmus, Charles M. "Varieties of Final Offer Arbitration." *Arbitration Journal* 37, no. 4 (December 1982): 4-6.

> A description of four kinds of final-offer arbitration: final offers certified in advance of arbitration, each party making two final-offer packages, giving a neutral a choice of three packages, and issue-by-issue arbitration.

1110. Brams, Steven J., and Samuel Merrill, III. "Binding versus Final-Offer Arbitration: A Combination Is Best." *Management Science* 32, no. 10 (October 1986): 1346-1355.

> Describes and espouses a new procedure which would combine elements of final-offer arbitration with conventional arbitration.

1111. Flanagan, Robert J., and Carl M. Stevens. "Socrates Confronts Final-Offer Selection; Comments." *Industrial Relations* 29, no. 3 (Fall 1990): 526-529.

> FOA viewed as an efficient way to resolve contract disputes.

1112. Black, Errol, Jim Silver, and Hugh M. Grant. "Contradictions and Limitations of Final-Offer Selection: The Manitoba Experience; A Comment." *Industrial Relations (Canada)* 45, no. 1 (Winter 1990): 146-168.

> The experiment in the use of FOA by private sector employers and unions in Manitoba is described. The FOA eroded the unions' willingness and capacity to strike, leading to its rejection.

1113. Kelly, Laurence. "Manitoba's Experience with Final Offer Selection." *Labor Law Journal* 42, no. 6 (June 1991): 381-384.

> This note describes the enactment of the Manitoba statute, its uses, provisions, and the political factors that led to its passage.

Impact on Bargaining Process
Theoretical and Experimental Studies

1114. Notz, William W., and Frederick A. Starke. "Final-Offer v. Conventional Arbitration as a Means of Conflict Management." *Administrative Science Quarterly* 23, no. 2 (June 1978): 189-203.

Report of experiment with male undergraduates that compares and contrasts the impact of each form of arbitration on key elements of the bargaining process.

1115. Anderson, John C. "The Impact of Arbitration: A Methodological Assessment." *Industrial Relations* 20, no. 2 (Spring 1981): 129-148.

The article concludes that the limited focus on effectiveness criteria and problems in research design leave unanswered the questions about the impact of interest arbitration.

1116. DiNisi, Angelo S., and James B. Dworkin. "Final-Offer Arbitration and the Naive Negotiator." *Industrial and Labor Relations Review* 35, no. 1 (October 1981): 78-89.

An experiment with undergraduate students demonstrates that with training even naive negotiators can effectively utilize final-offer procedures.

1117. Magenau, John M. "The Impact of Alternative Impasse Procedures on Bargaining: A Laboratory Experiment." *Industrial and Labor Relations Review* 36, no. 3 (April 1983): 361-377.

Results of a laboratory experiment: strikes were more effective than arbitration in producing agreement, and final-offer arbitration was more effective than conventional arbitration.

1118. Neale, Margaret A., and Max H. Bazerman. "The Role of Perspective-Taking Ability in Negotiating under Different Forms of Arbitration." *Industrial and Labor Relations Review* 36 (April 1983): 378-388.

In an experimental setting, investigates whether the ability of negotiators to adopt the perspective of their opponents is a key to success in negotiating under conventional and final-offer arbitration.

1119. Neale, Margaret A. "The Effects of Negotiation and Arbitration Cost Salience on Bargainer Behavior: The Role of the Arbitrator and Constituency on Negotiator Judgment." *Organizational Behavior and Human Performance* 34, no. 1 (August 1984): 97-111.

In this experimental study involving undergraduate students, the perception of costs associated with arbitration and with negotiations partially explains the frequency of use of arbitration.

1120. Bazerman, Max H., and Henry S. Farber. "Arbitrator Decision Making: When Are Final Offers Important?" *Industrial and Labor Relations Review* 39, no. 1 (October 1985): 76-89.

The article concludes that split-the-difference approach encourages the parties to adhere to extreme positions. Arbitrators do not follow this approach.

1121. Barr, Steve H. "Risk Aversion and Negotiator Behavior in Public Sector Arbitration." *Journal of Collective Negotiations in the Public Sector* 16, no. 2 (1987): 99-115.

> A study of final-offer arbitration based on a simulated bargaining situation.

1122. Treble, John G. "The 'Chilling Effect' of Conventional Arbitration: A Counterexample." *Bulletin of Economic Research (UK)* 41, no. 1 (January 1989): 59-67.

> The author shows by mathematical modeling how conventional, as compared to final-offer, interest arbitration may be used to avoid the chilling effect.

Empirical and Other Studies

1123. Long, Gary, and Peter Feuille. "Final-Offer Arbitration: 'Sudden Death' in Eugene." *Industrial and Labor Relations Review* 27, no. 2 (January 1974): 186-203.

> Analysis of first six negotiations under compulsory final-offer arbitration leads authors to conclude it preserved incentive to negotiate agreements.

1124. Wheeler, Hoyt N. "Compulsory Arbitration: A Narcotic Effect." *Industrial Relations* 14, no. 1 (February 1975): 117-120.

> Studies of fire fighters suggest that compulsory interest arbitration increases the reliance on impasse machinery and that it also chills negotiation. See also Wheeler's "How Compulsory Arbitration Affects Compromise Activity." *Industrial Relations* 17, no. 1 (February 1978): 80-84.

1125. Feuille, Peter. "Final-Offer Arbitration and the Chilling Effect." *Industrial Relations* 14, no. 3 (October 1975): 302-310.

> Reviews experience with FOA procedures in selected public jurisdictions and concludes that they have less of a chilling effect than conventional arbitration procedures.

1126. Feuille, Peter. "Final-Offer Arbitration and Negotiating Incentives." *Arbitration Journal* 32, no. 3 (September 1977): 203-220.

> Reviews experience in six jurisdictions. Finds that FOA induces negotiated settlements, although this effect seems to diminish over time.

1127. Olson, Craig A. "Final-Offer Arbitration in Wisconsin after Five Years." In 31 IRRA (1978): 167-169.

> Examines dependency on arbitration in Wisconsin.

1128. Lipsky, David B., and Thomas Barocci. "Public Employees in Massachusetts and Final-Offer Arbitration." *Monthly Labor Review* 101, no. 4 (April 1978): 34-37.

> The 1973 Massachusetts municipal employee statute allows FOA, and impasses from 1975 to 1976 increased nearly 70 percent.

1129. Kochan, Thomas A., and Jean Baderschneider. "Dependence on Impasse Procedures: Police and Fire Fighters in New York State." *Industrial and Labor Relations Review* 31, no. 4 (July 1978): 431-449.

>Presents model of impasse process and tests it using data on police and fire fighter negotiations in New York State between 1968 and 1975.

1130. Farber, Henry S., and Harry C. Katz. "Interest Arbitration Outcomes and the Incentive to Bargain." *Industrial and Labor Relations Review* 33, no. 1 (October 1979): 55-63.

>The authors found that uncertainties over costs and arbitrators' behavior were key factor in parties' response to arbitration.

1131. Farber, Henry S. "Does Final-Offer Arbitration Encourage Bargaining?" In 33 IRRA (1980): 219-226.

>Comparison of conventional and final-offer arbitration in terms of the degree of encouragement given to dispute through negotiation.

1132. Gerhart, Paul F., and John E. Drotning. "Do Uncertain Cost- Benefit Estimates Prolong Public-Sector Disputes?" *Monthly Labor Review* 103, no. 9 (September 1980): 26-30.

>Concludes that parties are more likely to push the impasse to the last step when that last step is arbitration or the strike.

1133. Bloom, David E. "Is Arbitration Really Compatible with Bargaining?" *Industrial Relations* 20, no. 3 (Fall 1981): 233-244.

>Constructs an "arbitrate-negotiate" decision model and concludes that one can calculate when a party will arbitrate rather than negotiate.

1134. Butler, Richard J., and Ronald G. Ehrenberg. "Estimating the Narcotic Effect of Public Sector Impasse Procedures." *Industrial and Labor Relations Review* 35, no. 1 (October 1981): 3-20.

>The authors question whether the existence of an arbitration alternative demotivates parties to negotiate settlements.

1135. Kochan, Thomas A., and Jean Baderschneider. "Estimating the Narcotic Effect: Choosing Techniques That Fit the Problem." *Industrial and Labor Relations Review* 35, no. 1 (October 1981): 21-28.

>Argues for a multidimensional methodological approach to measure whether interest arbitration decreases the motivation to bargain to settle.

1136. Bruce, Christopher J., and David E. Bloom. "The Compatibility of Arbitration and Bargaining/Reply." *Industrial Relations* 21, no. 3 (Fall 1982): 398-404.

>Discusses factors that would lead to negotiation rather than arbitration.

1137. Bazerman, Max H., and Margaret A. Neale. "Improving Negotiation Effectiveness under Final Offer Arbitration: The Role of Selection and Training." *Journal of Applied Psychology* 67, no. 5 (October 1982): 543-548.

> A negotiated resolution occurs more often if the last step is final offer arbitration. If the parties are trained to eliminate overconfidence, the approach works even better.

1138. Hirsch, Barry T., and Clifford B. Donn. "Arbitration and the Incentive to Bargain: The Role of Expectations and Costs." *Journal of Labor Research* 3, no. 1 (Winter 1982): 55-68.

> This study concludes that as the parties become more familiar with arbitration they may become more dependent on it and resort to it more frequently.

1139. Chelius, James R., and Marian M. Extejt. "The Impact of Arbitration on the Process of Collective Bargaining." *Journal of Collective Negotiations in the Public Sector* 12, no. 4 (1983): 327-336.

> Investigates the impact of arbitration on the process of collective bargaining, focusing on experience in Indiana and Iowa.

1140. Champlin, Frederic C., and Mario F. Bognanno. " 'Chilling' under Arbitration and Mixed Strike-Arbitration Regimes." *Journal of Labor Research* 6, no. 4 (Fall 1985): 375-387.

> Investigates whether arbitration "chills" the incentive to bargain using data from public sector collective bargaining activity in Minnesota. The data show a significantly lower settlement rate under arbitration as opposed to strikes.

1141. Currie, Janet. "Who Uses Interest Arbitration? The Case of British Columbia's Teachers, 1947-1981." *Industrial and Labor Relations Review* 42, no. 3 (April 1989): 363-379.

> Based on 35 years of interest arbitration for teacher bargaining units in British Columbia, the author reports that the only variable related to arbitration usage was previous experience with arbitration.

1142. Lester, Richard Allen. "Analysis of Experience under New Jersey's Flexible Arbitration System." *Arbitration Journal* 44, no. 2 (June 1989): 14-21.

> Interviews with arbitrators and advocates under New Jersey's interest arbitration system reveal that over two-thirds of the cases between 1978 and 1987 were settled without an award.

1143. Kleintop, William A., and J. Joseph Loewenberg. "Collective Bargaining, Compulsory Interest Arbitration, and the Narcotic Effect: A Longitudinal Study of

Delaware County, Pennsylvania." *Journal of Collective Negotiations in the Public Sector* 19, no. 2 (1990): 113-120.

> A study of bargaining in a single Pennsylvania county over a 10-year period shows that the narcotic effect operates in some relationships.

1144. Ashenfelter, Orley, and Janet Currie. "Negotiator Behavior and the Occurrence of Disputes." *American Economic Review* 80, no. 2 (May 1990): 416-420.

> The important causes of negotiation failures are divergent beliefs as to the likely outcome in arbitration, principal-agent problems, and uncertainty as to outcome and cost of arbitration.

Impact on Bargaining Results

Theoretical and Experimental Studies

1145. Subbarao, A. V. "The Impact of Binding Interest Arbitration on Negotiation and Process Outcome." *Journal of Conflict Resolution* 22, no. 1 (March 1978): 79-103.

> Experimental study of four variants of interest arbitration reveals total-package final offer generates bargaining while issue-by-issue subverts negotiations.

1146. Farber, Henry S. "An Analysis of Final-Offer Arbitration." *Journal of Conflict Resolution* 24, no. 4 (December 1980): 683-705.

> The author concludes that negotiated settlements under this process are skewed against the more risk-averse party.

1147. Starke, Frederick A., and William W. Notz. "Pre- and Post- Intervention Effects of Conventional versus Final Offer Arbitration." *Academy of Management Journal* 24, no. 4 (1981): 832-850.

> This experiment with college students shows that subjects anticipating FOA had lower aspirations and were closer to agreement than subjects anticipating conventional arbitration.

1148. Grigsby, David W., and William J. Bigoness. "Effects of Mediation and Alternative Forms of Arbitration on Bargaining Behavior: A Laboratory Study." *Journal of Applied Psychology* 67, no. 5 (October 1982): 549-554.

> An investigation of the effects of anticipated mediation and alternative modes of arbitration on bargaining behavior, using business students in a laboratory experiment. Bargaining under total package FOA left fewer unresolved issues.

1149. Bazerman, Max H. "Norms of Distributive Justice in Interest Arbitration." *Industrial and Labor Relations Review* 38, no. 4 (July 1985): 558-570.

A simulation-based study of the decision-making criteria that arbitrators employ in labor disputes. Maintaining the status quo by adjusting the present wage by average negotiated increase in industry is still the norm.

1150. Wittman, Donald. "Final-Offer Arbitration." *Management Science* 32, no. 12 (December 1986): 1551-1561.

An analysis, from a game-theory perspective, of the impacts of risk-aversion and of differing beliefs about the arbitrator on the parties' final offers.

1151. DuBose, Philip B., and William J. Bigoness. "A Test of Wheeler's Closed-Offer Arbitration System: An Experimental Study." *Journal of Labor Research* 8, no. 4 (Fall 1987): 385-393.

A simulation study with students. FOA was no more effective than conventional arbitration, except in prompting postnegotiation concessions.

1152. Samuelson, William F. "Final-Offer Arbitration under Incomplete Information." *Management Science* 37, no. 10 (October 1991): 1234-1247.

A model of FOA is presented in which each disputant has private information bearing on the true value of the case. The main conclusion is that FOA outcomes are crudely responsive to the underlying merits of the case.

1153. Olson, Craig A., Gregory G. Dell'Omo, and Paul Jarley. "A Comparison of Interest Arbitrator Decision-Making in Experimental and Field Settings." *Industrial and Labor Relations Review* 45, no. 4 (July 1992): 711-723.

This study compares the decisions made in an experiment with those made in actual cases by the same arbitrator. Only when wages were the only issue were the results in both situations substantially the same.

Empirical and Other Studies

1154. Loewenberg, J. Joseph. "Compulsory Arbitration for Police and Fire Fighters in Pennsylvania in 1968." *Industrial and Labor Relations Review* 23, no. 3 (April 1970): 367-369.

Reports on first year of compulsory arbitration statute and finds no difference in wages resulted from arbitrated as compared to negotiated settlements.

1155. Wheeler, Hoyt N. "Is Compromise the Rule in Fire Fighter Arbitration?" *Arbitration Journal* 29, no. 3 (September 1974): 176-184.

Study of 38 arbitration and fact-finding cases. Concludes that arbitrators do not commonly adopt "intermediate" positions.

1156. Rehmus, Charles M. "Binding Arbitration in the Public Sector." *Monthly Labor Review* 98, no. 4 (April 1975): 53-56.

Early results in Michigan show less wage dispersion among cities but no significant wage gains occurring as a result of interest arbitration.

1157. Feuille, Peter, and James B. Dworkin. "Final-Offer Arbitration and Intertemporal Compromise, or It's My Turn to Win." In 31 IRRA (1978): 87-95.

Analysis of the intertemporal compromise theory which states that arbitrators tend to satisfy both sides in final-offer arbitration by alternating the winners and losers over time.

1158. Lipsky, David B., and Thomas Barocci. "Final-Offer Arbitration and Salaries of Police and Firefighters." *Monthly Labor Review* 101, no. 7 (July 1978):

This study of three-year trial period of new Massachusetts arbitration statute concludes that no significant rise in salary levels resulted. See also "Final-Offer Arbitration and Public-Safety Employees: The Massachusetts Experience." 30 IRRA 65-76 (1977), by the same authors. Includes an analysis of the "chilling effect."

1159. Olson, Craig A. "The Impact of Arbitration on the Wages of Fire Fighters." *Industrial Relations* 19 (Fall 1980): 325-339.

A study of 72 cities with population over 100,000 reveals a modest positive relation between arbitration and wage level.

1160. Bloom, David E. "Collective Bargaining, Compulsory Arbitration, and Salary Settlements in the Public Sector: The Case of New Jersey's Municipal Police Officers." *Journal of Labor Research* 2, no. 2 (Fall 1981): 369-384.

The author concludes that the settlements under FOA were neither abnormally high nor low when compared to conventional arbitration.

1161. Farber, Henry S. "Splitting-the-Difference in Interest Arbitration." *Industrial and Labor Relations Review* 35, no. 1 (October 1981): 70-77.

Argues that it is because parties position themselves around expected award that splitting the difference occurs.

1162. Graham, Harry. "Arbitration Results in the Public Sector." *Public Personnel Management* 11, no. 2 (Summer 1982): 112-117.

The results of arbitration in the public sector during the 1970s are presented.

1163. Delaney, John Thomas, Peter Feuille, and Wallace Hendricks. "Interest Arbitration and Grievance Arbitration: The Twain Do Meet." In 36 IRRA (1983): 313-320.

This study concluded that selected environmental variables, especially the presence of an interest arbitration law, contribute to the strength of negotiated grievance procedures in police contracts.

1164. Pursell, Donald E., and William D. Torrence. "The Impact of Compulsory Arbitration on Municipal Budgets: The Case of Omaha, Nebraska." *Journal of Collective Negotiations in the Public Sector* 12, no. 2 (1983): 119-125.

>The authors found that arbitration had no significant impact on the city's ability to manage its budget.

1165. Delaney, John Thomas. "Strikes, Arbitration, and Teacher Salaries: A Behavioral Analysis." *Industrial and Labor Relations Review* 36, no. 3 (April 1983): 431-446.

>Study of outcomes in teacher bargaining in two states indicates that availability of arbitration has greater impact on wages than actual use and about the same impact as strikes.

1166. Ashenfelter, Orley, and David E. Bloom. "The Pitfalls in Judging Arbitrator Impartiality by Win-Loss Tallies under Final Offer Arbitration." *Labor Law Journal* 34, no. 8 (August 1983): 534-539.

>Based on New Jersey data, the article compares the outcomes under final-offer and conventional arbitration and urges against a simplistic analysis of win-loss records.

1167. Brams, Steven J., and Samuel Merrill, III. "Equilibrium Strategies for Final-Offer Arbitration: There Is No Median Convergence." *Management Science* 29, no. 8 (August 1983): 927-941.

>The authors' data suggest that FOA encourages parties to diverge rather than settle.

1168. Tallakson, Ruth, and Hoyt N. Wheeler. "Winning and Losing in Interest Arbitration." *Journal of Collective Negotiations in the Public Sector* 13, no. 2 (1984): 151-164.

>Presents an analysis of conventional interest arbitration cases involving Minnesota teachers and school boards. The analysis shows that the arbitration results were fairly evenly balanced.

1169. Delaney, John Thomas, and Peter Feuille. "Police Interest Arbitration: Awards and Issues." *Arbitration Journal* 39, no. 2 (June 1984): 14-24.

>Some of the findings were that: arbitrators have considerable discretion in fashioning awards, many cases present more issues than the process was designed to handle, most of the issues involve money, and arbitrators are reluctant to rewrite contracts.

1170. Delaney, John Thomas, Peter Feuille, and Wallace Hendricks. "Police Salaries, Interest Arbitration, and the Leveling Effect." *Industrial Relations* 23, no. 3 (Fall 1984): 417-423.

The authors conclude that arbitration has less of an effect on the dispersion of police salaries than market factors.

1171. MacManus, Susan A. "State-Mandated Collective Bargaining and Compulsory Binding Arbitration: The Fiscal Effect on Municipal Governments." *Public Administration Quarterly* 7, no. 4 (Winter 1984): 411-428.

This analysis of municipal worker contracts in 243 cities indicates that compulsory binding arbitration worsened municipal financial conditions.

1172. Delaney, John Thomas, and Peter Feuille. "Collective Bargaining, Interest Arbitration, and the Delivery of Police Services." *Review of Public Personnel Administration* 5, no. 2 (Spring 1985): 21-36.

With interest arbitration, the number of strikes has been reduced and greater protection has been given to employment interests, but the incentive to negotiate has been weakened, the cost of police services has risen, and the scope of managerial prerogatives has been limited.

1173. Feuille, Peter, John Thomas Delaney, and Wallace Hendricks. "The Impact of Interest Arbitration on Police Contracts." *Industrial Relations* 24, no. 2 (Spring 1985): 161-181.

More favorable union contracts have been negotiated in states with interest arbitration statutes than in states with no interest arbitration law.

1174. Feuille, Peter, John Thomas Delaney, and Wallace Hendricks. "Police Bargaining Arbitration and Fringe Benefits." *Journal of Labor Research* 6, no. 1 (Winter 1985): 1-20.

There is a strong positive relationship between police collective bargaining and fringe benefits, but the availability of arbitration has little or no influence on fringes.

1175. Connolly, Marie D. "The Impact of Final-Offer Arbitration on Wage Outcomes of Public Safety Personnel: Michigan vs. Illinois." *Journal of Collective Negotiations in the Public Sector* 15, no. 3 (1986): 251-262.

This statistical analysis of police unit wage levels in Michigan and Illinois indicates that compulsory arbitration buys labor peace at a price of about 5.5 percent higher wages.

1176. Feuille, Peter, and John Thomas Delaney. "Collective Bargaining, Interest Arbitration, and Police Salaries." *Industrial and Labor Relations Review* 39, no. 2 (January 1986): 228-240.

Data from 1971 to 1981 show that the availability of arbitration has a modest but positive impact on police salaries but that market factors exerted a stronger impact.

1177. Delaney, John Thomas. "Impasses and Teacher Contract Outcomes." *Industrial Relations* 25, no. 1 (Winter 1986): 45-55.

> A comparison of teacher strike rates and contract outcomes in Illinois, where there was no public employee collective bargaining law affecting teachers, and Iowa, which had an interest arbitration statute.

1178. Liebeskind, Arlyne K. "Compulsory Interest Arbitration for Public Safety Services in New Jersey: The First Three Years." *Journal of Collective Negotiations in the Public Sector* 16, no. 4 (1987): 343-361.

> This three-year study of police FOA in New Jersey reveals notable narrowing of the gap between awarded union positions and awarded employer positions.

1179. Graham, Harry. "Ohio's Experience with Interest Arbitration for Public Safety Forces." *Journal of Collective Negotiations in the Public Sector* 17, no. 2 (1988): 105-113.

> This study shows that police tended to go to arbitration more frequently than fire fighters; that arbitration focused on wage increases; and that both policy and fire fighters did well.

1180. Feuille, Peter, and Susan Schwochau. "The Decisions of Interest Arbitrators." *Arbitration Journal* 43, no. 1 (March 1988): 28-35.

> This analysis of 302 police interest arbitration awards finds that unions prevail for approximately 47 percent of the issues, especially salary, and employers prevail on about 40 percent of the issues, particularly in nonsalary areas.

1181. Subbarao, A. V. "Criteria in Arbitration of Wage Disputes: Theory and Practice in the Canadian Federal Public Service." *Industrial Relations (Canada)* 43, no. 3 (Autumn 1988): 547-569.

> This study shows that interest arbitration awards in Canadian federal public service wage disputes tend to be affected by intra-industry wage comparisons and by occupational wage increases at the time of the award.

1182. Schwochau, Susan, and Peter Feuille. "Interest Arbitrators and Their Decision Behavior." *Industrial Relations* 27, no. 1 (Winter 1988): 37-55.

> A study of police arbitration cases. Pay comparability seems to be the most important criterion to the arbitrators.

1183. Dell'Omo, Gregory G. "Wage Disputes in Interest Arbitration: Arbitrators Weigh the Criteria." *Arbitration Journal* 44, no. 2 (June 1989): 4-13.

> An examination of the criteria employed by Wisconsin public sector interest arbitrators. Internal wage comparisons were particularly important.

1184. Olson, Craig A., and Paul Jarley. "Arbitrator Decisions in Wisconsin Teacher Wage Disputes." *Industrial and Labor Relations Review* 44, no. 3 (April 1991): 536-547.

>The authors concluded that voluntary settlements in comparable jurisdictions had a substantial impact on arbitration decisions.

1185. Jarley, Paul. "The Effect of Interest Arbitration on Salary Dispersion among Employees." *Industrial Relations* 31, no. 2 (Spring 1992): 292-308.

>A Wisconsin study which reported that interest arbitration results in greater salary dispersion in teacher salaries across the state but less dispersion within small clusters of school districts.

1186. Ries, Edith Dunfee. "The Effects of Fact-Finding and Final-Offer Issue-by-Issue Compulsory Arbitration on Teachers' Wages, Fringe Benefits, and Language Provisions." *Journal of Collective Negotiations in the Public Sector* 21, no. 1 (Winter 1992): 45-67.

>Fact-finding is the terminal step in impasse proceedings for teacher negotiations in New Jersey, and in Connecticut it is compulsory interest arbitration. This study reported that teachers fare no better under arbitration than under fact-finding.

Impasse Procedures Other than Arbitration

Mediation

1187. Hoh, Ronald. "The Effectiveness of Mediation in Public Sector Arbitration Systems: The Iowa Experience." *Arbitration Journal* 39, no. 2 (June 1984): 30-40.

>This study suggested that the availability of compulsory arbitration in Iowa's impasse procedure has not impaired the ability of mediation to work effectively.

1188. Liebowitz, Jonathan S. "Public Sector Mediation: A Sequel." *Journal of Collective Negotiations in the Public Sector* 14, no. 4 (1985): 343-347.

>This article describes many of the problems confronted in the mediation of public employee contract disputes including the impact of interest arbitration.

1189. Hirlinger, Michael W., and Ronald D. Sylvia. "Public Sector Impasse Procedures Revisited." *Journal of Collective Negotiations in the Public Sector* 17, no. 4 (1988): 267-277.

>The authors conclude that mediation and fact-finding are generally ineffective, and employees should be offered a choice between the strike and arbitration.

1190. Gold, Alan B. "Mediation of Interest Disputes." In 41 NAA (1989): 9-21.

>A review of basic concepts pertaining to mediation in application to interest disputes.

Fact-Finding

1191. Wolkinson, Benjamin W., and Jack Stieber. "Michigan Fact Finding Experience in Public Sector Disputes." *Arbitration Journal* 31, no. 4 (December 1976): 225-247.

>Most participants, particularly those on the union side, found fact-finding effective in resolving impasses.

1192. Gerhart, Paul F., and John E. Drotning. "Is Fact Finding Useful in the Public Sector?" *Journal of Collective Negotiations in the Public Sector* 10, no. 3 (1981): 279-286.

>Considers two forms of fact-finding: advisory arbitration and supermediation.

1193. Gallagher, Daniel G., and M. D. Chaubey. "Impasse Behavior and Tri-Offer Arbitration in Iowa." *Industrial Relations* 21, no. 2 (Spring 1982): 129-148.

>Study of first years of experience with revised statute that allows arbitrator to choose fact finder's or either party's final offer. Most arbitrators choose fact finder's package.

1194. Gallagher, Karen S., and Donald L. Robson. "Factfinding in Indiana: A Study of Factfinding Frequency and Acceptance as an Impasse Resolution Procedure in Public School Negotiations." *Journal of Collective Negotiations in the Public Sector* 12, no. 2 (1983): 153-166.

>This statistical analysis of fact-finding in the public schools of Indiana seeks to identify variables positively correlated with acceptance of fact-finding recommendations.

1195. Dilts, David A. "An Examination of Fact-Finding as a Method of Dispute Settlement Training Grounds for Arbitrators." *Journal of Collective Negotiations in the Public Sector* 13, no. 3 (1984): 251-258.

>Dilts argues that once fact-finding is viewed as a dispute resolution technique in its own right, it becomes clear that experienced fact finders and arbitrators are not perfect substitutes for one another and experience in one area is not necessarily good training for the other.

1196. Gallagher, Daniel G., and Peter A. Veglahn. "The Effect of Statutory Impasse Schemes on the Acceptance of Factfinding Recommendations: Evidence from Iowa and New York." *Journal of Collective Negotiations in the Public Sector* 13, no. 2 (1984): 123-138.

A study of teacher disputes in Iowa and New York. The parties are more likely to accept fact-finding recommendations if the impasse resolution procedure also provides for arbitration.

1197. Helsby, Robert, Ken Jennings, David Moore, Steven Paulson, and Steven Williamson. "Union-Management Negotiators' Views of Factfinding in Florida." *Journal of Collective Negotiations in the Public Sector* 17, no. 1 (1988): 63-74.

A survey of the union and management representatives in Florida's "special master" (fact-finding) system.

1198. Magnusen, Karl O., and Patricia A. Renovitch. "Dispute Resolution in Florida's Public Sector: Insight into Impasse." *Journal of Collective Negotiations in the Public Sector* 18, no. 3 (1989): 241-252.

Florida's impasse procedures provide for nonbinding interest arbitration. The authors argue that while the arbitrator's reports are generally rejected, the recommendations are actually often adopted.

1199. Byrne, Dennis M. "An Analysis of Factfinding: Suggestions on How to Improve the Procedure." *Journal of Collective Negotiations in the Public Sector* 20, no. 2 (1991): 131-144.

In this critical analysis of fact-finding under the Ohio public sector labor relations statute, the author offers suggestions to improve the process.

1200. Nelson, Nels E. "How Factfinders View Criteria in Factfinding." *Journal of Collective Negotiations in the Public Sector* 21, no. 2 (1992): 159-170.

Ohio fact finders reported that they gave the greatest weight to comparisons with other public employers, previous collective bargaining agreements, ability to pay, the public interest, equity, and acceptability.

Mediation-Arbitration

1201. Kagel, Sam, and John Kagel. "Using Two New Arbitration Techniques." *Monthly Labor Review* 95, no. 11 (November 1972): 11-14.

Authors discuss use of mediation-arbitration (med-arb) in longshore and health care situations.

1202. Chvala, Charles J., and Michael Fox. "Final-Offer Mediation-Arbitration and Limited Right to Strike: Wisconsin's New Municipal Employment Bargaining Law." *Wisconsin Law Review* (1979): 167-189.

Outlines the history and procedures of Wisconsin's MERA and implications for municipal labor relations.

1203. Friedman, David R., and Stuart S. Mukamal. "Wisconsin's Mediation-Arbitration Law: What Has It Done to Bargaining?" *Journal of Collective Negotiations in the Public Sector* 13, no. 2 (1984): 171-190.

The authors report that Wisconsin's form of impasse resolution does prevent strikes, but it has seriously weakened collective bargaining.

1204. Allred, Stephen. "Med-Arb and the Resolution of the SSA-AFGE Bargaining Impasse: A Case Study." *Arbitration Journal* 39, no. 2 (June 1984): 46-54.

Describes successful use of med-arb in a large federal unit.

1205. Stern, James L. "The Mediation of Interest Disputes by Arbitrators under the Wisconsin Med-Arb Law for Local Government Employees." *Arbitration Journal* 39, no. 2 (June 1984): 41-45.

Author finds that half of all disputes were mediated successfully from 1978 to 1983. More experienced neutrals had better track records.

1206. Henry, Karen C. "Med-Arb: An Alternative to Interest Arbitration in the Resolution of Contract Negotiation Disputes." *Ohio State Journal on Dispute Resolution* 3, no. 2 (Spring 1988): 385-398.

A comparison of traditional dispute resolution methods, focusing on med-arb.

1207. Bartel, Barry C. "Med-Arb as a Distinct Method of Dispute Resolution: History, Analysis, and Potential." *Willamette Law Review* 27, no. 3 (Summer 1991): 661-692.

The author reviews the forms of med-arb, advantages and disadvantages, and its potential in dispute resolution.

Choice of Procedures

1208. Anderson, John C., and Thomas A. Kochan. "Impasse Procedures in the Canadian Federal Service: Effects on the Bargaining Process." *Industrial and Labor Relations Review* 30, no. 3 (April 1977): 283-301.

Reports chilling and narcotic effects for unions choosing arbitration rather than strike under Canadian choice-of-procedures impasse statute.

1209. Subbarao, A. V. "Impasse Choice and Wages in the Canadian Federal Service." *Industrial Relations* 18, no. 2 (Spring 1979): 233-236.

This study suggests that bargaining units that chose to strike gained higher average percentage salary increases than those which chose to arbitrate.

1210. Ponak, Allen, and Hoyt N. Wheeler. "Choice of Procedures in Canada and the United States." *Industrial Relations* 19, no. 3 (Fall 1980): 292-308.

This article describes the choice-of-procedures approach to FOA in Canada, Minnesota, and Wisconsin, and it offers several propositions for evaluating the performance of the system, behavior of the participants, and ability to reach agreement.

1211. Balkin, David B. "Strike Experience under Choice-of-Procedures in Minnesota Where the Public Employer Has the Choice." *Journal of Collective Negotiations in the Public Sector* 13, no. 2 (1984): 117-122.

> From 1974 to 1980, the Minnesota statute permitted management to make the choice between arbitration or allowing the employees to strike. Later, both parties were given the choice, and there was a dramatic increase in strikes.

1212. Subbarao, A. V. "Impasse Choice in the Canadian Federal Service: An Innovation and an Intrigue." *Industrial Relations (Canada)* 40, no. 3 (1985): 567-590.

> This article focuses on alternatives to the existing system of impasse resolution in the Canadian federal service.

1213. Goodman, John, and Joe Chattin. "Dispute Resolution in 'Essential Services': Procedural Experimentation in Canada." *Employee Relations (UK)* 8, no. 2 (1986): 8-12.

> A discussion of the Canadian Public Servants Staff Relations Act, which allows unions to choose between binding arbitration or a two-stage conciliation/strike path.

1214. Saunders, George. "Impact of Interest Arbitration on Canadian Federal Employees' Wages." *Industrial Relations* 25, no. 3 (Fall 1986): 320-327.

> Federal employees in Canada can choose between an "arbitration" path or a "conciliation/strike" path for settling disputes. This comparison of wage outcomes between the two paths suggests that the conciliation/strike route might have a wage advantage.

1215. Swimmer, Gene. "The Impact of the Dispute Resolution Process on Canadian Federal Public Service Wage Settlements." *Journal of Collective Negotiations in the Public Sector* 16, no. 1 (1987): 53-61.

> Statistical analysis suggests that unions choosing the latter route negotiated larger wage increases.

P. Nonunion Matters and Wrongful Discharge

Nonunion Complaint Procedures

1216. Ronner, Walter V. "Handling Grievances in a Non-Union Plant." In 14 IRRA (1961): 306-314.

> Study of the lack of use of grievance procedures in nonunionized industries, why they have not been utilized, and how grievance machinery should be utilized in nonunion sectors.

1217. Warren, William H. "Ombudsman Plus Arbitration: A Proposal for Effective Grievance Administration without Public Employee Unions." *Labor Law Journal* 29 (September 1978): 562-569.

> Proposes a grievance procedure for nonunion employees, including provision of representation and binding arbitration. Reviews experience with nonunion arbitration in universities.

1218. Miller, Ronald L. "Arbitration in Nonunion Grievance Procedures." *Employment Relations Today* 10, no. 4 (Winter 1983/1984): 393-406.

> This article examines the nonunion grievance procedures of 26 employers at one medical center.

1219. Balfour, Alan. "Five Types of Non-Union Grievance Systems." *Personnel* 61, no. 2 (March/April 1984): 67-76.

> Five systems are covered: open-door policy, ombudsman, peer decision, in-house hearing officers, and outside arbitrators.

1220. Florey, Peter. "A Growing Fringe Benefit: Arbitration of Nonunion Employee Grievances." *Personnel Administrator* 30, no. 7 (July 1985): 14-18.

> This article reports on an increasing use of grievance arbitration in nonunion firms and describes the various approaches taken.

1221. Feliu, Alfred G. "Legal Consequences of Nonunion Dispute-Resolution Systems." *Employee Relations Law Journal* 13, no. 1 (Summer 1987): 83-103.

> Analysis of the legal benefits and drawbacks to internal alternative dispute resolution (ADR) systems in nonunion settings and review of recent court rulings on finality and enforceability.

1222. McCabe, Douglas M. "Corporate Nonunion Grievance Arbitration Systems: A Procedural Analysis." *Labor Law Journal* 40, no. 7 (July 1989): 432-437.

> A survey of the grievance appeal systems in 78 nonunionized companies. Only six of the companies provided for the settlement of employee grievances through binding arbitration.

1223. Bakaly, Charles G., Jr. "Alternative Dispute Resolution of Employer-Employee Disputes in a Non-Union Setting." *Arbitration Journal* 45, no. 3 (September 1990): 47-49.

> The use of ADR resolution procedures in the nonunion setting is encouraged.

1224. Guidry, Greg, and Gerald J. Huffman, Jr. "Legal and Practical Aspects of Alternative Dispute Resolution in Non-Union Companies." *Labor Lawyer* 6, no. 1 (Winter 1990): 1-48.

> This article reviews the legal aspects of ADR, provides empirical data, and discusses the common forms of ADR.

1225. Walt, Alan, William E. Rentfro, and Shyam Das. "Employer Promulgated Arbitration." In 43 NAA (1991): 189-203.

> Three brief articles discuss nonunion arbitration systems.

1226. Plofchan, Thomas K., Jr. "Coming Home to Contract: Loosening the Death-Grip of Statutorily Created Rights on Arbitration in the Nonunion World." *Ohio State Journal on Dispute Resolution* 6, no. 2 (Spring 1991): 243-282.

> Arbitration is recommended for all nonunion employment agreements, and the author argues that arbitration will soon be compelled.

Wrongful Discharge

1227. Summers, Clyde W. "Individual Protection against Unjust Dismissal: Time for a Statute." *Virginia Law Review* 62 (April 1976): 481-532.

> Comprehensive examination of the "employment at will" doctrine under common law in the United States and a statutory proposal by the author.

1228. Hoffman, Eileen Barkas. "Mediation of Unfair Dismissal Grievances: The British Example." In 32 IRRA (1979): 171-179.

> Analysis of the operation of the British system of industrial tribunals and conciliation in protecting unorganized employees from unfair dismissals.

1229. Howlett, Robert G. "Due Process for Nonunionized Employees: A Practical Proposal." In 32 IRRA (1979): 164-170.

> Analysis of the political environment for the legislation of just-cause protection for unorganized employees. Includes an analysis of the possible use of mediation, arbitration, and fact-finding.

1230. Stieber, Jack. "The Case for Protection of Unorganized Employees against Unjust Discharge." In 32 IRRA (1979): 155-163.

> Includes a comparison of the mechanisms currently in place in common market countries, Sweden, and Norway. See also "Employment-at-Will: An Issue for the 1980s" in 36 IRRA 1-13 (1983) by the same author.

1231. Coulson, Robert. "Arbitration for the Individual Employee." *Employee Relations Law Journal* 5, no. 3 (Winter 1979/1980): 406-415.

> A discussion of the potential for a federal just-cause statute for at-will employees and nonunion employee grievance systems.

1232. Summers, Clyde W. "Protecting All Employees against Unjust Dismissal." *Harvard Business Review* 58, no. 1 (January/February 1980): 132-139.

The author advocates legislation that would protect nonunionized employees from wrongful discharge or discipline via a just-cause standard and neutral tribunal system.

1233. Hepple, Bob A., Lawrence R. Littrell, Theodore J. St. Antoine, and Henry B. Epstein. "Arbitration of Job Security and Other Employment-Related Issues for the Unorganized Worker." In 34 NAA (1982): 18-67.

Articles by Hepple on "the British experience with unfair dismissal legislation"; Littrell on "the Northrup experience"; and St. Antoine on "protection against unjust discipline: an idea whose time has long since come." Comment by Epstein.

1234. Hill, Marvin F., Jr. "Arbitration as a Means of Protecting Employees from Unjust Dismissal: A Statutory Proposal." *Northern Illinois University Law Review* 3 (1982): 111-185.

Explores the development of the employment-at-will rule and statutes in foreign countries and proposes a statute for the United States using arbitration.

1235. Briggs, Steven. "Beyond the Grievance Procedure: Factfinding in Employee Complaint Resolution." *Labor Law Journal* 33, no. 8 (August 1982): 454-459.

Traditional grievance procedures are narrow in scope. The scope of a review should be broadened for nonmanagerial employees who do not have access to a grievance procedure. To a limited extent, the same applies to managerial employees.

1236. Mennemeier, Kenneth C. "Protection from Unjust Discharges: An Arbitration Scheme." *Harvard Journal on Legislation* 19, no. 1 (Winter 1982): 49-96.

The author examines the merits of laws and court rulings to protect nonunionized at-will employees from unjust discharge.

1237. Catler, Susan L. "The Case against Proposals to Eliminate the Employment at Will Rule." *Industrial Relations Law Journal* 5, no. 4 (1983): 471-522.

Includes discussions of proposals for changes in the doctrine, including arbitration. The author argues against changes.

1238. Blumrosen, Alfred W. "Exploring Voluntary Arbitration of Individual Employment Disputes." *University of Michigan Journal of Law Reform* 16, no. 2 (Winter 1983): 249-275.

Outlines an arbitration process appropriate for individual employment contracts.

1239. Robins, Eva. "Unfair Dismissal: Emerging Issues in the Use of Arbitration as Dispute Resolution Alternative for the Nonunion Workforce." *Fordham Urban Law Journal* 12, no. 3 (1983-1984): 437-459.

> Explains differences in processes, concepts, standards and criteria, burden of proof, remedies, and authority of the decision-maker in termination cases in the nonorganized sector.

1240. Gould, William B., IV. "Reflections on Wrongful Discharge: Litigation and Legislation." In 37 NAA (1985): 31-51.

> A review of public policy issues in wrongful discharge cases and of the recommendations of a committee of the California Labor and Employment Law Section.

1241. Bierman, Leonard, and Stuart A. Youngblood. "Resolving Unjust Discharge Cases: A Mediatory Approach." *Arbitration Journal* 39, no. 1 (March 1985): 48-60.

> The authors report on mediation in resolving at-will disputes.

1242. Jauvtis, Robert L. "The Impact of Wrongful Discharge Suits on Grievance: Arbitration Procedures in Collective Bargaining Agreements." *Labor Law Journal* 36 (May 1985): 307-312.

> Examines the growth in state "wrongful discharge" statutes and recent court decisions which grant to unionized employees the right to file actions for wrongful discharge even though a grievance/arbitration process exists.

1243. Dupkin, David L. "Employment At-Will in the Unionized Setting." *Catholic University Law Review* 34, no. 4 (Summer 1985): 979-1019.

> The author concludes that the individual worker can challenge the dispute resolution procedure that the company and the union have built.

1244. Bedikian, Mary A. "Safeguarding the Interests of At-Will Employees: A Model Case for Arbitration." *Detroit College of Law Review* 1986, no. 1 (Spring 1986): 1-56.

> A general examination of at-will concepts of employment and how they have been modified over time.

1245. Koys, Daniel J., Steven Briggs, and Jay E. Grenig. "The Employment-At-Will Doctrine: A Proposal." *Loyola University of Chicago Law Journal* 17, no. 2 (Winter 1986): 259-264.

> After reviewing judicial exceptions to employment-at-will, the article proposes that employers adopt fair hearing procedures for the review of employee termination actions.

1246. Herman, Anthony. "Wrongful Discharge Actions after *Lueck* and *Metropolitan Life Insurance*: The Erosion of Individual Rights and Collective Strength." *Industrial Relations Law Journal* 9, no. 4 (1987): 596-659.

>The author examines court decisions through 1985 that bear upon the issue of wrongful discharge.

1247. Martin, Warren. "Employment at Will: Just Cause Protection through Mandatory Arbitration." *Washington Law Review* 62, no. 1 (January 1987): 151-172.

>The author proposes an administrative scheme with limited liability that centers on binding arbitration.

1248. Coleman, John J., III. "Muddy Waters: *Allis-Chalmers* and the Federal Policy Favoring Labor Arbitration." *Washington and Lee Law Review* 44, no. 2 (Spring 1987): 345-407.

>*Allis-Chalmers v. Lueck* expanded the scope of the pre-emptive policy, but boundaries are still uncertain.

1249. Gould, William B., IV. "Stemming the Wrongful Discharge Tide: A Case for Arbitration." *Employee Relations Law Journal* 13, no. 3 (Winter 1987/1988): 404-425.

>The author suggests statutory adoption of labor arbitration for nonunion cases of allegedly wrongful discharge.

1250. Levin, William. "The Individual Rights Explosion: Is There a Role for an Arbitrator?" *Labor Law Journal* 40, no. 8 (August 1989): 461-464.

>The author argues that unless a Uniform Employment Termination Act is passed, the forum for resolving individual rights disputes is not arbitration.

1251. Bakaly, Charles G., Jr., and Jeffrey I. Kohn. "Federal Preemption of State Law Wrongful Discharge Action by Agreements to Arbitrate." In Office of the General Counsel, American Arbitration Association. *Arbitration and the Law: AAA General Counsel's Annual Report: 1989-1990*, 149-177. New York: American Arbitration Association, 1990.

>An extensive examination of law, which has come to surround wrongful discharge action, and the employment-at-will doctrine.

1252. Krueger, Alan B. "The Evolution of Unjust Dismissal Legislation in the United States." *Industrial and Labor Relations Review* 44, no. 4 (July 1991): 644-660.

>A review of the law on this topic. A commentary on this article by Jack Stieber and Richard N. Block and a reply by the author are found in *Industrial and Labor Relations Review* 45, no. 4 (July 1992): 792-799.

1253. Block, Howard S. "Toward a Kinder, Gentler Society." In 44 NAA (1992): 12-25.

> Reviews the traditional doctrine of employment-at-will and recent court decisions. The author encourages legislative action that provides for arbitration.

Q. Arbitration in Selected Industries

Education

1254. Harter, Lafayette G., Jr. "Tenure and the Nonrenewal of Probationary Teachers." *Arbitration Journal* 34, no. 1 (March 1979): 22-27.

> When an arbitrator reinstates an improperly terminated teacher, the teacher might automatically qualify for tenure, and an undesirable teacher could receive tenure. This article examines how state courts have dealt with this situation.

1255. Lentz, Charles N. "Can Compulsory Arbitration Work in Education Collective Bargaining? A Second Look: The Teacher Organization Perspective." *Journal of Law and Education* 9, no. 1 (January 1980): 85-91.

> Focusing on Iowa, Minnesota, and Wisconsin public sector legislation, the article expresses reservations about the ability of conventional arbitration to motivate bargaining and produce fair results.

1256. Rynecki, Steven B. "Can Compulsory Arbitration Work in Education Collective Bargaining? A Second Look: A Management Advocate's View." *Journal of Law and Education* 9, no. 1 (January 1980): 93-101.

> Written from a management perspective, this article raises questions about the price paid for dispute resolution by this form of intervention.

1257. Russell, James S. "The Use of a Master Arbitrator in Strike Resolution: A Case Study." *Journal of Collective Negotiations in the Public Sector* 11, no. 2 (1982): 131-144.

> A study of a 1978 teacher strike at Lansing (Michigan) Community College. The court appointed a master arbitrator and it proved to be an effective means of impasse resolution in cases where the law prohibits strikes.

1258. Murrman, Kent F., and Bruce S. Cooper. "Attitudes of Professionals towards Arbitration." *Arbitration Journal* 37, no. 2 (June 1982): 12-17.

> A study that develops empirical measures of school principals' attitudes concerning the acceptability of arbitration.

1259. Rathburn, J. Eric. "Arbitrating Job Security Issues under the Public School

Code and Act 195: The Neshaminy Legacy." *Dickinson Law Review* 88, no. 3 (Spring 1984): 431-465.

> A discussion of a decision by the Pennsylvania Supreme Court that the dismissal of a professional employee of a school district was not arbitrable.

1260. Knight, Thomas R. "Public Policy and Arbitration of Tenure Decisions in New York State." *Journal of Collective Negotiations in the Public Sector* 14, no. 1 (1985): 25-44.

> This study finds that school administrators who make tenure decisions almost never encounter opposition from school boards and that the resulting gap in the collective bargaining rights of teachers requires legislative attention.

1261. Pashler, Peter. "Labor: Arbitration Award Reversing School District's Determination That Teacher's Performance Was Unsatisfactory Is Subject to a Narrow Scope of Review. (Case Note)." *Drake Law Review* 35, no. 1 (Winter 1986): 249-260.

> A review of a case in which the Iowa courts upheld an arbitration award that reversed a decision made by a school board to discipline a teacher.

1262. Annunziato, Frank R. "Grievance Arbitration in Connecticut K-12 Public Education." *Arbitration Journal* 42, no. 3 (September 1987): 46-57.

> This article examines all Connecticut public education awards conducted under the American Arbitration Association between 1977 and 1982 and includes interviews with 18 of the professional advocates involved.

1263. Gross, James A. "Standards of Behavior for Tenured Teachers; The New York State Experience." In 40 NAA (1988): 181-196.

> An exploration of New York State experiences in disciplining teachers for unbecoming conduct.

1264. Colon, Robert J. "Issues Brought to Grievance Arbitration by Iowa Public School Teachers: January 1982 through December 1986." *Journal of Collective Negotiations in the Public Sector* 18, no. 3 (1989): 217-227.

> Data from 1976 to 1981 was compared with data from 1982 to 1986. Evidence suggests that arbitration favors the employees.

1265. Colon, Robert J. "Job Security Issues in Grievance Arbitration: What Do They Tell Us?" *Journal of Collective Negotiations in the Public Sector* 19, no. 4 (1990): 243-251.

> This is an examination of the difficulties that issues such as seniority, reduction in force, transfer, and recall pose to administrators in Iowa public school systems.

Higher Education

1266. Edmonson, William F., and Alex J. Simon. "Arbitration in Higher Education." *Arbitration Journal* 29, no. 4 (December 1974): 217-224.

> This article compares arbitration in higher education with private sector arbitration and finds much similarity. It shows distribution of cases by type of grievance.

1267. Finkin, Matthew W. "The Arbitration of Faculty Status Disputes in Higher Education." *Southwestern Law Journal* 30 (Spring 1976): 389-434.

> Outlines the differences between industrial assumptions and decisional processes in institutions of higher education and how arbitrators have dealt with faculty grievances.

1268. Begin, James P. "Grievance Mechanisms and Faculty Collegiality: The Rutgers Case." *Industrial and Labor Relations Review* 31, no. 3 (April 1978): 295-309.

> This case study of Rutgers University concludes that grievances of procedural matters have no substantial impact on the collegial process.

1269. Douglas, Joel M. "An Analysis of the Arbitration Clause in Collective Bargaining Agreements in Higher Education." *Arbitration Journal* 39, no. 4 (December 1984): 38-48.

> This article examines 129 arbitration clauses and sets forth the findings with respect to 11 components such as the scope of arbitrability, limits on the power of the arbitrator, and the selection of arbitrators.

1270. Douglas, Joel M. "Arbitration Forums: Academia." In 41 NAA (1989): 331-346.

> Douglas discusses the similarities and differences between industrial and academic arbitration, focusing on the conflict between arbitration and notions of collegiality. James P. Begin comments.

1271. Purcell, Edward R. "Binding Arbitration and Peer Review in Higher Education." *Arbitration Journal* 45, no. 4 (December 1990): 10-15.

> A study of promotion, tenure, and reappointment disputes in the California State University system. Arbitrators tend to support peer decision-making rather than determinations made by campus presidents.

Federal Government

1272. Miserendino, C. Richard. "Arbitration in the Federal Service: The Deregulation of Remedies." *Arbitration Journal* 30, no. 2 (June 1975): 129-145.

> Focuses on review of arbitration awards.

1273. "Arbitration Awards in Federal Sector Public Employment: The Compelling Need Standard of Appellate Review." *Brigham Young University Law Review* 1977, no. 2 (1977): 429-446.

>This article advocates applying the compelling need standard not only to negotiability disputes but also to arbitration awards in the federal sector.

1274. Frazier, Henry B., III. "Labor Arbitration in the Federal Service." *George Washington Law Review* 45 (May 1977): 712-756.

>Experience with grievance arbitration under Executive Order 11491.

1275. Ferris, Frank D. "Remedies in Federal Sector Promotion Grievances." *Arbitration Journal* 34, no. 2 (June 1979): 37-43.

>Study of the limitations imposed by external law on the ability of arbitrators to offer remedies in federal sector promotion grievances.

1276. Sulzner, George T. "The Impact of Grievance and Arbitration Processes on Federal Personnel Policies and Practices: The View from Twenty Bargaining Units." *Journal of Collective Negotiations in the Public Sector* 9, no. 2 (1980): 143-157.

>This study finds no substantial impact because arbitration was not used frequently in the units studied.

1277. Goodwin, Van Allyn. "Federal Sector Arbitration under the Civil Service Reform Act of 1978." *San Diego Law Review* 17, no. 4 (July 1980): 857-893.

>A presentation of the standing of arbitration under the CSRA.

1278. Kagel, John. "Grievance Arbitration in the Federal Service: Still Hardly Final and Binding." In 34 NAA (1980): 178-217.

>Includes suggestion for statutory reform. Comments by James M. Harkless and John C. Shearer.

1279. Hayford, Stephen L. "The Impact of Law and Regulation upon the Remedial Authority of Labor Arbitrators in the Federal Sector." *Arbitration Journal* 37, no. 1 (March 1982): 28-37.

>Hayford points out that federal sector arbitrators are often given great latitude in the formulation of remedies but, he notes, they should be knowledgeable about relevant laws and regulations such as the Back Pay Act and the Federal Personnel Manual.

1280. Reischl, Dennis K., and Carl D. Moore. "Arbitrating Federal Sector Environmental Differential Pay Disputes Awarding Attorney's Fees in Federal Sector Arbitration." *Arbitration Journal* 37, no. 4 (December 1982): 32-47.

>This study examines the standards that arbitrators employ in differential

pay disputes in the federal sector, the burden of proof, remedies, and attorney's fees.

1281. Bufe, John F., and Frank D. Ferris. "A Second View of Awarding Attorney's Fees in Federal Sector Arbitration." *Arbitration Journal* 38, no. 1 (March 1983): 21-34.

    The statutory provisions and the standards for granting attorney's fees in federal sector arbitrations are discussed.

1282. Gentile, Joseph F. "Federal Sector Bargaining: Arbitration in the Federal Sector; Selected Problem Areas." *Labor Law Journal* 34, no. 8 (August 1983): 482-487.

    A practical examination of a number of advocacy issues in federal sector arbitration.

1283. Feigenbaum, Charles. "The Relationship between Arbitration and Administrative Procedures in the Discipline and Discharge of Federal Employees." *Labor Law Journal* 34, no. 9 (September 1983): 586-598.

    Stresses that federal sector arbitration operates in a unique context which must be respected by the arbitrator.

1284. White, Harold C. "The Review Process for Labor Arbitration in the Federal Sector." *Labor Law Journal* 35, no. 1 (January 1984): 35-43.

    Reviews the U.S. Court of Appeals at Washington, D.C., decision in *Devine v. White et al.* and concludes that the role of arbitration and the position of the collective bargaining agreement have taken on greater importance as a result of this decision.

1285. Blatch, Maralyn G. "The General Accounting Office's Jurisdiction and Federal Labor Relations Since Passage of the Civil Service Reform Act." *Arbitration Journal* 39, no. 1 (March 1984): 31-42.

    How the GAO has adapted its role in appropriations law to the statutory scheme established by the Civil Service Reform Act.

1286. Koren, Phillip F. "Adverse Action Arbitration in the Federal Sector: A Streamlining of the Appellate Procedures?" *Army Lawyer* (March 1984): 38-42.

    This article contends that, although existing procedures may protect employee rights, they are overly complex, too lengthy, and probably not consistent with the objectives of the CSRA.

1287. Koren, Phillip F. "Judicial Review of Federal Sector Adverse Action Arbitration Awards: A Novel Approach." *Army Lawyer* (November 1984): 22-38.

    This article draws the conclusion that reviewing courts should not automatically apply broad principles of deferral to arbitration decisions.

1288. Dawson, Richard T. "Federal Labor Relations Authority: Review of Arbitration Awards." *Air Force Law Review* 25, no. 2 (Spring 1985): 106-120.

> An examination of arbitration in the federal sector, concentrating on the Federal Labor Relations Authority review processes.

1289. Buxton, Val. "Pitfalls and Pratfalls of Impasse Resolution Procedures in the Federal Government: A Negotiator's Experience." *Labor Law Journal* 37, no. 3 (March 1986): 167-179.

> A review of impasse procedures in the federal government.

1290. Frazier, Henry B., III. "Arbitration in the Federal Sector." *Arbitration Journal* 41, no. 1 (March 1986): 70-76.

> A description of the arbitration requirements in the Civil Service Reform Act and the role played by the FLRA in determining if the award is contrary to law, rule, or regulation.

1291. Rudyk, Andrew. "The Relationship between Federal Sector Arbitration and the Merit Systems Protection Board." *Labor Law Journal* 37, no. 6 (June 1986): 372-377.

> This article provides a general survey of the relationship between arbitration and the Merit Systems Protection Board with an emphasis on describing the mission and function of the board.

1292. Nolan, Dennis R. "Federal Sector Labor Arbitration: Differences, Problems, Cures." *Pepperdine Law Review* 14, no. 4 (May 1987): 805-818.

> An examination of problems including the limited scope of bargaining; the applicability of external laws, rules, and regulations; and the need for better screening of grievances, better training for advocates, and more extensive preparation.

1293. Berry, Dean Clement. "*Cornelius v. Nutt* and the Current State of Arbitral Remedial Authority in the Federal Sector." *Oklahoma Law Review* 40, no. 4 (Winter 1987): 559-591.

> The areas of overlap and potential conflict between the Merit System Protection Board and arbitration. The author concludes that there should be one standard that is applied consistently by arbitrators and by the MSPB.

1294. Bowers, Mollie H. "Challenges to Arbitrability on Federal Sector Grievance Cases." *Hofstra Labor Law Journal* 5, no. 2 (Spring 1988): 169-196.

> Discusses arbitrability in the federal sector, screening and preparing a case, and procedural problems.

1295. Fishgold, Herbert, and Mary E. Jacksteit. "Implications of *Cornelius v. Nutt* for Federal Sector Arbitrators." *Arbitration Journal* 43, no. 1 (March 1988): 14-27.

>This article discusses a Supreme Court decision which held that the Merit Systems Protection Board standard on harmful error was binding on an arbitrator.

1296. Ross, Jerome H., William R. Kansier, William Dailey, John Mulholland, Frank D. Ferris, and James M. Harkless. "Arbitration in the Federal Sector." In 42 NAA (1990): 204-235.

>Ross provides the introduction, Kansier and Dailey offer the management perspective, and Mulholland and Ferris outline the union position. Harkless examines the FLRA review of arbitration awards.

1297. Ingrassia, Anthony. "Federal Sector Arbitration: A Management Viewpoint." In 43 NAA (1991): 203-214.

>This article describes the statutory framework for arbitration in the federal sector, the difference between the decisions of arbitrators and those of the MSPB, the limitations on the arbitrator's remedial power, and why awards are modified or set aside.

1298. Smith, Charles G. "The Resolution of Negotiation Impasses in the Federal Service." *Journal of Collective Negotiations in the Public Sector* 20, no. 4 (1991): 321-340.

>This article examines over 300 decisions made by the FSIP to resolve federal sector contract disputes.

1299. McKee, Jean. "Federal Sector Arbitration." In 44 NAA (1992): 187-206.

>The chair of the FLRA describes the federal sector arbitration caseload, the appeals process, and ways to reduce the number of appeals from arbitration awards. Jerome H. Ross and Earl J. Williams discuss problems.

Postal Service

1300. Cushman, Bernard. "Some Reflections upon the Postal Experience with Expedited Arbitration." In 27 IRRA (1974): 332-335.

>Analysis of the expedited arbitration process used by the postal unions and the postal service. See also Harvey Letter's "Expedited Arbitration in the Postal Service," 27 IRRA 336-339 (1974).

1301. Williams, J. Earl. "Arbitration in Specific Environments: The Postal Service." In 42 NAA (1990): 254-263.

>A discussion of the structure of arbitration, the forces that influence arbitration the arbitral caseload, the problems, and the complexity of the system.

Other Industries
Railroads and Airlines

1302. Daugherty, Carroll R. "Arbitration by the National Railroad Adjustment Board." In 8 NAA (1955): 93-126.

> Covers history, procedures, and experience of the NRAB. Discussions by Dudley E. Whiting and Paul M. Guthrie.

1303. Vernon, Gil. "Public Funding for the Arbitration of Grievances in the Railroad Industry." *Arbitration Journal* 38, no. 3 (September 1983): 22-23.

> Reviews the history of the NRAB and analyzes the argument for and against public funding. The article is followed by concurring and dissenting views from practitioners: "Response #1: Backlog Not the Issue—Public Funding Is; User Fees Questioned," by Jack Fletcher, pp. 34-37 and "Response #2: Public Funding Not the Issue—Backlog Is; Cost Sharing Supported," by Charles I. Hopkins, Jr., pp. 38-41.

1304. Wolf, Mary Jean. "Trans World Airlines Noncontract Grievance Procedure." In 39 NAA (1987): 27-33.

> The history, development, and structure of and experiences with TWA's grievance procedure for noncontract employees, including management.

1305. Eischen, Dana E., Seth D. Rosen, John M. Hedblom, Mary Clare Haskin, and Martin Soll. "Arbitration in the Airlines." In 42 NAA (1990): 189-203.

> Eischen presents the historical and legal background, and the other authors provide practitioner views.

1306. Scheinman, Martin F. "Arbitration in Specific Industries: The Railroads." In 42 NAA (1990): 263-267.

> A description of the structure of arbitration in this industry, the forces that influence it, the arbitral caseload, and the differences between railroad and other arbitration.

Sports

1307. Goldstein, Mark L. "Arbitration of Grievance and Salary Disputes in Professional Baseball: Evolution of a System of Private Law." *Cornell Law Review* 60 (August 1975): 1049-1074.

> Traces the maturation of labor relations in professional baseball and assesses the protection arbitration offers to players, owners, and fans.

1308. Dworkin, James B. "The Impact of Final-Offer Interest Arbitration on Bargaining: The Case of Major League Baseball." In 29 IRRA (1976): 161-169.

> Analysis of the use of FOA in professional baseball to test whether such use has a "narcotic" effect.

1309. Gessford, James B. "Arbitration of Professional Athletes' Contracts: An Effective System of Dispute Resolution in Professional Sports." *Nebraska Law Review* 55 (1976): 362-382.

> The author argues that grievance arbitration is the best way to resolve the increasing number of disputes in the sports industry.

1310. Dworkin, James B. "How Final Offer Arbitration Affects Baseball Bargaining." *Monthly Labor Review* 100, no. 3 (March 1977): 52-53.

> This study found that the availability of arbitration did not displace negotiations as the primary method of wage settlements.

1311. Staudohar, Paul D. "Player Salary Issues in Major League Baseball." *Arbitration Journal* 33, no. 4 (December 1978): 17-21.

> The impact of salary arbitration in major league baseball.

1312. Chelius, James R., and James B. Dworkin. "Arbitration and Salary Determination in Baseball." In 33 IRRA (1980): 105-112.

> A discussion of baseball arbitration.

1313. Chelius, James R., and James B. Dworkin. "Free Agency and Salary Determination in Baseball." *Labor Law Journal* 33, no. 8 (August 1982): 539-545.

> This article reviews the history of the reserve clause and the development of free agency in baseball, and it forecasts a dramatic increase in baseball salaries.

1314. Grebey, C. Raymond, Jr. "Another Look at Baseball's Salary Arbitration." *Arbitration Journal* 38, no. 4 (December 1983): 24-30.

> An advocate argues that in addition to causing cost increases, salary arbitration in baseball introduces further adversarial characteristics into the player-club relationship.

1315. Miller, Marvin J. "Arbitration of Baseball Salaries: Impartial Adjudication in Place of Management Fiat." *Arbitration Journal* 38, no. 4 (December 1983): 31-35.

> This article describes conditions in major league baseball before salary arbitration, disputes the claim that free agency eliminated the need for salary arbitration, and makes suggestions for improving the salary arbitration procedures.

1316. Luskin, Bert, Thomas T. Roberts, John Donlan, and Richard Moss. "Arbitration in Professional Sports." In 36 NAA (1984): 155-189.

> Commentaries on arbitration in professional football and baseball by arbitrators and union representatives.

1317. Dworkin, James B. "Salary Arbitration in Baseball: An Impartial Assessment after Ten Years." *Arbitration Journal* 41, no. 1 (March 1986): 63-69.

> An arbitrator concludes that baseball's final-offer arbitration procedure has enticed the parties into bargaining in good faith, but arbitrators are now being forced to choose between two unreasonable final offers.

1318. Wong, Glenn M. "A Survey of Grievance Arbitration Cases in Major League Baseball." *Arbitration Journal* 41, no. 1 (March 1986): 42-62.

> This survey concludes that the system is working well, the rulings have had a profound impact on the sport, and arbitration has become an effective policy-making tool.

1319. Wong, Glenn M. "Major League Baseball's Grievance Arbitration System: A Comparison with Nonsports Industry." *Employee Relations Law Journal* 12, no. 3 (Winter 1986/1987): 464-490.

> A comprehensive comparison of arbitration in baseball with arbitration in nonsports industry.

1320. Wong, Glenn M. "Major League Baseball's Grievance Arbitration System: A Comparison with Nonsport Industry." *Labor Law Journal* 38, no. 2 (February 1987): 84-99.

> The author shows how many of the same issues that come to arbitration in nonsports industries are the topic of arbitration in major league baseball.

1321. Ensor, Richard J. "Comparison of Arbitration Decisions Involving Termination in Major League Baseball, the National Basketball Association, and the National Football League." *Saint Louis University Law Journal* 32, no. 1 (Fall 1987): 135-169.

> Ensor concludes that arbitration decisions are influenced by the facts in the case, procedural requirements, and the parties' lack of knowledge of the collective agreement. The principles applied in one sport are often applicable in another.

1322. Roberts, Thomas T. "Sports Arbitration." *Industrial Relations Law Journal* 10, no. 1 (1988): 8-11.

> Developments relating to drug testing in major league baseball.

1323. Meyer, Jeffrey D. "The NFLPA's Arbitration Procedure: A Forum for Professional Football Players and Their Agents to Resolve Disputes." *Ohio State Journal on Dispute Resolution* 6, no. 1 (1990): 107-128.

> The National Football League Players Association has developed an arbitration process to cover disputes between players and their agents. This article reviews how the process has worked.

1324. Faurot, David G., and Stephen McAllister. "Salary Arbitration and Pre-Arbitration Negotiation in Major League Baseball." *Industrial and Labor Relations Review* 45, no. 4 (July 1992): 695-710.

>The variables that influence an arbitrator's decision are shown to be the player's performance during the previous season, career performance, previous compensation, his position, and the club's recent performance.

Public Safety

1325. LaVan, Helen, and Cameron Carley. "Analysis of Arbitrated Employee Grievance Cases in Police Departments." *Journal of Collective Negotiations in the Public Sector* 14, no. 3 (1985): 245-254.

>This article describes many of the distinctive characteristics of police grievance cases and the factors that influence win ratios.

1326. Wolkinson, Benjamin W., Kenneth Chelst, and Lo Ann Shepard. "Arbitration Issues in the Consolidation of Police and Fire Bargaining Units." *Arbitration Journal* 40, no. 4 (December 1985): 43-54.

>The article describes various forms of consolidation, the problems, and the arbitration of issues such as the assignment of personnel to nontraditional work, contracting out, minimum staffing requirements, and safety.

Coal

1327. Blalock, Larry W. "The Current State of Grievance Arbitration in the Coal Industry." *West Virginia Law Review* 82, no. 4 (Summer 1980): 1401-1423.

>The article focuses on the problems of ineffective screening, fair representation, delay, and cost in coal industry arbitration, and the development of the Arbitration Review Board.

1328. Barkey, Fred A. "Recent Initiatives in Grievance Arbitration Screening by United Mine Worker District in the Soft Coal Industry." *Labor Law Journal* 37, no. 6 (June 1986): 350-356.

>This article discusses the use of arbitration screening boards in the soft coal industry and concludes that these boards were effective in screening out weak cases and lessening the vulnerability of elected union leaders.

1329. Bourne, Steve. "The Rise and Fall of the Arbitration Review Board." *Labor Law Journal* 39, no. 8 (August 1988): 470-475.

>A study of the evolution and the demise of the Arbitration Review Board in the bituminous coal industry.

1330. Sharpe, Calvin William. "A Study of Coal Arbitration under the National Bituminous Coal Wage Agreement between 1975 and 1990." *West Virginia Law Review* 93, no. 3 (Spring 1991): 497-598.

The article analyzes the features of the coal industry that influence the arbitration process. The National Bituminous Coal Wage Agreement provides clear guidelines that govern most of the issues.

Miscellaneous

1331. Jensen, Vernon H. "Dispute Settlement in the New York Longshore Industry." *Industrial and Labor Relations Review* 10, no. 4 (July 1957): 588-608.

> Analysis of arbitration agreement in 1955 between International Longshoremen's Association and employers and its impact on reducing job actions.

1332. Bain, Trevor. "Arbitration: An Alternative to Crisis Bargaining." *Arbitration Journal* 23, no. 2 (1968): 102-109.

> Study of effects of arbitration in the flat glass industry. Arbitrators, in a crisis atmosphere, are less likely to solve work rule disputes than the parties themselves.

1333. Fischer, Ben. "Arbitration: The Steel Industry Experiment." *Monthly Labor Review* 95, no. 11 (November 1972): 7-10.

> Examines early experience with expedited arbitration of routine cases.

1334. Denenberg, Tia Schneider. "The Application of Labor-Management Dispute Settlement Procedures to Prison Inmate Grievances." In 29 IRRA (1976): 170-176.

> Analysis of the use of arbitration procedures in resolving prisoner grievances, based on an empirical analysis of procedures in Wisconsin, Maryland, and California prisons.

1335. LaVan, Helen, Cameron Carley, and J. Marshall Jowers. "The Arbitration of Employee Grievances in Health Care Institutions: An Empirical Study." *Arbitration Journal* 35, no. 4 (December 1980): 33-36.

> A study of 72 arbitration decisions influenced by the 1974 amendment to the Taft-Hartley Act. Arbitration was not significantly affected by the law.

1336. Dybeck, Alfred C., Jared H. Meyer, and Robert Kovacevik. "Arbitration in Specific Environments: The Steel Industry." In 42 NAA (1990): 236-253.

> A panel discussion about arbitration in this industry. Dybeck provides historical background and an analysis of significant patterns; Meyer and Kovacevik provide a management and union viewpoint.

SUBJECT INDEX

The numbers are for citations unless indicated by p. or pp. before them.

Ability to pay   1029, 1067, 1068, 1069, 1070
Absenteeism   403, 573, 574, 575, 644
Abuse, verbal and physical   653
Acceptability of the arbitrator   56, 219, 221, 222, 223, 225, 227, 228, 234
Accounts receivable   363
Adjournments   350
Adverse actions   1286, 1287
Advocacy   18, 48, 51, 69, 70, 71, 72, 73, 74, 75, 76, 79, 85, 88, 144, 147, 372, 373, 374, 375, 386
AFL-CIO internal disputes plan   756
AFL-CIO v. U.S. Postal Service   809
African-American heritage   236
Age Discrimination in Employment Act   979, 981, 982, 984, 985, 986
AIDS   576, 577, 578
Airlines   150, 1304, 1305
Alcohol   103, 104, 105, 579, 581, 582, 583, 585, 586, 587, 588, 590, 591, 595, 596
Alexander v. Gardner-Denver   818, 820, 821, 822, 823, 824, 825, 827, 888, 964, and p. 25
Alford v. General Motors   p. 31
Allis-Chalmers Corporation v. Lueck   134, 1248
Americans with Disabilities Act   969
Arbitrability   89, 193, 194, 491, 492, 493, 494, 495, 497, 498, 500, 501, 502, 517, 1294
Arbitration, future   60, 260, 261, 262, 263, 264, 268, 347
Arbitration, gender effects   477, 483, 595
Arbitration, general   3, 6, 9, 11, 14, 15, 16, 17, 18, 19, 20, 35, 36, 38, 39, 41, 42, 44, 47, 48, 49, 50, 68, 77, 78, 88, 155, 156, 158, 159, 166, 168, 171, 174, 182, 215, 288, 309, 311, 351, 782
Arbitration, history   46, 59, 61, 62, 110, 246, 247, 251, 252, 254, 255, 256, 257, 258, 259, 260, 265, 266, 268
Arbitration, law of   1, 7, 13, 43, 46
Arbitration literature   181

229

SUBJECT INDEX

Arbitration, law of   1, 7, 13, 43, 46
Arbitration literature   181
Arbitration reporters   161, 175, 177
Arbitration, scope of   524
Arbitration systems   162
Arbitration, teaching materials   37, 52, 53, 54
Arbitrator advertising   292
Arbitrator bias   365, 657
Arbitrator errors   800
Arbitrators, availability and utilization   45, 224
Argentina   33, 202
Atkinson v. Sinclair Refining   p. 19
AT&T Technologies v. Communication Workers   499, 500, 814, and p. 19
Attitudes   167, 220, 1046, 1258
Attorney's fees   1280, 1281
At-will employees   *See* Unjust dismissal
Australia   29, 31, 33, 120, 200, 202, 203, 204, 208
Award clarification   367

Back pay   743, 745
Bankruptcy   519, 520, 521
Bargaining units   1326
Barrentine v. Arkansas Best Freight   843 and p. 31
Baseball   1307, 1308, 1310, 1311, 1312, 1313, 1314, 1315, 1316, 1317, 1318, 1319, 1320, 1324. *See also* Professional sports
Bechtel Construction v. LIUNA   p. 19
Bethlehem Steel Company   247, 693
Boards of Arbitration   305, 342, 343, 344, 345
Borden v. AAA; RHDSU   p. 20
Bowen v. U.S. Postal Service   449, 452, 453, 455, 456, and p. 30
Boys Markets v. Retail Clerks   p. 19
Briefs and closing arguments   348, 387
Buffalo Forge Co. v. Steelworkers   p. 19

California   1075, 1240, 1271
Calling the grievant as adverse witness   352, 354
Canada   4, 30, 35, 36, 65, 83, 108, 120, 122, 124, 125, 131, 180, 198, 204, 339, 340, 571, 634, 674, 697, 767, 768, 858, 859, 860, 1021, 1024, 1032, 1056, 1141, 1181, 1208, 1209, 1210, 1212, 1213, 1214, 1215
Carbon Fuel Co. v. United Mine Workers of America   842
Caseloads and earnings   58, 210, 217, 262, 263, 291, 296, 297
Characteristics of arbitrators   58, 210, 212, 213, 214, 217, 218, 227, 234
Chicago Teachers Union v. Hudson   457

SUBJECT INDEX 231

Chrysler 249
Chrysler v. Allied Industrial Workers p. 27
Civil Rights Act of 1991 969
Civil service 201, 431, 434
Closed offer arbitration 1151
Coal 4, 279, 807, 842, 1327, 1328, 1329, 1330
Code of professional responsibility 245, 366, 759
Collyer Insulated Wire 921, 922, 923, 924, 925, 926, 930, 931, 943, and p. 22
Comparable worth 696, 697, 698
Compelling need standard 1273
Compensatory damages 742
Conciliation 27, 28, 29, 30, 34
Connecticut 193, 1076, 1077
Constitutional rights 430
Construction 4, 157
Contract interpretation 101, 265, 467, 522, 523, 524, 525, 526, 527, 528, 551, 554
Cornelius v. Nutt 1293, 1295, and p. 24
Cost 172, 275, 276, 290, 297, 305, 306, 307, 308, 310, 312, 316, 317, 318, 319, 320
Criminal charges 559, 618
Criteria, grievance arbitration 474, 681
Criteria, interest arbitration 1040, 1067, 1181

Darr v. NLRB p. 22
Decision-making 12, 160, 169, 183, 214, 459, 460, 461, 462, 464, 465, 466, 470, 471, 472, 473, 475, 476, 477, 478, 479, 481, 482, 1120, 1149, 1182, 1184
Declaratory awards 321
Deferral 778, 843, 844, 864, 886, 887, 888, 889, 890, 891, 892, 893, 894, 895, 897, 898, 899, 900, 901, 902, 903, 904, 905, 906, 907, 908, 909, 910, 911, 912, 913, 914, 915, 916, 917, 918, 919, 920, 921, 922, 923, 924, 925, 926, 927, 928, 929, 930, 931, 932, 933, 934, 935, 936, 937, 938, 939, 940, 941, 942
Delay 172, 303, 305, 306, 308, 310, 315, 316, 317, 318, 320, 322, 323
Del Costello 449
Delta Air Lines v. ALPA pp. 28, 29
Delta Queen v. MEBA p. 23
Department stores 66
Devine v. Pastore and Estrella p. 24
Devine v. White 1284
Discharge 91, 95, 98, 101, 108, 336, 558, 560, 562, 563, 564, 566, 567, 571, 584, 595, 649, 656, 802, 873, 960, 1283
Discipline 91, 92, 93, 94, 95, 96, 97, 98, 99, 100, 101, 112, 149, 403, 410, 436,

232 SUBJECT INDEX

    584, 595, 649, 656, 802, 873, 960, 1283
Discipline   91, 92, 93, 94, 95, 96, 97, 98, 99, 100, 101, 112, 149, 403, 410, 436, 557, 559, 561, 565, 568, 570, 571, 614, 649, 652, 657, 659, 660, 855, 1263, 1283
Disclosure   236, 360, 361, 362, 363, 366
Discourtesy   663
Discovery   356, 357, 358
Discrimination   625, 628, 657, 817, 819, 837, 840, 944, 945, 946, 947, 948, 949, 950, 951, 952, 953, 954, 955, 956, 957, 958, 959, 960, 961, 963, 965, 966, 967, 968, 969, 977
Discrimination, age   840, 979, 980, 981, 982, 983, 984, 985, 986. *See also* Gilmer v. Interstate
Discrimination, handicap   988, 989, 990, 991, 992, 993, 994
Discrimination, national origin   995
Discrimination, religious   987
Discrimination, sex   970, 971, 972, 973, 974, 975, 976, 978
Disloyalty   621
Disparate treatment   657, 665
Dispute settlement   2, 4, 5, 8, 14, 15, 55, 168, 207, 1020, 1036, 1052, 1076, 1080, 1081, 1257
Disqualification of the arbitrator   348
Diversity   422, 423, 424
Drake Bakeries v. Bakery and Confectionery Workers   p. 19
Drugs   103, 105, 185, 402, 580, 583, 584, 585, 586, 587, 589, 590, 591, 593, 595, 598, 599, 601, 602, 603, 604, 605, 606, 607, 1322
Due process   84, 135, 149, 314, 425, 426, 428, 429, 431, 432, 435, 436, 442, 445, 1229

Earnings   *See* Caseloads and earnings
Education   *See* Schools
Employee assistance programs   183, 587, 592, 600
Employee privacy   90, 401, 414, 421, 606
Employee Retirement Income Security Act   716, 717, 719, 720, 724, 725, 728
Employer handbooks   523
Employment applications   660
Employment testing   419, 679, 681
Enforcement   517, 723, 780, 858, 874
Ethical dilemmas   19, 349, 364, 366, 368, 369, 370, 371
Evidence   74, 82, 83, 84, 348, 352, 353, 354, 390, 396, 397, 399, 400, 401, 402, 403, 428, 527
Expedited arbitration   290, 305, 332, 333, 334, 335, 336, 337, 338, 339, 341, 1300
External law   267, 523, 630, 762, 764, 765, 766, 770, 771, 772, 774, 775, 776, 777, 778, 779, 783, 784, 785, 787, 798, 806, 817, 818, 819, 820, 821, 822,

823, 824, 825, 826, 827, 828, 829, 830, 831, 832, 833, 834, 835, 836, 837, 838, 839, 840, 841, 865, 866, 867, 870, 872, 875, 888, 896, 952, 957, 962, 964, 967, 969
Fact-finding   121, 128, 129, 131, 132, 1007, 1041, 1069, 1081, 1092, 1186, 1189, 1191, 1192, 1193, 1194, 1195, 1196, 1197, 1198, 1199, 1200
Fair Labor Standards Act   869, 888
Fair representation   115, 165, 440, 441, 442, 443, 444, 445, 446, 447, 448, 449, 450, 451
Fair Share   *See* Union security fee arbitration
Fall River v. NLRB   p. 21
Family obligations   623
Federal Arbitration Act   845, 980
Federal sector   143, 144, 145, 146, 147, 396, 943, 1272, 1273, 1274, 1275, 1276, 1277, 1278, 1279, 1280, 1281, 1282, 1283, 1284, 1285, 1286, 1287, 1288, 1289, 1290, 1291, 1292, 1293, 1294, 1295, 1296, 1297, 1298, 1299
Fighting   654
Final-offer arbitration   121, 126, 127, 851, 1065, 1072, 1082, 1083, 1084, 1089, 1090, 1098, 1099, 1100, 1101, 1102, 1103, 1104, 1105, 1106, 1107, 1108, 1109, 1110, 1111, 1112, 1113, 1114, 1116, 1118, 1120, 1121, 1123, 1126, 1127, 1128, 1131, 1137, 1142, 1146, 1147, 1148, 1150, 1151, 1152, 1157, 1158, 1160, 1166, 1167, 1178, 1186, 1308, 1310
Fire fighters   127, 128, 1085, 1086, 1095, 1096, 1129, 1154, 1155, 1179, 1326
First contract arbitration   124, 125, 1056
Flat glass   1332
Florida   454, 1197, 1198
France   32, 196

Gambling   667
Garments   4
Garnisheed   622
General Electric   332
General Motors   250, 304
Germany   33, 196, 202
Gilmer v. Interstate   837, 839, and p. 26
Great Britain   27, 30, 33, 120, 198, 201, 202, 1228, 1233
Grievance and grievances   269, 270, 271, 272, 273, 378, 508
Grievance arbitration, abroad   207, 209
Grievance mediation   65, 274, 275, 276, 277, 278, 279, 280, 281, 282, 283, 284, 285, 286, 287, 635
Grievance procedure   21, 63, 64, 67, 304, 439
Grievances, causes of   63, 67
Grievant's personal problems   463

Hair 608, 609, 610, 611
Hammontree v. NLRB p. 22
Handbooks *See* Employer handbooks
Handicapped employees 106, 988, 992, 994
Harding et al. v. U.S. Postal Service p. 31
Hawaii 93, 851
Health care 151, 152, 153, 154, 1021, 1335
Hearing procedures 83, 290, 348, 352, 353, 355, 402
Higher education 1266, 1267, 1268, 1269, 1270, 1271
Hill v. Norfolk and Western p. 23
Hines v. Anchor Motor Freight p. 30
Holiday pay 701
Horseplay 655
Hosiery industry 59
Hospitals 66, 151, 152, 153, 154, 1021, 1335
Hours of work 687, 758
Howard Johnson v. Local Joint Executive Board 515, 516, and p. 21

Illinois 128, 1078, 1177
Immunity 299, 300, 301
Incentives 690, 691, 692
Independent participation by employees 427, 433
India 34
Indiana 850, 852, 853, 1194
Individual rights 165, 427, 433, 437, 438, 440, 443, 444, 538, 771, 781, 838, 869, 895, 898, 902, 1238, 1250
Industrial courts 7
Industrial engineering 87, 543
Insubordination 403, 612, 613, 650, 653
Interest arbitration, abroad 120, 200, 204, 208, 1024
Interest arbitration, experimental studies 1016, 1119, 1130, 1145, 1153
Interest arbitration, fiscal aspects 122, 1066, 1068, 1069, 1070, 1164, 1171
Interest arbitration, general 116, 118, 121, 123, 129, 195, 380, 847, 996, 998, 999, 1000, 1001, 1002, 1005, 1006, 1007, 1008, 1009, 1013, 1021, 1022, 1023, 1026, 1028, 1030, 1031, 1032, 1033, 1034, 1035, 1037, 1038, 1039, 1041, 1042, 1043, 1044, 1045, 1047, 1053, 1054, 1055, 1059, 1060, 1061, 1062, 1063, 1064, 1071, 1073, 1074, 1075, 1078, 1079, 1085, 1086, 1087, 1088, 1091, 1093, 1094, 1095, 1096, 1097, 1118, 1141, 1154, 1156, 1163
Interest arbitration, impact 380, 1047, 1065, 1115, 1117, 1121, 1139, 1145, 1159, 1164, 1170, 1173, 1175, 1176, 1186
Interest arbitration, outcomes 1051, 1160, 1161, 1162, 1168, 1169, 1172, 1174, 1179, 1180, 1182, 1183, 1185
Interest arbitration, political aspects 1003, 1004, 1027, 1048, 1049, 1050, 1075

Interest arbitration, private sector   117, 997, 1010, 1011, 1012, 1014, 1015, 1017, 1018
International Paper Company   332
Internship   240, 241, 242
Interrogation   356, 410, 412, 428
Iowa   123, 852, 1033, 1079, 1080, 1081, 1177, 1187, 1193, 1255, 1261, 1264, 1265
Iowa Electric v. IBEW   p. 28
Israel   33, 202, 205
Italy   32, 33, 202

Jamaica   120
Japan   33, 202
Job classification and evaluation   110, 546, 693, 694, 695
Job security   540, 1233, 1259, 1265
John Deere   248
John Wiley v. Livingston   p. 21
Judicial review   170, 183, 193, 435, 761, 769, 774, 780, 791, 795, 796, 797, 798, 799, 800, 801, 802, 803, 804, 805, 806, 807, 808, 809, 810, 811, 813, 814, 815, 816, 826, 845, 846, 847, 848, 849, 850, 856, 857, 860, 865, 866, 875, 878, 958, 1284, 1287, 1288
Jurisdictional disputes   157, 757
Just cause   96, 102, 568, 569, 570, 571, 572, 579, 594, 618, 1231, 1232, 1247

Kenya   34

Labor courts   32, 197
Last chance agreements   600
Late arbitration awards   788
Lawyers and legalisms   302, 322, 324, 325, 326, 327, 328, 329, 330, 331
Lingle v. Norge   p. 32
Litton v. NLRB   p. 20
Local 106, SEIU v. Evergreen Cemetery   p. 19
Logging   4
Longshore   199, 1331
Loser-pays arbitration   313
Lueck v. Metropolitan Life Insurance   1246

Management rights   90, 194, 306, 536, 537, 538, 539, 540, 541, 542, 551, 859
Massachusetts   123, 192, 1065, 1082, 1128
Mass transit   332, 1012
McDonald v. City of West Branch   790 and p. 31

236 SUBJECT INDEX

Med-Arb   206, 1201, 1202, 1203, 1204, 1205, 1206, 1207
Mediation   9, 30, 129, 130, 635, 1148, 1187, 1188, 1189, 1190, 1192, 1205
Medical condition   106, 988
Medical evidence   90, 404, 405, 406, 407, 408
Mental illness   587, 591, 989, 990, 991, 993
Merit Systems Protection Board   145, 1291, 1293, 1295, 1297
Michigan   123, 1026, 1033, 1084, 1085, 1086, 1087, 1191
Minnesota   123, 1033, 1168, 1210, 1255
Minority Group Members   657
Misco   814, 828, 829, 830, 831, 832, 834, 835, 883. *See also* Paperworkers v. Misco
Monetary awards   743, 745, 747
Multi-Employer Pension Plan Amendments   726, 727, 728, 729
Municipal governments   189, 1164, 1171

Narcotic effect   1124, 1127, 1129, 1130, 1133, 1134, 1135, 1136, 1138, 1143, 1208
National Academy of Arbitrators   216, 245
National Labor Relations Board   731, 863, 869, 885
National Radio Co.   p. 22
National Railroad Adjustment Board   149
Nebraska   1042, 1164
Nevada   1088
New Jersey   117, 123, 854, 855, 1089, 1090, 1142, 1166, 1178
Newsday, Inc. v. L.I. Typographical Union   p. 27
Newspaper publishing   1012
New York   123, 332, 1091, 1129, 1260, 1263
New York City   123, 204, 1026, 1030, 1067
New Zealand   28, 30, 199, 206, 208
NLRB v. Bildisco   p. 32
NLRB v. Burns   p. 21
Nolde v. Bakery Workers   505, 506, 507, 513, and p. 20
Nonunion   135, 136, 1216, 1217, 1218, 1219, 1220, 1221, 1222, 1223, 1224, 1225, 1226, 1229, 1230, 1231, 1233, 1236, 1304
Nonpunitive disciplinary systems   99
Northwest Airlines v. ALPA   p. 28
Norway   196, 1230
No-spouse rule   974

Occupational Safety and Health Act   707, 708, 711, 869, 888
Off-duty conduct   107, 614, 615, 616, 617, 618
Oklahoma   1092
Olin Company   932, 934, 935, 936, 937, 938, 939, 940, 941, and p. 22

SUBJECT INDEX 237

Paperworkers v. Misco   p. 27. *See also* Misco
Past misconduct   656
Past practice   90, 525, 548, 549, 550, 551, 552, 553, 554, 555, 556
Paul Felix Warburg Union Catalog of Arbitration   40
Pay guarantees   687
Pennsylvania   117, 123, 857, 1026, 1093, 1095, 1096, 1097, 1143, 1154
Pension   716, 718, 719, 722, 724
Pensions, trustee   721, 722
Performance ratings   658, 1261
Perjury   390
Philippines   34
Plant closing and relocation   736, 737, 738
Police   127, 1058, 1085, 1086, 1095, 1096, 1129, 1154, 1169, 1170, 1172, 1173, 1174, 1175, 1176, 1178, 1179, 1180, 1325, 1326
Political aspects   191, 192
Polk Brothers v. Chicago Truck Drivers et al.   p. 24
Polygraphs   90, 409, 412, 413, 414, 415, 416, 417, 418, 420
Post reinstatement performance   668, 669, 670, 671, 672, 673, 674, 675
Postal   332, 339, 1300, 1301
Postal Workers v. U.S. Postal Service   p. 23
Post-contract arbitrability   503, 504, 505, 506, 507, 508, 509, 510, 511, 512, 513, 514
Postreinstatement performance   108
Practice of arbitration   289, 291, 294, 295, 298
Precedent   88, 529, 530, 531, 532, 533, 534, 535
Predictability of awards   470, 480
Pregnancy   978
Prehearing   356, 357, 358, 359, 376, 568
Preparation and presentation   69, 71, 72, 75, 76, 85, 377, 379, 381
Prison inmate   1334
Privacy   *See* Employee privacy
Productivity   87, 542, 543, 732
Professional sports   1309, 1316, 1321, 1322, 1323. *See also* Baseball
Promotion   960, 1275
Proof   74, 81, 82, 395, 398, 584
Public policy exception   267, 780, 786, 793, 808, 829, 864, 867, 868, 869, 870, 871, 872, 873, 874, 875, 876, 877, 878, 879, 880, 881, 882, 883, 884
Public sector   21, 22, 23, 24, 25, 26, 66, 107, 119, 130, 170, 186, 187, 189, 190, 191, 192, 194, 195, 272, 293, 445, 454, 458, 468, 495, 510, 511, 512, 612, 616, 773, 849, 851, 852, 854, 855, 857, 942, 1019, 1025, 1029, 1040, 1055, 1057, 1064, 1077, 1088, 1132, 1187, 1188, 1189
Public utility   117
Punishment theory   561

238   SUBJECT INDEX

Railroads   64, 148, 150, 1302, 1303, 1306
Refusal to cross a picket line   640
Refusal to do hazardous work   713, 714, 715
Reinstatement   108, 668, 669, 670, 671, 672, 673, 674, 675, 744, 746, 748, 753
Religious practice   661, 662
Remedies   112, 183, 402, 597, 740, 741, 742, 743, 747, 749, 750, 751, 752, 753, 754, 1272, 1279, 1280
Representational issues   356, 757
Retention of jurisdiction   354, 759
Rhode Island   856
Rockville Training Center v. Alvin Peschke   853
Role of arbitration and arbitrators   10, 22, 160, 164, 173, 176, 178, 179, 184, 185, 207, 231, 463, 467, 597, 763
Russell Memorial Hospital v. Steelworkers   pp. 29, 30

Safety   706, 707, 708, 709, 710, 711, 712, 994
Schneider v. Robbins   723 and p. 33
Schools   66, 132, 138, 139, 140, 141, 142, 281, 617, 669, 1024, 1141, 1165, 1177, 1186, 1194, 1254, 1255, 1256, 1258, 1259, 1260, 1261, 1262, 1263, 1264, 1265
Scope of arbitration   163
S. D. Warner Co. v. United Paperworkers   846
Search and searches   90, 401
Section 301 of the LMRA   450, 789, 792, 794
Security risks   619, 620
Selection of arbitrator   56, 210, 220, 226, 228, 229, 230, 232, 233, 234, 235, 468
Seniority   180, 544, 672, 676, 677, 678, 680, 682, 683, 958, 960, 961
Sexual harassment   624, 625, 626, 627, 628, 629, 630, 631, 632, 633, 634, 635, 636, 637, 638
Shortened work week   758
Sinclair Refining v. Atkinson   p. 19
Sleeping on the job   666
Slowdowns   644, 1058, 1172
Smoking   111, 704, 705
Spielberg Mfg. Co.   898, 916, 917, 918, 919, 920, 926, 928, 929, and p. 22
Split the difference   1016, 1120, 1161
St. Anne-Nackawic v. Paperworkers   861, 862
State and local government   24, 123, 188, 431, 1073
Stead Motors v. IAM   p. 29
Steel   66, 110, 332, 1333, 1336
Steelworkers Trilogy   114, 550, 760, 769, 773, 791, 804, 805, 811, 814, 825, 854, 859
Steelworkers v. American Manufacturing Co.   p. 17
Steelworkers v. Enterprise Wheel & Car Corp.   p. 17

SUBJECT INDEX 239

Steelworkers v. Warrior & Gulf Navigation Co. p. 17
Strike misconduct 640, 641, 642, 645, 648
Strikes 190, 647, 842, 1032, 1047, 1053, 1054, 1057, 1060, 1061, 1062, 1063, 1064, 1074, 1132, 1144, 1165, 1172, 1202, 1211, 1257
Strikes, sympathy 646
Strikes, wildcat 639, 643
Stroehmann v. Local 776, Teamsters p. 27
Subcontracting 730, 731, 732, 733, 734, 735, 739
Subpoenas 348, 382, 383, 384, 385
Suburban Motor Freight 927, 928, 929
Successor employer 89, 515, 516, 517, 518
Supervisory performance of bargaining unit work 755
Supply of arbitrators 211
Surveillance 90, 410, 411, 412, 421
Sweden 32, 33, 196, 197, 202, 1230

Taylor, George W. 61
Teachers *See* Schools
Teamster Joint Grievance Committee 902
Technological change 544, 545, 546, 547, 695
Tennessee Valley Authority 773
Tenure 254, 1260, 1263, 1271
Testing *See* Alcohol; Drugs; Employment Testing
Textiles 4
Textile Workers v. Lincoln Mills 113 and pp. 10, 15
Theft 410, 588, 664
Timeliness 369
Training and development 55, 57, 80, 93, 137, 179, 237, 238, 239, 240, 241, 242, 243, 244, 253
Transfer of work 737, 739
Troubled employee 583, 594, 597

Umpireships 248, 249, 250, 346
Union business on company time 651
Union representatives, discipline 641, 647, 650, 652
Union security fee arbitration 457, 458
United States Steel Corporation 110
United Steelworkers 110
United Technologies Corp. 932, 933, 934, and p. 22
Unjust dismissal 133, 1227, 1228, 1230, 1232, 1233, 1234, 1235, 1236, 1237, 1239, 1241, 1242, 1243, 1244, 1245, 1246, 1247, 1248, 1249, 1251, 1252, 1253
U.S. Postal Service v. Letter Carriers p. 29

United States Steel Corporation   110
United Steelworkers   110
United Technologies Corp.   932, 933, 934, and p. 22
Unjust dismissal   133, 1227, 1228, 1230, 1232, 1233, 1234, 1235, 1236, 1237, 1239, 1241, 1242, 1243, 1244, 1245, 1246, 1247, 1248, 1249, 1251, 1252, 1253
U.S. Postal Service v. Letter Carriers   p. 29

Vacation   699, 700
Vermont   812

Wage arbitration   109
Wage comparisons   1029, 1045
Wage rates   684, 686, 688, 689
Wage reopeners   685
Waiver of the right to arbitrate   496
Wallen, Saul   10, 12
War Labor Board   252, 256, 257, 259
Washington   281
Waterfront   199
West Germany   32
Win-loss rates   468, 469
Wisconsin   123, 189, 1026, 1033, 1098, 1099, 1127, 1183, 1184, 1203, 1205, 1210, 1255
Witnesses   85, 86, 348, 354, 388, 389, 391, 392, 393, 394
Work assignments   540
Work rules   702, 703
Working conditions   551
W. R. Grace v. Rubber Workers   865, 867, and p. 25

AUTHOR INDEX

The numbers are for citations unless indicated by p. or pp. before them.

Aaron, Benjamin 32, 60, 256, 349, 484, 548, 558
Abrams, Roger I. 166, 169, 176, 191, 251, 252, 263, 300, 301, 378, 489, 563, 569, 578, 682, 687, 688, 700, 701, 732
Abramson, Elliott M. 588
Ackerman, Lawrence J. 619
Ackerman, Robert M. 1044
Adair, J. Leon 625
Adair, Thomas S. 764
Adams, Arvil V. 145
Adams, George W. 95
Adams, John A. 888
Adams, Meryl 654
Adell, Bernard 154
Adelman, Richard 414, 441, 627
Aggarwal, Arjun P. 634
Aksen, Gerald 818
Alexander, Gabriel N. 250, 373, 648, 676
Allen, A. Dale, Jr. 217, 297, 598
Allen, Robert E. 713
Alleyne, Reginald 331, 925, 926
Allotta, Joseph J. 398, 399
Allred, Stephen 1204
Anderson, Arvid 204, 777, 782, 1026, 1034, 1063, 1091
Anderson, John C. 227, 1115, 1208
Anderson, Wayne F. 128
Andiappan, Palaniappan 978
Andrews, J. David 328
Andrewson, Dale E. 582
Annunziato, Frank R. 1262
Ashcraft, William O. 372
Ashe, Bernard F. 445, 806
Ashenfelter, Orley 478, 1144, 1166

Asher, Lester 440
Ashmore, Robert W. 625
Attia, Gilles Simon 1075

Babcock, Linda C. 1052
Babjak, Betty Ann 855
Backhouse, Constance 1056
Baderschneider, Earl R. 151
Baderschneider, Jean 121, 1129, 1135
Baer, Walter E. 11, 68, 73, 88, 530, 649
Bagby, Thomas R. 134
Bailer, Lloyd 548, 551
Bain, Trevor 527, 1332
Bairstow, Frances 204
Bakaly, Charles G., Jr. 1223, 1251
Balfour, Alan 1219
Balkin, David B. 1211
Banta, Don A. 836
Barber, Sherry 339
Barden, James E. 922
Barken, Marlene 408
Barker, C. Paul 922
Barkey, Fred A. 1328
Barkston, Eddie W. 473
Barlow, Wayne E. 872
Barnacle, Peter J. 108
Barnett, George E. 9
Barocci, Thomas 1128, 1158
Barr, Steve H. 1121
Barreca, Christopher A. 57, 80, 414
Barrette, Thomas L., Jr. 864
Bartel, Barry C. 1207
Bartlett, Anthony F. 327, 957
Barton, David 989
Barton, Douglas H. 46
Baxter, Ralph H., Jr. 981
Bazerman, Max H. 1118, 1120, 1137, 1149
Beatty, David M. 35
Bedikian, Mary A. 383, 874, 1244
Begin, James P. 21, 1268, 1270
Bell, Cathleen G. 605
Bemmels, Brian 481, 483
Benar, Herbert 222

Bendixsen, Glen M. 724
Benetar, David L. 538
Benewitz, Maurice C. 161, 395
Benjamin, Edtard B., Jr. 296
Bennett, Charles P. 869
Ben Scheiber, Israel 305, 619
Berger, Ralph S. 519
Berkeley, Arthur Eliot 232, 233, 234, 298, 322, 666
Berkowitz, Monroe 1029
Berlowe, Amanda J. 871
Bernhardt, Herbert N. 731
Bernstein, Ira P. 903
Bernstein, Irving 109, 740
Bernstein, Merton C. 8, 175
Bernstein, Michael I. 839
Bernstein, Stuart 344
Berry, Dean Clement 1293
Bickner, Mei L. 245
Bierman, Leonard 1241
Bigoness, William J. 477, 1148, 1151
Bingham, Lisa B. 1077
Bird, Richard B. 423
Black, Errol 1112
Black, Hugo L., Jr. 411
Blackburn, John 43, 133
Blaine, Harry R. 338
Blalock, Larry W. 1327
Blatch, Maralyn G. 1285
Bloch, Richard I. 16, 96, 292, 352, 394, 528
Block, Howard S. 575, 1253
Block, Richard N. 175, 323, 330, 972, 1252
Block, S. Lester 550
Bloom, David E. 380, 1090, 1133, 1136, 1140, 1166
Blumrosen, Alfred W. 1238
Blutrich, Michael D. 350
Bocher, Sheri L. 526
Bognanno, Mario F. 58, 218, 1060, 1140
Bohlander, George W. 273
Bornong, Joseph H. 911
Bornstein, Tim 47, 386, 387, 590, 596, 636, 1031
Bosch, Frederick J. 645
Bourne, Steve 1329
Bowers, Mollie H. 276, 705, 1025, 1028, 1294

Brams, Steven J. 1110, 1167
Brannen, Dalton E. 225
Braun, Kurt 2
Breitenbach, Thomas A. 517
Brennan, William J., Jr. 267
Brett, Jeanne M. 278, 279
Brice, Amy L. 725
Briggs, Felicity D. 1070
Briggs, James I., Jr. 932
Briggs, Steven 227, 245, 1235, 1245
Briscoe, C. Chester 295
Bressenden, Paul F. 29
Britton, Raymond L. 708
Brodie, Donald W. 140, 817
Brotman, Billie Ann 643, 689, 907
Brown, Donald J. M. 35
Brown, Henry K. 212
Brown, Susan R. 547
Bruce, Christopher J. 1136
Brundage, Albert 325, 376
Brusch, Stephen Anthony 955
Bucheit, Scott E. 1044
Bufe, John F. 1281
Burkey, Lee M. 409, 410
Burris, William 339
Burroughs, John 737
Burstein, James A. 837, 984
Bush, Barbara A. 963
Bush, Raymond G. 938
Butler, Richard J. 1134
Butt, Elizabeth Rae 65
Buxton, Val 1289
Byrne, Dennis M. 1199

Cahn, Marc H. 239
Cain, Joseph P. 464
Cairnie, James 1024
Calkins, Benjamin 496
Canan, Robert H. 325
Caraway, John F. 361
Caraway, John M. 284
Carley, Cameron 1325, 1335

Carmell, William A. 964
Carr, David J. 415
Carter, Donald D. 571
Castagnera-Cain, James 772
Castle, Robert C. 896
Casto, William R. 773
Catler, Susan L. 1237
Cattel, Thomas A. 1085
Cavanagh, Christopher L. 380
Celmer, Albert B. 147
Cerbone, Richard R. 683
Chamberlain, Neil 536, 539, 540
Champlin, Frederic C. 1060, 1140
Chandler, Timothy 816
Chang, Ducksoo 27
Chattin, Joe 1213
Chaubey, M. D. 1193
Chauhan, D. S. 25, 1050
Chelius, James R. 1139, 1312, 1313
Chelst, Kenneth 1326
Christensen, Andrea S. 349
Christensen, Thomas G. S. 410, 795, 867
Chvala, Charles J. 1202
Clark, Leroy D. 593, 963
Clark, R. Theodore, Jr. 118, 128, 129, 733, 1053, 1068
Clarke, Jack 396
Clemow, Brian 1076
Clume, William H., III 1099
Cohen, David M. 1028
Cohen, Donald W. 572
Cohen, George H. 185, 373
Cohen, Hyman 333
Cohen, Martin A. 608
Cohen, Stuart 354
Cohen, Victor 847
Cole, David L. 3, 5, 155, 157
Cole, Howard A. 175, 249
Coleman, Charles J. 58, 194
Coleman, John J., III 1248
Collins, Daniel G 594
Collins, Wilbur L. 492
Colon, Robert J. 1264, 1265
Colosimo, Robert 339

Committee on Research and Education   210
Compton-Forbes, Patricia   1093
Conlon, Mark T.   846, 966
Connolly, Marie D.   1175
Cooner, Donna   381
Cooper, Bruce S.   1258
Cooper, Jerome R.   640
Cooper, Kenneth B.   402, 589
Cooper, Laura J.   359
Corbitt, Leslie   175
Corcoran, Kevin J.   1071
Costello, Edward J.   635
Cotton, John L.   735
Coulson, Robert   18, 105, 142, 178, 314, 370, 455, 471, 566, 662, 944, 1231
Couser, Ann   663
Covington, Robert N.   924
Cox, Archibald   3, 159
Cox, Garylee   235
Cramer, Dorothy J.   991
Crane, Louis A.   249, 493
Craver, Charles B.   39, 412, 849, 1036
Crawford, Donald A.   730
Crawford, Vincent P.   1107, 1108
Creo, Robert A.   147
Cromwell, Cynthia A.   919
Crone, Allison Stoddard   501
Crow, Stephen M.   638
Cuberley, Mark David   554
Culhane, John G.   918
Cuomo, Andrew M.   350
Currie, Janet   1141, 1144
Curry, Earl M., Jr.   175, 475
Cushman, Bernard   1300

Dailey, William   1296
Das, Shyam   1225
Dash, G. Allan, Jr.   62, 302
Datz, Harold J.   1018
Daugherty, Carroll R.   1302
Davey, Harold W.   248, 311, 342, 460, 491, 543
Davidoff, Philip K.   603
Davis, Lisa   654, 655

Davis, Pearce   548, 691, 702
Davy, Jeanette A.   273
Dawson, Donald   615
Dawson, Richard T.   1288
Day, Jack G.   257
Daykin, Walter L.   699, 703
Decker, Kurt H.   25, 358, 1096
DeCoste, F. C.   1005
Deitsch, Clarence R.   26, 181, 329, 456, 469, 479, , 850, 852, 853, 931
Delaney, John Thomas   1163, 1165, 1169, 1170, 1172, 1173, 1174, 1176, 1177
Dell'Omo, Gregory G.   599, 665, 1153, 1183
Dempster, George D.   1082
Denenberg, Richard V.   103, 600, 601, 602
Denenberg, Tia Schneider   103, 580, 586, 600, 601, 602, 1334
Dennehy, Daniel T.   413
Dennis, Rodney E.   669
Diamond, Bertram   559
Diekemper, Jerome A.   453
DiLauro, Thomas J.   576, 1064
Dilts, David A.   26, 181, 329, 367, 369, 403, 456, 468, 469, 479, 850, 852, 853, 931, 1045, 1195
DiNisi, Angelo S.   1116
DiRocco, Anthony P.   138
Dobbelaere, Arthur, Jr.   556
Dobranski, Bernard   660, 720
Doering, Barbara W.   295
Doering, Rick R.   607
Doherty, Robert E.   1062
Dohrmann, Robert M.   915
Dolson, William F.   80
Donlan, John   1316
Donn, Clifford B.   1004, 1105, 1138
Doolan, Robert J.   537
Dorr, John Van N., III   237
Dorsey, James E.   768
Doty, Ethan Allen   1094
Douglas, Joel M.   1269, 1270
Douglas, Robert L.   240
Downey, Laurie Eiler   357
Doyle, C. T.   529, 552
Driver, Claudia L.   721
Drotning, John E.   466, 1132, 1192
DuBose, Philip B.   477, 1151

Dunau, Bernard 440
Dunham, Robert E. 1055
Dunlop, John T. 157, 184
Dunn, John K. 1040
Dunne, James T. 304
Dunsford, John E. 179, 430, 437, 572, 828
Duran, Rowena M. 711
Durkin, David L. 1243
Dworkin, James B. 416, 1116, 1157, 1308, 1310, 1312, 1313, 1317
Dybeck, Alfred C. 265, 1336

Easterbrook, Frank H. 786
Edmonson, William F. 1266
Edwards, Harry T. 172, 428, 798, 818, 876, 904, 945, 951
Ehrenberg, Ronald G. 121, 1134
Ehrlich, Howard Leslie Abraham 860
Eischen, Dana E. 1305
Eisenhofer, Jay 844
Elarbee, Fred W., Jr. 640
Elder, Celia J. 936
Elkin, Randyl D. 51
Elkouri, Edna Asper 44
Elkouri, Frank 44, 143, 260
Elliott, David 490
Elliott, Sheldon D. 37
Elson, Alex 366, 489, 549
Elwell, Karen 824
Emerson, Catharine 391
Englander, William H. 495
Ensor, Richard J. 1321
Epp, Daniel L. 511
Epstein, Henry B. 1233
Epstein, Lee 364
Estes, R. Wayne 79, 835
Ewing, David 136
Extejt, Marian M. 1139

Fairweather, Owen 42, 198, 691
Fallon, William J. 289, 1068
Farber, Henry S. 1120, 1130, 1131, 1146, 1161
Farley, Larry D. 398, 399

Faurot, David G.   1324
Feigenbaum, Charles   1104, 1283
Feild, Hubert S.   286
Feinberg, I. Robert   503
Feinsinger, Nathan P.   157, 160, 249
Feliu, Alfred G.   1221
Feller, David E.   344, 743, 750, 751, 760, 765, 766, 886, 1011
Ferentino, Joseph M.   153
Ferris, Frank D.   1275, 1281, 1296
Feuille, Peter   126, 815, 816, 824, 1051, 1101, 1123, 1125, 1126, 1157, 1163, 1169, 1170, 1172, 1173, 1174, 1176, 1180, 1182
Figuero, José R.   145
Finkin, Matthew W.   1267
Finston, Felicia A.   892
Fischback, Charles P.   656
Fischer, Ben   163, 1333
Fischer, Robert W.   560
Fisher, Carrie G.   520
Fisher, Patrick J.   745
Fisher, Robert W.   622
Fishgold, Herbert   1295
Fitzgibbon, Susan A.   633
Flagler, John J.   354, 418
Flanagan, Robert J.   1111
Fleischli, George R.   232, 738, 783, 1072
Fleming, R. W.   6, 197, 261, 306, 426, 1066
Fletcher, Betty Binns   170
Fletcher, Jack   1303
Florey, Peter   458, 1220
Fogel, Walter   802
Forkosch, Morris D.   203
Fortado, Bruce   466
Foster, Howard G.   621, 1069
Fowler, Aubrey R., Jr.   174, 825, 965
Fox, Carie   881
Fox, M. J., Jr.   381, 905, 928
Fox, Michael   1067, 1202
Fox, Thomas R.   928
Francis, Thomas S.   452
Franklin, Geralyn McClure   831
Fraser, Bruce   423, 424, 485, 626
Frazier, Henry B., III   1274, 1290
Freedman, Yvonne F.   581, 585

Freiden, Jesse   743, 760
Friedman, Clara H.   254
Friedman, David R.   1203
Friedman, George H.   800
Friedman, Joel W.   165
Friedman, Milton   388
Friedman, Sheldon   733
Fryer, John   733
Fuller, Lon L.   160
Furlong, Gary   384
Furniss, Edgar S.   30

Gallagher, Daniel G.   681, 1033, 1079, 1081, 1193, 1196
Gallagher, Karen S.   1194
Gandz, Jeffrey   270
Garbutt, Cynthia Horvath   664
Garrett, Robert F.   377
Garrett, Sylvester   62, 250, 325, 467, 784
Gates, Conrad J.   936
Gear, Richard   786
Gellens, Kathryn A.   710
Gentile, Joseph F.   353, 1282
Gerhart, Paul F.   1132, 1192
Gershenfeld, Walter J.   362, 1035
Geslewitz, Irving M.   507
Gessford, James B.   1309
Getman, Julius G.   43, 168, 430
Giacalone, Robert A.   371
Giacobbe, Jane   1041
Gifford, Courtney D.   45
Gill, Lewis M.   258
Gillin, Leslie M.   982
Gillis, L. P.   180
Gilroy, T. P.   1020
Gilson, C. H. J.   180
Glass, Jerrold A.   648
Glasser, Joseph   290
Glick, Leslie Alan   365
Goetz, Raymond   504
Goff, Wayne H.   461
Goggin, Edward P.   44
Gohmann, John W.   150

Gold, Alan B.   1190
Gold, Charlotte   55, 482, 669
Goldberg, Arthur J.   536
Goldberg, Mitchell D.   105
Goldberg, Stephen B.   277, 278, 279
Goldsmith, Willis J.   593
Goldstein, Elliott H.   346, 401
Goldstein, Mark L.   1307
Gomberg, William   691
Gomez, Angel   629, 630
Goodman, John   1213
Goodwin, James C.   371
Goodwin, Van Allyn   1277
Gordon, John A.   793
Gorsky, M. R.   83, 859
Gosline, Ann   47, 392
Gotbaum, Victor   1035
Gottesmal, Michael H.   423, 778, 833
Gottlieb, Ira   812
Gould, William B., IV   795, 814, 1240, 1249
Graham, Harry   167, 293, 1162, 1179
Graham, Joseph C., III   612, 669
Grant, Hugh M.   1112
Grebey, C. Raymond, Jr.   1314
Greenbaum, Marcia L.   421, 463, 539, 626, 627, 1035
Greenberg, Murray   476
Greenfield, Patricia A.   712, 787, 939
Greer, Charles R.   1034, 1092
Gregorich, John E.   893
Gregory, David L.   958
Gregory, Gordon A.   275, 284
Grenig, Jay E.   79, 523, 535, 739, 783, 810, 1245
Griffin, Charles J., Jr.   336
Grigsby, David W.   1148
Grodin, Joseph R.   1048, 1049, 1088, 1100
Grody, Donald   85
Gromfine, I. J.   343
Gross, Ernest   137
Gross, James A.   432, 472, 712, 763, 1263
Grossman, Mark M.   89, 729
Gruenberg, Gladys W.   704
Gruhn, Brian   881
Guckeen, Alice   894

Guidry, Greg   1224
Gullett, C. Ray   461
Gunderson, Morley   122
Guthrie, Paul M.   1302

Haber, Lawrence J.   1045
Hafferty, Carole A.   856
Haggard, Thomas R.   521
Hall, Gary A.   686, 1016
Hamilton, Arthur   884
Handsaker, Morrison   53, 1009
Harkless, James M.   1278, 1296
Harper, Michael C.   889
Harris, Michael M.   416
Harris, Philip   476, 531, 755
Harrison, Alan J.   71
Harter, Lafayette G., Jr.   1254
Haskin, Mary Clare   1305
Hassler, Allison   715
Hatch, D. Diane   872
Hauck, Vern E.   577, 637, 960, 974, 988
Haughton, Ronald W.   691
Hayford, Stephen L.   431, 434, 942, 1279
Hays, Paul R.   114
Healy, James J.   676
Heath, Charles M.   376
Hedblom, John M.   1305
Heenan, Roy L.   733
Heinen, Mark   284
Heinsz, Timothy J.   382, 385, 811
Helburn, I. B.   295, 465, 661, 671, 672, 675, 1006
Helsby, Robert   1197
Helsby, Wayne L.   454
Hendricks, Wallace   1163, 1170, 1173, 1174
Heneman, Herbert G., III   214
Henkel, Jan W.   933
Henry, Karen C.   1206
Heppel, John   559
Hepple, Bob A.   1233
Herman, Anthony   1246
Herrick, John Smith   213, 215
Heshizer, Brian P.   167, 293

Hewitt, Thomas L.   51
Hexter, Christopher T.   882
Hildreth, W. Bartley   25
Hilgert, Raymond L.   54
Hill, John R.   661
Hill, Marvin F., Jr.   72, 84, 90, 112, 375, 393, 597, 615, 618, 820, 948, 949, 1234
Hillock, Laura R.   968
Hines, R. J.   1021
Hirlinger, Michael W.   1189
Hirsch, Barry T.   1004, 1138
Hobgood, William P.   45
Hodapp, Paul F.   514
Hoellering, Michael F.   332, 334, 449
Hoffman, Eileen Barkas   33, 202, 1228
Hoffman, Joan   663
Hogan, John A.   549
Hogler, Raymond L.   435, 436, 813
Hoh, Ronald   1187
Holden, Lawrence T.   1065
Holley, William H., Jr.   286, 658
Holly, J. Fred   558, 686
Hopkins, Charles I., Jr.   1303
Hopkins, Ronald   790
Horlacher, John Perry   538
Horton, Raymond D.   1003, 1027
Houseman, K. A.   1023
Howan, Lillian T.   752
Howard, Wayne E.   677
Howlett, Robert G.   762, 863, 1037, 1229
Hoyman, Michele M.   823
Hubek, Philip J.   758
Huffman, Gerald J., Jr.   1224
Hunt, Evelyn M.   981
Hunter, John E.   672
Hyman, Warren H.   1074

Ichniowski, Casey   1058
Igoe, Joseph A.   138
Imundo, Louis V.   52
Ingrassia, Anthony   1297
Irving, John S., Jr.   568, 833, 887

Jackson, R. L. 132
Jacksteit, Mary E. 1295
Jacobs, Roger B. 356, 450, 821
Jaffee, Samuel H. 307
Janisch-Ramsey, Kimberly 417
Jarley, Paul 1153, 1184, 1185
Jascourt, Hugh 783
Jauvtis, Robert L. 1242
Jeannette, Michael W. 908
Jenab, Deena B. 969
Jennings, Daniel F. 217, 297
Jennings, Ken 532, 562, 567, 653, 654, 655, 657, 663, 1197
Jennings, Thomas W. 320, 347
Jensen, Vernon H. 678, 1331
Jick, Todd 121
Johnsen, Julie E. 116
Johnson, David B. 167
Johnson, Richard 1059
Jones, Dallas L. 81, 91, 288, 745
Jones, Edgar A., Jr. 462, 765, 804, 805
Jones, Harry E. 148, 1073
Jones, James E., Jr. 355, 430, 665
Jordan, James H. 320
Jowers, J. Marshall 1335
Juliussen, James H. 667
Justin, Jules J. 491

Kaden, Lewis B. 801
Kadish, Sanford H. 559
Kagel, John 46, 318, 1201, 1278
Kagel, Sam 76, 328, 760, 1201
Kahn, Mark L. 351, 618, 678, 730
Kahn, Steven C. 897
Kandel, William 952
Kansier, William R. 1296
Kaplan, Roger P. 144
Karim, Ahmad 403
Katz, Harold A. 503
Katz, Harry C. 1130
Katz, Marsha 231, 272
Katz, Robert S. 751
Kauffman, Nancy L. 230, 341

Keim, James A. 644
Kelley, Kevin W. 832
Kelliher, Peter M. 493
Kelly, Kathy 318
Kelly, Laurence 1113
Kelly, Mark 933
Kennedy, Thomas 59, 678
Kerr, Robert W. 861
Kerur, Sharad 131
Kilberg, William J. 308
Killingsworth, Charles C. 162, 186, 247, 541, 695
King, Brian L. 220
King, Geoffrey R. 544
King, Otis H. 754
Kirk, Geoffrey T. 606
Kirsner, Kenneth M. 734
Kittle-Kamp, Thomas L. 940
Klaas, Brian S. 599
Kleeb, Robert H. 440
Kleiman, Bernard 219
Kleintop, William A. 1143
Knight, Thomas R. 522, 565, 1260
Kochan, Thomas A. 121, 264, 1129, 1135, 1208
Koen, Clifford M. 638
Koff, David E. 510
Kohn, Jeffrey I. 1251
Kohrs, El Dean V. 679
Kolb, Deborah M. 283
Koren, Phillip F. 1286, 1287
Kostyack, John F. 962
Kotin, Leo 440, 427
Kouf, Kim M. 508
Kovacevik, Robert 1336
Kovarsky, Irving 974, 988
Koven, Adolph M. 102, 104, 289
Koys, Daniel J. 1245
Kramer, Andrew M. 779
Krashinsky, Stephen 98
Krause, Loren A. 1063
Kriksciun, Curt 505
Krinsky, Edward B. 189, 1070
Krislov, Joseph 188, 211, 756, 1003
Kromm, Gene M. 419

Krotseng, Richard Van M. 736
Krueger, Alan B. 1252
Kruger, Daniel H. 1073, 1087
Kurlantzick, Lewis S. 86, 389
Kutell, Diane 1071

Labig, Chalmer E., Jr. 671
Labor Committee, American Public Transit Association 64
LaCugna, Charles S. 78
Laffer, Kingsley 200
Lafferty, Linda 404
Lampkin, Linda 594
Lamprati, Luigi M. B. 31
Landau, Jeffrey M. 518
Landis, Brook I. 12
Laner, Richard W. 1078
Lansing, Paul 896
Larkin, John Day 62
La Rue, Homer C. 236, 1008
Lataille, Ralph H. 137
LaVan, Helen 195, 272, 953, 1325, 1335
Lawson, Eric W., Jr. 74, 228
Lawson, Eric W., Sr. 74
Layton, Robert 969
Lazar, Joseph 149
Leahy, William H. 439, 556, 639, 650, 451
Leap, Terry L. 106, 994
Lehoczky, Paul N. 695
Lentz, Charles N. 1255
Lenz, Laurence H., Jr. 842
Leonard, Arthur S. 506
Leonard, Edwin C., Jr. 468
Leonard, John W. 614
LeRoy, Michael 815, 816
Lester, Richard Allen 123, 1038, 1142
Letter, Harvey 1300
Levin, Anne S. 857
Levin, Edward 85, 580, 642
Levin, William 448, 1250
Levine, Marvin J. 826
Levinson, David 199
Levitt, Mark E. 454

Lewin, David 66
Lewis, Daniel E. 321
Liberson, Dennis H. 975, 1017
Liden, Robert C. 419
Lieberman, Michael 983
Liebes, Richard 376
Liebeskind, Arlyne K. 1178
Liebowitz, Jonathan S. 1188
Lind, Kate H. 937
Linenberger, Patricia 713
Lipsitz, Richard 411
Lipsky, David B. 1128, 1158
Lister, Phyllis 723
Littrell, Lawrence R. 1233
Lockett, Cheryl L. 111
Loevi, Francis J. 144
Loewenberg, J. Joseph 120, 171, 207, 1026, 1095, 1097, 1143, 1154
Long, Gary 1101, 1123
Loomis, Lloyd 592
Lovell, Ned B. 141
Lovo, Mario M. 646
Luskin, Bert 1316
Lynch, Dennis O. 913
Lynch, Lawrence T. 927
Lyons, Ruth E. 55

Macdonald, Alastair Peter 124
Macey, Barry E. 528
Mack, Curtis L. 903
MacKay, Duncan Ross 879
MacManus, Susan A. 1171
MacMillan, Alexander 295
Magee, James Michael 877
Magenau, John M. 1117
Magnusen, Karl O. 1198
Malin, Martin H. 422, 457, 967
Malinowski, Arthur Anthony 670
Mangum, David G. 757
Manning, Julia W. 1078
Manson, Julius J. 156
Mapes-Riordan, Lynne D. 984
Marchione, Anthony R. 443

Marcus, Richard L. 353
Marett, Pamela C. 313
Marion, Phyllis 698
Markowitz, James R. 408
Marmo, Michael 107, 587, 591, 611, 616, 617, 623, 624, 990
Martin, Christopher C. 603
Martin, Cindy 532
Martin, Edward F. 296
Martin, Warren 1247
Marx, Herbert L., Jr. 153, 368
Mason, Ronald L. 789
Masters, Richard L. 589
Mathis, Benton J., Jr. 555
Matkov, George J. 402
Mayo, Thomas W. 1013
McAllister, Stephen 1324
McAvoy, Joan Zeldon 1022
McCabe, David A. 9
McCabe, Douglas M. 135, 1222
McCammon, Marlise 735
McCarthy, Kevin M. 836
McCormick, Mary 1030
McDermott, Thomas J. 224, 494, 608, 680
McDonagh, Thomas J. 689
McDonald, Paula L. 497
McGill, Linda D. 873
McGinnis, William, Jr. 1043
McGuckin, John J., Jr. 610
McHugh, William A., Jr. 593
McIntosh, Kristin E. 878
McKee, Jean 1299
McKee, William L. 230
McKelvey, Jean T. 3, 113, 115, 210, 451, 676, 970, 971
McKenna, Ian B. 697
McKersie, Robert 268
McLaughlin, Richard P. 553
McPherson, Donald S. 287
McPherson, William H. 196
Mead, John 756
Meiners, Roger S. 1086
Meltzer, Bernard D. 761, 762, 780, 819, 870
Mennemeier, Kenneth C. 1236
Merrifield, Leroy S. 39

Merrill, Samuel, III   1110, 1167
Metzger, Norman   153
Metzler, John H.   679
Meyer, Jared H.   1336
Meyer, Jeffrey D.   1323
Meyers, Frederic   289
Mignin, Robert J.   572
Miller, Allen K.   221
Miller, David P.   405
Miller, Erin-Aine   70
Miller, Gerald L.   25
Miller, Gerry M.   344
Miller, Marvin J.   1315
Miller, Paul F.   151
Miller, Richard U.   685, 1010
Miller, Ronald L.   206, 1218
Miller, Thomas R.   594
Mills, Miriam K.   659
Minami, Wayne   1068
Mironi, Mordehai   121, 1032
Miscimmara, Phillip A.   776
Miserendino, C. Richard   1272
Mittenthal, Richard   266, 268, 316, 370, 528, 549, 575, 762
Moberly, Robert E.   14
Monat, Jonathan S.   629, 630
Mooney, Thomas B.   1076
Moore, Carl D.   1280
Moore, David   1197
Moore, Sir John   204
Moran, James P.   880
Morley, C. Val   868
Morris, Charles J.   765, 769, 899, 906, 1001
Moses, Mary Helen   898
Moss, Richard   1316
Mouser, Deanna J.   883
Mukamal, Stuart S.   1039, 1203
Mulholland, John   1296
Murphy, Betty Southard   872
Murphy, Frank J.   693
Murphy, Michael E.   717
Murphy, William P.   255, 445, 625
Murray, Matthew E.   336
Murray, Robert Emmet   1034

Murrman, Kent F. 1258
Myers, Jewell L. 370

Naffziger, Fred J. 923
Nager, Glen D. 969
Nakamura, Edward H. 170
Nash, Peter G. 921, 922
Neal, Mollie W. 819
Neale, Margaret A. 1118, 1119, 1137
Nelson, Anne H. 56
Nelson, Nels E. 229, 475, 1102, 1200
Nelson, W. B. 613, 628
Neuborne, Helen R. 636
Newman, Harold 1034
Newman, Winn 818
Nichol, Victor 323
Nichols, Robert H. 344
Nicolau, George 320, 353, 402
Nolan, Dennis R. 13, 176, 208, 251, 252, 263, 300, 301, 489, 569, 578, 682, 687, 688, 700, 701, 732, 759, 1292
Northrop, Michael K. 914
Notz, William W. 1114, 1147
Nowlin, William A. 244, 632
Nuffer, Brian E. 513
Nussbaum, Karen 421

O'Connell, Francis A., Jr. 163
O'Dea, Raymond 31
Office of the General Counsel, American Arbitration Association 1, 449, 455, 662, 785, 809, 827, 840, 865, 969, 1251
O'Grady, James P., Jr. 274
O'Hara, John F. 376
Oldham, James 915
Oliver, Anthony T. 915
Oliver, Susan M. 594
Olson, Craig A. 1052, 1057, 1061, 1127, 1153, 1159, 1184
Oppenheimer, Margaret 953
Oral History Project, National Academy of Arbitrators 62
Ordman, Arnold 863
Ornati, Oscar A. 545, 995
Ostrander, Kenneth H. 139

Ostrin, H. Howard   537
Ottolenghi, Smadar   205
Overton, Craig E.   1040
Owens, Stephen D.   822, 947

Page, Rosemary S.   809, 827, 865
Palmer, Bruce Murdoch   36
Palmer, Earl Edward   36
Parker, Joan   829
Pashler, Peter   1261
Patterson, Diane L.   125
Patton, Craig Dow   941
Paulson, Steven   1197
Pearce, Thomas G.   637
Peck, Cornelius J.   901
Pecori, John V.   866
Pegnetter, Richard   431, 434, 1081
Perkovich, Robert   502
Peters, Edward   15
Peters, Robert M.   188
Petersen, Donald J.   152, 177, 226, 231, 269, 291, 487, 758
Petersen, Paul F.   994
Peterson, Richard D.   66
Petrie, James S.   421
Phelps, James C.   536
Phelps, Orme W.   998
Phillips, John R.   566, 1080
Plass, Stephen   253
Platt, Harry H.   62, 219, 249, 551
Plofchan, Thomas K., Jr.   1226
Polasek, Robert G.   20
Ponak, Allen   674, 0210
Popper, Seth Michael   794
Pops, Gerald M.   22
Porter, Alexander B.   363
Porter, J. M., Jr.   557
Power, James F.   309
Prashker, Herbert   219, 445
Prasow, Paul   15
Primeaux, Walter J.   225
Pritzker, Malcolm L.   727
Provost, Glendel J.   581, 585

Purcell, Edward R. 1271
Pursell, Donald E. 1164

Quigg, David L. 644
Quinn, Francis X. 759
Quinn, Thomas J. 287

Rabin, Jack 25
Rabin, Robert J. 714
Raffaele, Joseph Antonio 326
Rahnama-Moghadam, Mashalah 403
Rains, Harry H. 1054
Raits, Vivian I. 895
Raposa, John Francis 728
Raskin, Abraham H. 780
Rathburn, J. Eric 1259
Ratner, Mozart G. 770
Ray, Douglas E. 830, 845, 934
Reardon, Jack 556
Reavley, Martha 978
Redeker, James R. 97, 99
Reed, Keith A. 152
Rehmus, Charles M. 343, 759, 1026, 1047, 1084, 1109, 1156
Reid, Candace 642
Reiner, Martha L. 371
Reinhardt, Stephen R. 780
Reischl, Dennis K. 146, 943, 1280
Renovitch, Patricia A. 1198
Rentfro, William E. 1225
Rezler, Julius 152, 177, 226, 291, 487
Richard, Loretta Rhodes 509
Ries, Edith Dunfee 1186
Roberts, Benjamin C. 619, 795
Roberts, Matthew T. 286
Roberts, Thomas T. 400, 405, 1316, 1322
Robins, Eva 241, 1239
Robinson, Cammie R. 917
Robinson, James W. 50, 317
Robinson, William L. 819
Robitzer, William D. 1083
Robson, Donald L. 1194

Rock, Eli   187
Rodenberg, Thomas D.   979
Rodgers, Robert C.   465, 671, 672, 1006
Roebker, Maria T.   875
Ronner, Walter V.   1216
Rooney, Robert E., Jr.   275
Rose, Joseph B.   340
Rosen, Seth D.   648, 1305
Rosenbaum, Mark   287
Rosenberg, Marvin   161
Rosenberg, Sheldon   973
Rosenthal, R.   573
Rosenzweig, Linda E.   916
Ross, Arthur M.   303, 559, 668
Ross, David B.   1019
Ross, Jerome H.   1296, 1299
Rothschild, Donald P.   39, 294
Rothstein, Mark A.   185
Roumell, George T., Jr.   803, 993
Rubenfeld, Stephen A.   954
Rubins, Alvin B.   299
Rudyk, Andrew   1291
Rueschhoff, M. Susan   1042, 1046
Rule, William S.   631
Russell, Craig   791
Russell, James S.   1257
Rutledge, Ivan C.   524
Ryder, Meyer S.   219, 742
Rynecki, Steven B.   72, 1256

Sachs, Theodore   766
Sack, Jeffrey   98
Sacks, Barbara B.   193
Sacks, Howard R.   86, 389
Salter, Robert   684
Samavati, Hedayeh   1045
Samuelson, William F.   1152
Sanderson, John P.   75
Sandler, Andrew   897
Sandver, Marcus H.   214, 338
Sargrad, Gita D.   855
Saunders, George   1214

Scharman, Clifford   1015
Scheinholtz, Leonard L.   776
Scheinman, Martin F.   82, 1306
Schmedemann, Deborah A.   280
Schneider, Randy J.   719
Schnepp, Roger H.   343
Schoen, Sterling H.   54
Schoonhoven, Ray J.   42
Schwartz, Adolph E.   708
Schwartz, Kenneth D.   837
Schwartz, Rosalind   70
Schwochau, Susan   1180, 1182
Scott, Clyde   527
Scott, K. Dow   574
Sears, Don W.   405
Seeber, Ronald L.   276
Seide, Katherine   38, 40
Seidman, Joel   93, 652
Seifman, Donald H.   716
Seitz, Peter   173, 223, 241, 315, 335, 472, 533, 743, 748, 1002
Sembower, John F.   302
Severson, James   516
Seward, Ralph T.   3, 62, 539, 540
Seybold, John W.   690
Shank, Mark A.   900
Sharfman, I. L.   246
Sharpe, Calvin William   259, 909, 1330
Shaw, Lee C.   503, 766
Shawe, Earle K.   379
Shearer, John C.   319, 753, 1278
Sheffield, Barbara   567
Shepard, Lo Ann   1326
Sherman, Herbert L., Jr.   110, 360, 366, 438, 922
Sherman, James J.   346
Shils, Edward B.   61
Shister, Joseph   250
Shore, Richard P.   164
Shulman, Harry   158
Sibbernsen, Richard D.   546
Sigal, Benjamin C.   538, 851
Sigler, John C.   282
Silberman, Allan D.   285
Silberman, David   786

Silerman, R. Gaull 636
Silver, Jim 1112
Silver, S. 978
Simkin, William E. 62, 673
Simmons, Gordon 154
Simon, Alex J. 1266
Simons, Jesse 151, 402
Sims, Andrew C. L. 862
Sinicropi, Anthony V. 84, 90, 112, 183, 242, 375, 597, 751, 949, 1020
Sink, D. Scott 1034, 1092
Sirefman, Joseph 741
Siwica, Richard P. 771
Skelton, B. R. 313
Skratek, Sylvia P. 281
Slobodin, Megan 154
Small, Jeffrey 216
Smith, A. J., Jr. 411
Smith, Barry F. 726
Smith, Charles G. 1298
Smith, Clifford E. 218
Smith, J. Martin 709
Smith, N. Gregory 446
Smith, Ralph R. 146
Smith, Russell A. 39, 288, 493
Smith, Russell H. 1029
Smith, Susan L. 102, 104
Smolensky, William R. 585
Snow, Carlton J. 525, 588, 788, 854
Sobel, Irvin 426
Soll, Martin 1305
Somers, Gerald G. 579
Sovern, Michael I. 764
Spelfogel, Evan J. 410
Spencer, Janet Maleson 583
Sprehe, J. Timothy 216
Srb, Jozetta H. 994
St. Antoine, Theodore J. 268, 762, 799, 910, 1233
Stahl, Michael J. 464
Stallworth, Lamont E. 276, 422, 664, 823, 967
Stanley, Douglas C. 767
Stanton, David W. 499
Stark, Steven 488
Starke, Frederick A. 1114, 1147

Staudohar, Paul D.   23, 119, 190, 749, 1103, 1311
Steen, Jack E.   374
Stein, Bruno   542, 620
Stein, Emanuel   492, 517, 550, 740
Stein, Mark H.   502
Steinberg, Michael   83
Steiner, Julius M.   48
Stephens, Elvis C.   808, 831
Stephens, Richard C.   581, 585
Stern, James L.   127, 201, 1026, 1057, 1098, 1205
Stessin, Lawrence   337
Stevens, C. M.   999
Stevens, Carl M.   1111
Stewart, Henry G.   836
Stewart, Thomas H.   986
Stieber, Jack   133, 175, 262, 323, 330, 1000, 1191, 1230, 1252
Stochaj, John M.   1089
Stockman, Abram H.   425, 427
Stone, Morris   49, 94, 429, 746
Strouble, Dennis D.   954
Stutin, Cathy M.   647
Stutz, Robert L.   742
Subbarao, A. V.   1145, 1181, 1209, 1212
Sulzner, George T.   1276
Summa, Joseph B.   706
Summers, Clyde W.   344, 440, 1227, 1232
Sweeney, Michael T.   840
Swenson, Leanne M.   935
Swimmer, Gene   1215
Syer, Frank   154
Sylvia, Ronald D.   1189
Szymanski, Patrick J.   318

Tabler, Susan B.   528
Tallakson, Ruth   1168
Taylor, Brian S.   920
Taylor, Carl L.   568
Taylor, George W.   3, 996
Taylor, G. Stephen   574
Teele, John W.   459, 744
Tener, Barbara Z.   245
Tener, Jeffrey B.   1034

Teple, Edwin R.   14, 922
Theeke, Herman A.   420
Theeke, Tina M.   420
Thompson, Douglas H.   100
Thompson, Mark   1024
Thompson, Scott C.   192
Thornicroft, Kenneth William   595
Thornton, Robert J.   470, 480
Tideman, Curtis   722
Tidwell, Gary L.   390
Tilove, Robert   718
Tobias, Paul H.   324
Tobias, Robert M.   607
Tobin, John E.   92
Toole, Judith H.   848
Torrence, William D.   1164
Treble, John G.   1122
Tremiti, Joseph F.   834
Trotta, Maurice S.   41, 63
Trower, Christopher   69
Trumka, Richard L.   807
Tucker, Mark M.   609
Tufano, Paul A.   645

Ullman, Joseph C.   21
Unterberger, S. Herbert   690, 692, 694, 695
Updegraff, Clarence M.   7
Usery, W. J.   310

Vacura, Julie R.   929
Valtin, Rolf   608
Van de Water, John B.   997
Vause, W. Gary   24
Veglahn, Peter A.   345, 604, 681, 884, 1196
Venuti, Michael D.   891
Ver Ploeg, Christine D.   698, 781
Vercruysse, Robert   1035
Vernon, Gil   1303
Vetter, Jan   833
Vladeck, Judith P.   349
Vocino, Thomas   25

Volz, Marlin M. 44
Vorro, Elizabeth A. 836

Wachter, Michael L. 264
Waite, William W. 690
Waks, Jay W. 885
Waldman, Seymour M. 441
Wallace, Anne 858
Wallen, Saul 114, 162, 539, 551
Walsh, Joseph 683
Walt, Alan 1225
Warner, Elizabeth F. 792
Warns, Carl A., Jr. 289, 640
Warren, William H. 1217
Watkins, John L. 641
Wayland, Robert F. 831
Weatherill, J. F. W. 77, 339
Webster, Carol 950
Webster, James J. 448
Weise, John T. 128
Weisel, Martha S. 838, 841
Weitzman, Allan H. 153
Weitzman, Joan 1089
Werner, Charles A. 354
Wertheimer, Barbara M. 56
Werther, William B., Jr. 312
Westerkamp, Patrick R. 221, 843, 964
Westin, Alan F. 421
Wheeler, Hoyt N. 561, 1106, 1124, 1155, 1168, 1210
White, Harold C. 312, 1284
Whiting, Dudley E. 742, 1302
Widenor, Marcus R. 715
Wiggins, Ronald L. 87
Willcoxon, Michael 516
Williams, J. Earl 1299, 1301
Williams, Jerre S. 427, 534
Williams, Peg A. 140
Williams, Robert E. 134
Williams, Wendy W. 819
Williamson, John D. 589
Williamson, Steven 1197
Willig, Deborah R. 977

Wilson, Andrea 406
Wirtz, W. Willard 425
Wisniewski, Stanley C. 696
Witt, Glenna M. 908
Witte, Edwin 3
Wittman, Donald 1150
Wolf, Mary Jean 1304
Wolff, David A. 249
Wolff, Sidney A. 536, 743
Wolfson, Beth Anne 707
Wolfson, Steven R. 956
Wolkinson, Benjamin W. 930, 975, 987, 989, 992, 1191, 1326
Wollett, Donald H. 445, 564, 912
Wolsteil, Sheldon A. 905
Wolters, Roger S. 286, 562, 567
Wong, Glenn M. 1318, 1319, 1320
Wood, Lynelle M. 942
Woods, H. D. 4, 198
Woods, Noel S. 28
Woolf, Donald A. 474
Woyar, Mark N. 338
Wright, James A. 393
Wrong, Elaine Gale 959, 961, 976, 980
Wynns, Pat 584

Yaffe, Byron 10
Yarowsky, Jonathan 797
Yedwab, Janet G. 774
Youngblood, Stuart A. 1241
Youngdahl, James E. 433, 946

Zack, Arnold M. 16, 17, 19, 96, 101, 130, 209, 238, 243, 343, 346, 370, 407, 1007, 1029
Zack, Norma W. 407
Zacur, Susan Rawson 234
Zalas, George J. 373
Zelek, Mark E. 182
Zimmerman, Gregory E. 902
Zimny, Max 80
Zirkel, Perry A. 271, 284, 470, 480, 498, 510, 512, 570, 775
Ziskind, David 426

ABOUT THE CONTRIBUTORS

Paul Barron (J.D., University of Pittsburgh) is a professor of law at the Tulane University Law School.

Mei Liang Bickner (Ph.D., U.C.L.A.) is a professor in the School of Business Administration and Economics at California State University, Fullerton.

Charles J. Coleman (Ph.D., State University of New York at Buffalo) is a professor of management at Rutgers University School of Business at Camden.

Gerald C. Coleman (J.D. and LL.M., Georgetown University) is an adjunct professor of law at Rutgers University School of Business at Camden.

Greg Dell'Omo (Ph.D., University of Wisconsin) is an assistant professor of management at St. Joseph's University.

Theodora T. Haynes (M.B.A. and M.L.S., Rutgers University) is an associate professor in the Paul Robeson Library of Rutgers University at Camden.

Stanley J. Schwartz (Ed.D., Temple University) is an associate professor of management in the School of Business at Rider College.

Perry Zirkel (J.D., University of Connecticut; LL.M., Yale) is University Professor of Education and Law at Lehigh University.